Why Constitutions Matter

Why Constitutions Matter

edited by

Niclas Berggren
Nils Karlson
Joakim Nergelius

Transaction Publishers
New Brunswick (U.S.A.) and London (U.K.)

Third printing 2009
Published in 2002 by Transaction Publishers, New Brunswick, New Jersey by arrangement with City University Press, Stockholm, Sweden.

This book is printed on acid-free paper that meets the American National Standard for Permanence of Paper for Printed Library Materials.

Library of Congress Catalog Number: 2001053506
ISBN: 0-7658-0924-9
Printed in the United States of America

Library of Congress Cataloging-in-Publication Data

Why constitutions matter / edited by Niclas Berggren, Nils Karlson, Joakim Nergelius.
p. cm.
Originally published: Stockholm: City University Press, 2000.
Includes bibliographical references.
ISBN: 0-7658-0924-9 (paper. : acid-free paper)
1. Constitutional law. 2. Rule of law. 3. Democracy. I. Berggren, Niclas. II. Karlson, Nils. III. Nergelius, Joakim.

K3171 .W49 2002
342'.02—dc21 2001053506

Contents

Introduction, p VII

James Buchanan
Why Do Constitutions Matter? p 1

Aleksander Peczenik
Why Constitution? What Constitution? Constraints on Majority Rule, p 17

Mats Lundström
The Moral Standing of Democracy, p 61

Joakim Nergelius
Parliamentary Supremacy under Attack: the British Constitution Revisited, p 107

Sverker Härd
Arbitrary Democracy, p 137

Niclas Berggren and Peter Kurrild-Klitgaard
Economic Effects of Political Institutions, with Special Reference to Constitutions, p 167

Wolfgang Kasper
The Evolution of Constitutional Qualities under the Influence of Global Competition, p 213

Erik Moberg
Competition in Government by Federalism, p 233

The authors, p 289

Introduction

The rule of the people is the essence of democracy. So why should there be formal constraints that regulate and even limit this rule? When and why do constitutionalism and democracy go hand in hand? Could constitutionalism even be seen as an essential component of modern democracy? And what are the effects of these constitutional rules? Why do constitutions matter?

The theme of the present volume, *Why Constitutions Matter*, makes clear that the basic political institutions play an important role for how a society and a political system function. For instance, the design of the constitution affects who gets to exercise power and who does not, who wins and who loses in the political game. The rules deciding the type of electoral system used, as well as how votes in the legislature are to be run and how governments are to be appointed and discharged, have fundamental effects on the political game.

But the constitution means more than this. Its design also affects how laws and policies are formed, irrespective of who is in power. It introduces limits on and legally binds political power. It affects how the political process functions and its results.

The constitution is thus an important (or even *the* most important) part of society's basic system of rules. Its rules constitute a kind of basic norm for other laws and rules, for the judicial system and legal application, and therefore also for citizens' sense of justice and for the forming of norms. Most importantly, perhaps, the constitution regulates the relationship between the state and the individuals in a society and can hence be seen as a kind of contract between those in office and the people.

Consequently, the constitution is of great importance for how the political system, the economy, the rule of law, and the formation of norms work in a society. A society's long-term welfare seems highly dependent on its institutions. If suitable institutions are missing, or if present institutions are designed in a faulty manner, a society functions worse than otherwise. Such a conclusion receives strong support from research results in the neo-institutional tradition in the social sciences.

Consequently, there is a growing international interest in constitutional issues. The new democracies in Eastern Europe, Asia and Southern Africa are in a process where the recently introduced democratic institutions find their form and content. Several well-established democracies, such as Italy, the UK and New Zealand, have made major constitutional revisions in later years. "Constitutional social engineering" is increasingly seen as one of the most important methods to improve the working properties of democracies, economies, and the rule of law.

This does not, of course, imply that constitutions are the only things that matter for how the political process, or society, functions. Ideas, ideologies, technological developments and so on, are of course also of major importance. The point is that institutions and constitutions do matter, to some non-negligible extent, and that they, therefore, are suitable objects of study in the social sciences.

Still, scientific knowledge of these issues is unsatisfactory. Admittedly, an increased interest is noticeable, but not much research has been done as yet, especially not with an interdisciplinary approach. To help counter this, the City University of Stockholm has initiated the research project *Democracy and Constitutionalism*, sponsored by The Foundations of Torsten and Ragnar Söderberg (Torsten och Ragnar Söderbergs Stiftelser). The project has five central starting-points.

Firstly, the project is *interdisciplinary*. Constitutional problems are analysed from three different and complementary fields: law, political science, and economics. This broad approach seems particularly apt when analysing such an encompassing institution as the constitution, as its design has repercussions on many areas of society.

Secondly, the project has a *historical dimension*, *i e*, it tries to connect the discussion on real-world constitutions to concrete constitutional traditions. Without necessarily requiring that future constitutional reforms be contingent on earlier arrangements, we think it is essential to be able to make use of earlier experiences and insights, not least to increase the proposed reforms' prospects of gaining legitimacy and acceptance.

Thirdly, the project strives towards a *systems perspective*. A constitution consists of several different but mutually dependent parts. Looking at these in isolation is, in our view, not very fruitful; rather, one should consider how today's system functions in its totality and which components in this constitutional construction can be exchanged for new ones. In such a venture, it is important to take into consideration how different components interact and how this affects the functioning of the constitution in itds entirety.

Fourthly, the project tries to combine *different kinds of analyses*: some contributions are theoretical, some are empirical, some try to clarify concepts, some focus on the consequences of various constitutional arrangements, whereas others launch specific reform proposals.

Fifthly, the project also contains *general arguments*. Although focus is on the Swedish constitution, several contributions are applicable to other contexts and contain general reasoning on constitutional matters.

The project is run on a network model, with three "core researchers" (Berggren, Karlson and Nergelius) and a number of "network researchers" who write individual contributions. In total, about 15 scholars are participating from law, political science and economics—in writing papers and attending research seminars as well as a broad, public seminar series on constitutional issues. The present book is the second collection of contributions from this group of scholars. Each author is responsible only for his own contribution. Let us now turn to the individual chapters.

Nobel laureate and economist *James Buchanan* answers the question "Why Do Constitutions Matter?" by reiterating some familiar arguments for constraining the available choice-set, such as the weakness-of-will argument and the argument that having too many options is costly in a world where the decision-makers have limited cognitive capacities. He then goes on to clarify the difference between procedural and substantive constraints, where the former operate directly on the means through which choices are made, while not directly impinging on the set of options open to selection, and where the latter act directly on the set of options among which the selections are to be made. A constitution may specify that some physically feasible outcomes are simply "out of bounds," regardless of the procedures through which they may be reached. Lastly, and as the main contribution, two new ways of answering the title question are presented. First, the idea of "rules as rationality" is presented, stating that rules may impose structural rationality on choice situations by forcing the decision-makers to pay attention to all relevant aspects of an issue. It would seem highly unlikely that the interdependencies or externalities among the differing legislative choices would be fully internalized within the calculus of individual participants. Absent a rule or requirement that all of the interdependencies be reckoned with, that all margins of adjustment be simultaneously considered, there would seem to be no basis for predicting even tolerable "efficiency" in collective or political decision-making, even as evaluated by any single person. An example: having a budget process. Second, the idea of "rules as default options" is introduced, which states that rules are needed to cover situations where choices are not explicitly confronted; rules provide back-up or default means for selecting among alternatives when attitudinal or institutional considerations intervene to make deliberative decisions impossible or, at the least, inconvenient. In all, this explains the reason for rules.

Legal scholar *Aleksander Peczenik*, in his "Why Constitution? What Constitution? Constraints on Majority Rule," argues that constitutionalism requires that majority power be constrained by legal rules. It also requires that the same majority cannot easily change the constraints. This idea faces, however, the following objections. First, it appears to be undemocratic to constrain majority power. Second, the rules constraining the majority appear to be unjust, unless limited by weighing and deliberation. If thus limited, they appear to be too obscure to constrain the majority. Third, the constraints must be justifiable by recourse to something else than majority power. Whatever this justification is, it appears to be controversial. Fourth, the constraints must be changeable. It is not clear who can justifiably make the changes.

This paper presents the following answers to those objections: First, the modern concept of democracy is not the same as majority power. It is a constrained majority power. Second, limitations of the rules constraining majority power are inevitable, since all (or almost all) rules are defeasible, and thus open to limitations. Yet, rules are possible and they can be efficient. Third, justification of rules is possible by having recourse to normative moral theory. Normative moral theory is contestable, yet possible. Fourth, the changes of rules constraining the majority must pass a double check: they must be acceptable to the majority and they must be reasonable. Reasonableness is a matter of deliberation that is not arbitrary. The final conclusion of the paper is that to facilitate this deliberation, we need both strong courts and strong legal dogmatics.

In his article "The Moral Standing of Democracy," political scientist *Mats Lundström* discusses the question of how to justify democracy. He relates the question to three issues: definitions of "democracy", arguments for or against democracy and arguments for or against constitutional restraints on democracy. Lundström takes up the debate from the days of Herbert Tingsten, the founder of modern Swedish political science, on how to define "democracy." He argues that a definition of "democracy" should only be defended on semantic or conceptual grounds, not on the basis of political reasons. Lundström maintains that the concept of democracy could and should be stated in naturalistic, factual terms. "Democracy" refers to the distribution of power over decisions and actions of a state. Drawing on Charles Beitz, Lundström discusses three kinds of normative theory of democracy: *a.* procedural theories, *b.* best-result theories, and *c.* popular-will theories. The first ascribes an intrinsical value to democracy, while the other two defend democracy in terms of its outcomes. A best-result theory argues that democracy is the best way of achieving a just society, while a popular-will theory only focuses on democracy's ability to achieve collective rationality regarding political decisions. Lundström suggests that a best-result theory provides the most reasonable argument for democracy. This argument for democracy also applies to constitutions in general. Therefore, the domain of democratic decision-making is an open question, and should be judged according to an outcome-oriented moral standard. This standard must, according to Lundström, meet the demand of Kantian second-order universalism, *i e* a standard that no one has a reasonable argument to reject.

The above-mentioned articles are all exponents of a principled point of view, where the emphasis is put on finding general analytical schemes for discussing democracy and constitutionalism. The next set of articles is more empirically oriented, where the focus of the analysis is on the impact of constitutional rules in various areas.

Legal scholar *Joakim Nergelius'* contribution "Parliamentary Supremacy Under Attack: the British Constitution Revisited" analyses the impact, theoretically and constitutionally, of the recent constitutional reforms in the United Kingdom, initiated by the Labour Party after its landslide victory in the parliamentary election in 1997. The enactment of the so-called Human Rights Act from 1998, which incorporates the European Convention of Human Rights into British law, is of particular interest in this context since it means a clear challenge to the traditional concept of parliamentary supremacy, the main principle in British constitutional law for more than three hundred years. A new element of the separation of powers may therefore be said to have been introduced. The importance of this constitutional reform should thus not be underestimated. In fact, it is of general importance since it stresses some flaws or shortcomings in the concept of parliamentary supremacy, *i e* unlimited parliamentarism. The fact that the United Kingdom, the homeland of parliamentarism, now places restrictions and limitations on the traditional omnipotence of the Parliament may even be seen as yet another example of the global tendency towards a *judicialisation* of politics. Besides that, the incorporation of the European Convention of Human Rights also has important implications for the conception of human rights, the role of the courts and some other aspects of British law.

In "Arbitrary Democracy," political scientist *Sverker Härd* focuses on the electoral system, one of the most important instruments in the constitutional toolbox of a democracy. According to the theories of collective decision-making, there are several ways of reaching collective decisions. Consequently, there are various ways of distributing seats in parliament. These alternative decision methods and electoral systems are equally democratic. These theories of collective decisions emphasise the arbitrary nature of decision methods, which means that all democratic decision methods fall short of clearly naming a winning alternative.

When the decision methods are transferred to electoral systems it can be shown that the election results, and the allocation of parliamentary seats, are equally arbitrary. Different electoral systems will distribute parliamentary seats differently, although the preferences of the electorate remain the same.

What is the relevance of arbitrary decision methods to Swedish politics? The analysis rewrites modern Swedish political history. The voters are allowed to return to the ballot boxes and the votes are counted according to different electoral systems. This is done, practically, by conducting several analyses of the material in opinion surveys. Four electoral systems are discussed, all generated from the theoretical discourse: the proportional plurality method, approval voting, the Borda count, and the standardized utility method. The main result is that the election results differ with alternative electoral systems, also when the voter preferences are held constant. Differences in the distribution of parliamentary seats have effects on several central aspects of parliamentary politics.

In their contribution "Economic Effects of Political Institutions, With Special Reference to Constitutions," economist *Niclas Berggren* and political scientist *Peter Kurrild-Klitgaard* try to explain why there are theoretical reasons—stemming from new institutional economics and constitutional economics—to believe that there are relationships between political institutions, especially constitutional ones, and economic performance. At base, human action is considered sensitive to the incentives provided by the institutional structure. A survey of empirical studies which seems to lend support to this hypothesis is included, *e g* of the economic effects of institutions that entail economic and political freedom, of the rule of law, of various decision rules, of electoral systems, and of the separation of powers (*e g* federalism, popular initiatives, and bicameralism). Although the overall results are still inconclusive in some areas, the protection of private property rights seems central to economic growth, budget processes seem important to sound fiscal policies, and mandatory referendums on new spending programmes seem to limit government expansion. Also, in some settings, the division of power—both horizontally and vertically—exerts a positive influence on economic variables.

Finally, two articles, which express quite different views, deal with the issues of federalism and institutional competition.

Economist *Wolfgang Kasper*, in his "The Evolution of Constitutional Qualities under the Influence of Global Competition," adopts an evolutionary perspective, rooted in new institutional economics, on the issue of constitutional change. He notes that changing circumstances typically elicit experimentation with alternative institutional arrangements. If successful, imitation and the gaining of the critical mass will lead to the emergence of new internal institutions. If sufficient numbers of rules are altered, then the overriding rules—the constitutional provisions—will also be adapted for the sake of rule consistency. But institutional adjustment to new circumstances is far from inevitable, especially when we deal with external rules. This is so because the information feedback to the rule-makers from the impact of changed circumstances which individuals experience is more roundabout, because it involves cumbersome collective choices and hard-to-reach compromises, and because "lumps" of organized interests are involved.

Political scientist *Erik Moberg*, in his "Competition in Government by Federalism" discusses and evaluates the claim that government will benefit by competition within a federal structure. According to this argument such an arrangement will impede an exploitation of the citizens, and foster innovative legislation. He starts by making a few basic and crucial distinctions. One is between hierarchies and federations, which are both multilevel systems, but otherwise fundamentally different. The other is between real federalism and quasi-federalism. In a real federation legislation occurs at both levels. Quasi-federalism prevails when only other public decisions than legislative ones are allocated to different levels. After these distinctions have been made the discussion is limited to government competition within real federations. At the heart of all discussions on governmental competition are, according to Moberg, ideas about variety and mobility. The different states of a federation provide the variety, and the common federal level makes it is easy for the citizens to move between those states, and thus ensures mobility. In a unitary state, such as for instance Sweden, federalism can be achieved in two ways. The one is by fission, which means that the original state divides itself into a number of parts—the mobility is there from the beginning and the variety is created. The other is by fusion, which means that the original state, together with other independent states, creates a federation, such as for instance the European Union—the variety is there from the beginning and the mobility is added.

On the whole Moberg's conclusions do not favour the ideas of competition in government. For fission it is claimed that the risk of negative interaction between the levels, for instance federal subsidizing of the state level, and ensuing "races to the bottom", is substantial. It is also argued that the created legal system is likely to have low transparency and that therefore the incentives for rent-seeking and tricky behaviour in general will be great. Some of the expected good results of fission may rather, it is claimed, be obtained by decreasing the public domain and by giving ample room for private activities, for instance by vouchers. As for fusion it is claimed that high mobility, which certainly may be valuable, may be obtained through ordinary international co-operation and agreements, and thus without creating a real federation, and that this is preferable.

What these articles have in common is that they all deal with problems in modern democracies and that they illustrate the main topic of this book, namely, that constitutions do indeed matter. Many issues and all political systems are open to an evaluation in the constitutional dimension. No area of state activities may as such be considered too important, ancient or established to be questioned and analysed in rational constitutional terms, including the possibility of constitutional change. Thus, it is our hope that these articles will all contribute to, and maybe even initiate, further important constitutional discussions.

Stockholm and Lund in May, 2000
Niclas Berggren
Nils Karlson
Joakim Nergelius

*Why Do Constitutions Matter?**

James M Buchanan

I. Introduction

Let me say, at the outset, that I am encouraged by the very fact of this conference and by the several other initiatives that have been organized, and are ongoing, both in Sweden and in other parts of Europe. These efforts embody a gathering recognition that constitutions and constitutional structures are the instruments through which reforms must be effected if ultimate improvements in patterns of political outcomes are to be expected. Both as a career-long contractarian-constitutionalist and as a classical liberal advocate of tightened constraints on majoritarian politics, I can only express my personal satisfaction at this opportunity to participate in the dialogue. And as an academic observer, rather than a hands-on participant in politics itself, I join my fellows in holding to the faith that ideas can exert an ultimate influence on the course of events. We cannot let go of the belief that we do, indeed, have a raison d'être.

As you know, I have advanced various and familiar answers to the question posed by my title. I shall restrict my discussion here of these most familiar "reasons of rules" to a minimum, represented by the summary treatment covered in Section II. In

* This text was also the contents of a lecture by James Buchanan at the City University of Stockholm conference "The Constitutional Challenge", on 1 September, 1999.

Section III, I clarify the distinction that must be made between procedural and substantive constraints that describe any constitutional order. After these introductory arguments, I devote the major portion of this lecture to a treatment of two elements in an inclusive "logic" of constitutions that have not been adequately recognized. These separate elements are generally applicable, both at the level of individual and of collective choice. First, I suggest that constitutions matter because rules for making choices are themselves essential components of rationality. Second, constitutions matter because patterns of action are not fully determined through conscious choices.

II. Reasons for Rules

At the level of the individual, there are two broadly familiar reasons why a personal "constitution" may be deliberately designed and implemented—a rule or rules aimed specifically at constraining the set of available options that are predicted to be open.

First there is the argument derived from a "weakness of will," represented in the classical myth of Ulysses and the Sirens.[1] Practical modern illustrations are discussed variously under such rubrics as the economics of self-control, addiction, and temptation.[2] In a planning or prospective stage of rational reflection, the individual may recognize his or her own vulnerability to the then-attractive but ultimately damaging options that may be presented as possible. Protections or barriers may be erected that will exclude some or all such options from arising.

The second familiar argument applicable to the individual psychology of choice stems from the recognition that choosing is itself costly, and that there are quite rational reasons for restricting the number of options to be evaluated to a manageable set. This argument finds analytical and empirical support in the concept of bounded rationality associated with the long-continuing emphases of Herbert Simon.[3] As the discussion in Section V will indicate, the second of the "new" arguments to be developed in this lecture is closely related to, but is in another sense quite different from, this familiar logic of constitutional structure.

As attention is shifted from the level of the individual to that of the collectivity, or to the choices of members of and agents for coalitions who are authorized to act on behalf of the inclusive membership of a defined group, these reasons are supplemented by another that is surely more dominant in any consideration of political constitutions. An individual, as a citizen in an organized polity, may not be concerned about any weakness of her own will, and, further, she may be quite willing to leave all options open as they emerge. Support for the imposition of constraints on the operation of the political process may stem exclusively from the fear that a coalition of other persons may act, in the name of the collective unit with powers of enforceability, in ways that harm her own interests. Constitutional constraints are, in this setting, aimed at limiting the range and scope of actions that may be taken by others without the consent of the person in question but actions to which the person is locked in by the fact of collective unity.

This reason for rules arises in any collective organization that allows actions to be taken without any explicit consent of the individuals who are affected. Its importance is directly related to the difficulty that the members may face in leaving or exiting from the group. The by-laws or constitutions of organizations, or "clubs," that are competitors for voluntary membership need not be carefully examined. If, however, the exit is costly, or even effectively prohibited, as with national political units, constitutional constraints against exploitation assume critical significance. Political environments with intergovernmental mobility, as in federal structures, occupy in-between positions on the potential exploitation spectrum.

III. Procedural and Substantive Constraints

Before discussing the other reasons for rules, which I promised in the Introduction, it is useful to keep in mind that there are two basic forms or types of constraints, both of which may be described under the constitutional rubric.

Procedural constraints, as the modifying adjective suggests, operate directly on the means through which choices are made, while not directly impinging on the set of options open for selection. For example, a constitution, whether formal or informal, may specify that decisions made on behalf of an organized political unit must be authorized by a defined number or proportion of elected legislators in assembly. Such a provision may range from simple majority to approach Wicksellian unanimity. Any such a requirement is purely procedural; it places no boundaries at all on the set of feasible outcomes.

Substantive constraints, by comparison, act directly on the set of options among which selections are to be made. A constitution may specify that some physically feasible outcomes are simply "out of bounds," regardless of the procedures through which they may be reached. Either a simple or qualified majority in a legislative assembly or a parliament may act unconstitutionally, in most jurisdictions, if it enacts laws (including tax laws) that overtly discriminate against designated groups through the use of non-justifiable criteria, such as gender, race, or religion.[4]

These two conceptually distinct means of constraining actions, the procedural and the substantive, are often confused and intermingled in popular and political discourse. And the term *constitutional* tends sometimes to be reserved to apply only to substantive rules, thereby leaving both existing and potential procedural rules in unexamined limbo.

I want to emphasize, first, that everyone is a constitutionalist in one or both of these two stances. The ardent advocate of parliamentary majoritarianism, who rejects any and all efforts to restrict the choice set that defines the options open for majority coalitions, remains, at the same time, a strong constitutionalist in implicit advocacy of the procedural requirement that majority rule must, in fact, be honored, and, further, that majorities must be organized from representatives and /or parties that submit to periodic elections with an open franchise. Such a majoritarian is a constitutionalist no less than the person who supports, say, a rule that restricts the public sector growth to a stipulated share of the national product.

At one level or another, we agree: "Yes, constitutions do matter." The issue that remains involves the extent of the parameters within which political action is allowed to take place. The current relevance of the question: Why do constitutions matter? lies in the underlying supposition that the traditional and long-acknowledged constraints have, somehow, failed to prevent political overreaching, and, by implication, that we now need to reexamine the prospects for some nontraditional constitutional limits, whether these be procedural or substantive in nature.

IV. Rules as Rationality

In the Introduction I promised to discuss more fully two reasons for rules that are not widely recognized, as such, or at least in any explicit sense. The first of these reasons calls attention to the relationship between the critical characteristics of rational choice itself and the operative presence of learned rules.

Economists work within a conventional definition of rationality. There need be no explicit definition of a maximand, but whatever serves this role, its value is maximized when that which is scarce is allocated among competing claims or ends so that marginal increments to value, measured in the dimension of the maximand, are equal. The mathematics is that of the differential calculus. If utility is the term used for "that which is maximized," and the scarce resource is measured by a fixed amount of some numeraire (dollars), utility is maximized only when a dollar spent on each of the separately valued goods yields the same increment to utility.

Economists use this model of choice behavior both as a norm and as an explanation. The model offers normative advice as to how any chooser must choose in order to maximize utility. At the same time, and often simultaneously, the model is used as a description of the behavior itself, and hypotheses derived therefrom are subjected to empirical testing. A falsification of these hypotheses is often interpreted to reflect a failure properly to specify the maximand rather than any rejection of the postulate of rationality itself.

I want to suggest, however, that persons do not "naturally" behave in accordance with the norm so defined. In the first place, individual utility functions may not exist separately from the process of choice, and the *ex post* derivation of such functions may be misleading in suggesting that alternatives are, somehow, ordered on some unidimensional scalar. Conventional rationality need not be built into our psychological makeup, as if it is somehow genetically hard-wired. In order to act as dictated by the precepts of structural rationality, persons must *adopt a rule*; they must impose a "constitution" on themselves, one that will require that all of the relevant margins or dimensions of adjustment be simultaneously adjusted, that each choice be informed by the relevant opportunity costs of all options. Without the operative presence of such a learned rule, persons may naturally tend toward melioration rather than "as if" maximization, as some empirical evidence suggests.

As an illustration, think of a person in a supermarket. What will guide her purchases among the separate items? Does it not seem plausible that she might tend to equalize the *average* value from each outlay rather than marginal increments to value? Does the tangency position so beloved by economists meet the test of descriptive accuracy, especially in a setting of behavior that is naive or unlearned?

Perhaps the personalized constitution that dictates consideration of marginal adjustments is so familiar to us that we neglect its existence, but can the postulate of fully integrated personal behavior be quite so universal as economics seems to imply? Perhaps economists should pay more attention to the findings of psychologists.[5]

As we extend the examination of this reason for rules to the collective unit, its relevance becomes more apparent. Governments are not monolithic entities, the choices of which are best modeled as if emanating from a single mind. Governmental decision-making may be essentially processed through legislative assemblies, the actions of which reflect contrived consensus among members of separate coalitions. As observed, the legislatures are responsive to the demands made upon them by coalitions of differing composition. It would seem highly unlikely that the interdependencies or externalities among the differing legislative choices would be fully internalized within the calculus of individual participants, whether these be legislators themselves, as agents, or voters, as indirect choosers. Absent a rule or requirement that all of the interdependencies be reckoned with, that all margins of adjustment be simultaneously considered, there would seem to be no basis for predicting even tolerable "efficiency" in collective or political decision-making, even as evaluated by any single person.

Viewed in this light, we may interpret governmental budgets and budgetary processes, which are aimed to bring all of the fiscal accounts into the open as some sort of summary reckoning, to be essentially constitutional documents and requirements. These elements of the collective decision structure introduce integration among the separate components without, at the same time, imposing any requirement that the budgetary processes be modeled as if any defined maximand even exists.

Note that, as outlined here, this reason for rules, for a budgetary constitution that limits or constrains individual or collective choice behavior, does not find its logical support in either some predicted weakness of will, a desire to reduce or eliminate the choice options, or in some fear that others may impose damages to personal interests. The limits or constraints that are dictated by the rule of structural rationality are suggested as necessary means to the attainment of any objective, whatever this might be. As such, this reason for rules operates solely on the procedural level, but, even by comparison with other procedural constraints, this reason remains totally nonspecific.

Note also that the inclusively defined political constitution which embodies budgetary institutions that explicitly require simultaneous consideration of relevant taxing and spending margins need not be adjudged to validate the presumption that either individual utility functions or a "social welfare function" exists in any meaningful sense. All that is required is that each and every member of the body politic, and each as a potential member of some or another coalition, express preferences among the alternatives that reflect proper reckoning of genuine opportunity costs, as impacting on that person. The emergent patterns of outcomes from political processes may ultimately reflect no consistent ordering on any dimensional scalar. Recognition of this post-Arrow understanding of political processes does not, however, carry the implication that within any person's calculus of choice, as a participant in collective decisions, there remains no value in rules that require an explicit acknowledgment of the interdependencies or externalities among separately valued end objects.[6]

V. Rules as Default Options

There is a second "reason for rules," a second argument in response to the "constitutions matter" query that has not, to my knowledge, been sufficiently recognized. And, again, the argument seems equally to be applicable to an individual or a collective choice setting. Rules are needed to cover situations where choices are not explicitly confronted; rules provide back-up or default means for selecting among alternatives when attitudinal or institutional considerations intervene to make deliberative decisions impossible or, at the least, inconvenient.

As I noted in the Introduction, this logical basis for rules or limits is closely related to, but different from, that which concentrates attention on the efficacy of reducing the number of choice options, thereby obviating the necessity of balancing off an unmanageable number of adjustment margins. The reason for the adoption of rules as default options is not derived from the complexity of choice, as such. It is, instead, derived from the observed fact that, for any of many causes, actions may be taken without an explicit choice having been made or confronted. Rules serve, in this conceptualization, not as a means of economizing on costly choices by bounding the set of choice alternatives, but, instead, as *substitutes* for choice in those settings where, advertently or inadvertently, a choice situation does not or is not allowed to emerge.

As applied to individual or personal choice, this argument suggests the efficacy of the deliberative adoption of habits or conventions in behavior patterns. As the standard treatment of these behavioral attributes indicate, such rules may emerge non-consciously through an evolutionary process. But I am suggesting here that, quite apart from the evolutionary aspects, deliberative selection of and promotion of habits and conventions, as attributes of personal constitutions that define, direct, and determine behavior in certain settings, may be utility enhancing.

The reason for rules identified by this argument may seem, and may be, of trivial significance as applied to individual choice behavior. But it can become quite important when we consider collective or political actions, and especially when dynamic developments are brought into account. In many situations, collective decisions assume the form of establishing programs based on parametric criteria that do not, and cannot, be expected to remain stable through time. The results are that the effects chosen to apply to an existing choice environment become quite different as the underlying parameters change. In order to satisfy the presumed rationality criteria that informed the initial choice of program, continuous adjustments, period-by-period, would be required. But it is understood that such adjustments rarely, if ever, are observed to take place. And some default option, whatever this may be, takes the place of choice, and without a conscious sense of what is happening.

The argument may be specifically illustrated by examples from familiar settings in modern welfare democracies. The government, through its legislature, sets a structure of tax on personal incomes—a structure that incorporates some degree of progression in rates on a measured base. Let us say that this structure is chosen in year Y_0. It is allowed to stay in place through, say, years, Y_1, Y_2, . . ., Y_{10}. But suppose that, over the decade, real income increases, generally across all classes; for example, say that incomes double over the period. With the unchanged tax rate schedule, the revenue generated by the income tax will increase *disproportionately* more than the base itself. Personal incomes, for everyone, will be taxed at a higher rate; tax revenue will become an ever larger share in the total value of the economy's product. In this scenario, the default or back-up option, without explicit tax-rate adjustments period-by-period, is an increasing relative size of the public sector.

Such a result, if deemed to be undesirable at the time of the initial selection of the tax structure, can be prevented or forestalled only if a constitutional rule is put in place that defines an alternative default result in the absence of a period-by-period adjustment in structure. For example, the progressive rate structure may be modified to insure rough constancy in the overall share of the income taken in taxation, while preserving the tax-price differentials among the income classes, presumably motivated by distributional objectives. In a sense, some such rule would "constitutionalize" the tax structure by incorporating predicted dynamic patterns of change in the economy, thereby obviating any need for continuous adjustments.[7]

A second example involves built-in adjustments in spending or outlay patterns in modern welfare states. Pay-as-we-go systems of tax support for pensioners are in trouble almost everywhere because of a failure to project age cohort patterns accurately, leaving default options that create fiscal results that approach crises. A constitutional recognition of such prospects at the time of the programs' inception might have provided for built-in rules that would have made pension commitments dependent on the relationship among the cohort group sizes. The point made here should be evident. Properly drawn rules can provide default options for contingencies that may not explicitly enter the current choice calculus of the legislators during the debates on program initiation. This reason for rules takes on more relevance to the extent that the rent-seeking motivation of special interest beneficiary groups are taken into account. The agents for such groups, including those in legislatures, are strongly motivated to offer underestimates of future-period program costs, in the hope that, once approved, the default option will act so as to insure a program continuance at levels that would never have secured initial period approval.

During the several post-World War II decades in which governments, everywhere, have increased in size relatively to the nongovernmental sector, this reason for rules has come to be widely recognized. And measures have been introduced that may, effectively, be called "constitutional," such as sunset provisions, and requirements for a periodic reevaluation and a renewed approval of specific programs.

VI. Why Do Constitutions Matter?

In the preceding two sections, I have sketched out arguments in support of constitutional rules, inclusively interpreted, that are less familiar than those that explicitly inform the political, legal, and analytical discussion. The very term "constitutionalist" is often used pejoratively, as if, somehow, the position defined is "anti-democratic." The first step, therefore, in any response to the query as to why constitutions matter is that of emphasizing the fact that, indeed, we are all constitutionalists and in any of the several senses outlined above. Whether applied to private or to public choices, we want to pursue our objectives rationally, and some default options are surely preferred to others. Also, in reverting to the familiar set of arguments, we acknowledge a possible weakness of will in some situations, and we may also want to reduce the complexity involved in some choices. Further, the politics that we observe, anywhere and everywhere, does operate without the existing constitutional parameters, few of which we should want to repeal or to eliminate.

What and where, then, is the locus of the debate, dispute, and controversy? Disagreement arises only at the margins where extensions or contractions in constitutional constraints or limits become alternatives for action. As regards private choices, persons may or may not choose to impose more or less binding rules on their own behavior. Issues of relevance for discussion here only arise when collective action is involved, when the question becomes one of defining appropriate limits on the procedures of selecting political agents, on the actions of these agents, and on the range and scope of the collective action.

There is little or no basis for any claim that the now-existing set of constitutional parameters defining the boundaries for political action in any country is necessarily optimal or efficient, simply because such a set exists. And this conclusion should apply to any political unit, whatever may be its organizational-institutional structure or its political history. If the naive evolutionist norm that "everything that exists is efficient" is rejected, then constitutional reform becomes a subject matter for a critical and continuing discourse. And, as noted previously, in such a discourse useful distinctions may be drawn between procedural and substantive constraints, both as existent and as potential.

In one sense, constitutions must be seen to matter because, otherwise, we find ourselves, willy-nilly, in a setting of constitutional drift, where inattention to rules and rules' structures may allow patterns of results to emerge that are preferred by no one, then, now, and in the future.

The great game of politics, as it is observed to be played out in any jurisdiction, may not be operating within rules that anyone would have chosen in an explicit selection among constitutional alternatives. Evolutionary institutionalism is simply not enough to justify a continuing failure to look critically at the structural status quo. An explicit attention to constitutional rules, as such, may, of course, yield a defense of stasis, and, in some cases, may even suggest a loosening of the restrictions on the in-period political action by the legislative authorities. But we should also expect, and especially given the observed excesses of modern fiscal appetites, that some missing pieces might take the form of additional procedural and substantive limits.

In any case, the relevant dialogue should be carried on within the discourse of the constitutionalists and not between those who defend and those who criticize the existing status quo. Furthermore, it is important that the dialogue remain constitutional, as opposed to the ever-present temptation to engage political adversaries on the appropriateness of this or that political alternative, without any reference to the constraining rules.

Critics will have noted that, in this whole lecture, I have made no effort to respond to the simplistic claim that constitutions cannot matter because preselected rules can never prove to be enforceable against the emerging interests, whether those of an individual or of a dominant political coalition. Constitutional rules have the effect of increasing the costs of taking certain actions. It is more costly to take an action in violation of a rule than it is to take that same action in the absence of the rule. If this much be acknowledged, then rules must matter if the basic law of economics is accepted. An increase in the cost of any choice alternative will reduce the resort to that alternative. Demand curves do, after all, slope downward. Demand curves are neither horizontal (*e g*, constitutional rules work perfectly) nor vertical (*e g*, constitutional rules never work).

Constitutional structure and strategy must be informed, first, by a definition of those patterns of outcomes that are deemed undesirable and, second, by an implementation of limits on the procedures or results designed to forestall such patterns. A failure to think that "constitutions matter" can only produce attitudes of permissiveness that have proved damaging over far too many dimensions of modern social existence.

Postscript

A colleague who read the draft of this lecture suggested that my argument that the particular constitutionalism espoused is universal rather than American/provincial may not hold. It is suggested that the protection of individual liberty, including economic liberties, that seems to be embedded in American thinking about constitutions, need not be central to constitutional thinking more universally considered. The promotion of "justice," however defined, may take precedence over personal liberties. Perhaps I am naive in my implicit presumption that an acceptance of the argument that rules are needed to protect against the coercion of others through collective auspices implies a recognition of the fact that intrusions on liberties through the promotion of collective purposes (like social justice) are necessarily limited, perhaps severely.

Notes

1. For a seminal treatment, see Elster, 1979.
2. Thomas Schelling (Schelling, 1978) was an early contributor to this discussion.
3. See Herbert Simon, 1957.
4. In a recent book, written jointly with Roger Congleton, we have argued that generality, as a constitutional principle, is not as inclusively descriptive of existing constitutional practice as would be warranted by properly interpreted efficiency criteria (Buchanan & Congleton, 1998).
5. The argument summarized in the preceding paragraphs is more fully developed in Buchanan & Yoon (forthcoming).
6. From Arrow's impossibility theorem we know that any collective choice rule less than unanimity may fail to generate a fully consistent ordering of social outcomes. Under the standard assumptions, any outcome in the emergent set is Pareto-efficient (nondominated). But these assumptions impute rationality to each person as a participant in the collective choosing process. If, contrary to these assumptions, persons fail to internalize the potential externalities among the separate collective outcomes, the voting rule may generate outcomes that are Pareto-dominated by others that embody internalization within the individuals' choice processes.
7. National tax structures are, to an extent, normally treated as being constitutional, in that they are expected to be reformed only at periodic intervals rather than continuously. See Brennan & Buchanan, 1983.

References

Arrow, Kenneth, 1951, *Social choice and individual values.* New York: Wiley, 1951.

Brennan, Geoffrey & Buchanan, James M, 1983, "The tax system as social overhead capital : a public choice perspective on fiscal norms", in *Public Finance and Economic Growth* (*ed* Karl Roskamp) Detroit: Wayne State University Press, 1983, pp 46-56. [Proceedings of the 37th Congress of the International Institute of Public Finance, Tokyo, 1981.]

Buchanan, James M & Congleton, Roger D, 1998, *Politics by principle, not interest : toward nondiscriminatory democracy.* Cambridge & New York: Cambridge University Press, 1998.

Buchanan, James M & Yoon, Yong J, "Rationality as prudence : another reason for rules", in *Constitutional Political Economy*, vol 10 (3), pp 211-218.

Elster, Jon, 1979, *Ulysses and the sirens.* Cambridge: Cambridge University Press, 1979.

Schelling, Thomas, 1978, "Egonomics, or the art of self-management", in *American Economic Review,* 68 (May 1978), pp 290-94.

Simon, Herbert, 1957, *Models of Man.* New York: John Wiley & Sons, 1957.

Wicksell, Knut, 1896, *Finanztheoretische Untersuchungen.* Jena: Gustav Fischer, 1896.

Why Constitution? What Constitution? Constraints on Majority Rule

Aleksander Peczenik

I. Majority Rule and its Problems

Majority Rule Should be Constrained

Majority rule is at the core of democracy.

Yet, the majority rule can lead—and historically has sometimes led—to evil results. Several examples, *inter alia* the history of the French revolution, show that unlimited power of a democratically elected legislative assembly does not prevent oppression. So is the case for several well-known reasons. First of all, the majority can be tempted to unjustly further its own interests, at the expense of other persons. Second, the majority can make irrevocable decisions under the influence of a momentary passion. Third, the majority is subject to political action, at best argumentative, but often also manipulative. Politics is a struggle for power, not a debate over public good. The key participants in this struggle are organized in parties and interest groups. Unorganized individuals are thus handicapped. Fourth, majority rule is almost always executed *via* representatives. A consistent direct democracy can work in small states like ancient Athens or Swiss cantons, but hardly in big and complex ones. This opens the problem of political representation of interests. One of the most important properties of democracy consists in the fact that those in power protect the common interests of the citizens and weigh various particular interests against each other.[1] Yet, the representatives are also tempted to serve particular interests, not to merge them into the common good. Fifth, modern democracy is inextricably linked to nations, to nationalism and to the nation state. Majority decisions made within a state can be detrimental to important interests localized outside of it, for instance to the survival of refugees etc. Sixth—and this is the most profound objection:

> Formal democracy substitutes voting for moral judgement: it destroys ethical assessment. In a pure liberal-democratic system, there are no values, only competing opinions. Some democrats evade this objection, by simply saying that everything decided democratically is right. This claim seems logically untenable, since it can be applied to any regime of government.[2]

For these reasons, it is attractive to impose constraints on the majority rule.

Criteria and Values of Democracy

Indeed, the constraints are shown in the political language. Democracy is synonymous with the power of the people. This is the main idea of democracy. To be sure, the expression "the power of the people" is vague. Nevertheless, a study of the political language shows that it makes sense to proffer some facts as reasons for the conclusion that a state or a social order is democratic. These criteria of democracy make the central idea of the power of the people clearer. *Inter alia*, one may consider the following, partly overlapping, criteria: 1) political representation of the interests of the citizens, 2) majority rule, 3) participation of citizens in politics, 4) freedom of opinion, 5) some other human and political rights, 6) legal certainty, 7) division of power and 8) responsibility of those in power. Each criterion corresponds to a different value, which can be realized to a certain degree, more or less.[3] It follows that there are degrees of democracy.[4] On the other hand, no single criterion is sufficient for democracy.[5]

The criteria of democracy constitute a kind of a check list, making it easier to test whether a state is democratic. They also show a need of rules, promoting democracy. Thus, democracy is promoted when there are rules increasing the degree of political representation of the interests of the citizens, the influence of the majority of citizens, the participation of citizens in politics, the legal certainty, the division of power and the responsibility of those in power.

The Constraint of Generality

James Buchanan and Roger Congleton[6] proposed a more principled constraint on the majority rule, namely a generality constraint on the political process. Under this requirement, majorities would be prohibited constitutionally from treating different persons and groups differently. The generality principle is familiar in application to law; legal systems incorporate the ideal that all persons are to be treated equally. Buchanan and Congleton extend the generality norm to politics.

No doubt, generality is essential to both fairness and political efficiency. However, the requirement of generality is hopelessly vague. How general must political decisions be? One can construct a literally infinite set of general norms, justifying any political decision. Which norm is to be preferred then?

Consociational Democracy

The so-called consociational theory of democracy attempts to avoid some problems of majoritarian rule. The most important characteristic features of consociational democracy are the executive power-sharing and the government by grand coalitions.[7] Consociational democracy is approximated in the Swiss political system. According to Weiler *et al*:[8]

> The essential characteristic of consociational democracy is not so much any particular institutional arrangement as the deliberate joint effort by the elites to render the system functional and stable. The key element is what Dahrendorf has termed a cartel of elites.
> The pay-off of consociationalism seems to be the achievement of stability in the face of a high degree of social fragmentation which normal pluralist models cannot achieve. There are, naturally, implications for self-understanding of democracy in the polity. The democratic justification of consociationalism begins with the acceptance of deep and permanent fragmentation in the polity. Even in traditional constitutional pluralist democracies there is an acceptance that certain "high stake" decisions, such as constitutional amendments, require "super majorities" or other mechanisms which would be more inclusive of minorities. Consociationalism rejects the democratic legitimacy of permanent minorityship which is possible, even likely, for a fragmented polity operating a pluralist, majoritarian election and voting system. Consociationalism seems, thus, to enhance legitimacy in its inclusiveness and the broadening of ultimate consent to government. Theoretically, there is a strong case to be made for a consociational type of inclusiveness also in relation to at least certain areas of Union governance. If the international mode is, in fact, consociational, this would be a justification not from an efficiency and stability perspective but from a normative representational one as well.

Yet, the authors do not consider consociationalism to be a proper model for the European Union, because there are, of course, obvious problems.

> It will often be discovered that some elites, within the consociational cartel of elites, have very deficient internal democratic structures of control and accountability... Second, consociational power sharing is favourable to "status" social forces, those whose elites participate in the cartel. It excludes social forces that are not so recognized.[9]

Moreover, what happens when a consensus of the elites cannot be reached by reasoned argumentation? Is a desperate consensus, reached under the threat of a collapse of the whole system, always something good? Are the consensual mechanisms within a very broad political elite of the supermajority transparent enough? For example, do European citizens know enough about what reasons decide on an agreement reached within the Commission?

II. Majority Rule Constrained by Rights

A List of Rights

Back to more principled problems regarding the majority rule. Majority rule must be justifiable and constrained by something else than majority power. Human and political rights appear to be good candidates for constraining the majority rule. The protection of rights is in the focus of contemporary political philosophy.

Passing from philosophy to the law, it can be said that constitutions can, should and often do include rules making it difficult for the parliamentary representation of the majority to restrict political and human rights. Such rules are constraints on the power of the majority.

To be sure, the list of rights may vary in time and space. But in the Western world, there is a widespread consensus as regards rights. Who would protest against freedom of opinion, freedom of the press, freedom of information, freedom of movement, freedom of assembly, freedom of demonstration, freedom of association, freedom of religion; right to life, protection of physical integrity, right to privacy, protection of family life, right of private property, protection of correspondence; freedom from inhuman or denigrating treatment, freedom from compulsory labour, freedom from discrimination, right to due process of law; and equality before the law?[10]

Limitation of Rights

There is, however, a practical problem. The rules expressing rights and thus constraining majority appear to be unjust, unless limited by weighing and deliberation. They may also collide with each other—and this leads to difficult problems of their weighing and balancing. If thus limited, the rights appear to be too obscure to constrain majority. Moreover, there is a tendency to invent more and more rights, including social and economic ones. The inflation of rights makes the problem of limitation even more difficult.

The idea that the rights must be limited is accepted by international and national treaties and laws that seek to protect human rights. Here are some examples.[11]

- The Universal Declaration of Human Rights permits limitations "as are determined by law, solely for the purpose of securing due recognition and respect for the rights and freedoms of others and of meeting the just requirements of morality public order and the general welfare in a democratic society" (Article 29(2)).

- The European Convention of Human Rights permits limitations that are "necessary in a democratic society", in addition to other considerations related to the right in question.
- In the United States, the Supreme Court has developed a jurisprudence of limitation which requires laws interfering with certain rights having a "preferred position"—notably non-discrimination on the grounds of race and free speech—to be subjected to a superior level of scrutiny, "strict scrutiny".
- Article 19(2) of the German Basic Law states: "In no case may the essence (*Wesensgehalt*) of a basic right be encroached upon". The meaning of the "essential content" of a right has been much debated by legal scholars.

Such terms as "necessary in a democratic society", "preferred position", "strict scrutiny" and "essential content" indicate that there is a core of rights that should not be limited.

However, this core is defined in a vague manner, open to (moral) deliberation. In brief: Rights are constrains on the constitution, yet these constraints are open to limitations and the scope of limitations is open to deliberation.

The Need of Changeable Fixed Points

Last but not least, only advocates of a strong Natural Law philosophy would claim that contentually rich constraints on majority rule can be eternal. The constraints must be changeable—and they must be changeable in another way than *ad hoc*.

If the constitution could be changeable by simple majority decisions, the constraints would be too weak. In such a case, the constitution would simply be an advice to the majority not to abuse its own unlimited power. To make the constraints strong, one must make them more fixed than the majority decisions. This can be done by introducing qualified majority requirement for constitutional changes and/or by checking and balancing (the division of powers), especially by judicial review. The state would then be organized around the majoritarian principle, but its core institutions would be organized around the consociational principle.

The key insight is this: Constitutional constraints must be justifiable and difficult to change, yet flexible. We need constraints but we also need a non-arbitrary way to create, limit and change them.

III. Philosophical Underpinning 1: Justification of Majority Rule

A Relativist Justification of Majority Rule

The majority rule has a powerful moral justification. But this justification is controversial.

One can justify majority rule, *inter alia*, as follows. Political views compete with each other and it might be practically impossible to prove which is the right one. A majority decision is then a good means to achieve a peaceful solution.[12] Furthermore, one can justify majority rule as promoting some values that people usually respect, *e g* freedom and equality.[13]

A relativist justification of this kind is eminently plausible. It is, however, philosophically shallow. Here and now, majority rule appears to be a good conflict-solving device. However, in many centuries, since the Antiquity until the modern times, democracy had a bad reputation, precisely because it was regarded as promoting conflicts rather then solving them. Moreover, majority rule would be superior compared to such conflict-solving devices as a universal prescription of sedatives, even if the latter proved to be more efficient.

An appeal to values that people usually respect is not more profound, unless completed with some philosophical underpinning. For surely, the slaves living in a society where everybody is a slave of the king, would arguably respect the royal peace more than political competitions in a democratic system. Would this make slavery superior to majority rule?

Majority Rule in the Light of Preference Utilitarianism

Another way to justify the majority rule is to base it on preference utilitarianism. Majority rule is justifiable as an approximation of the calculus of human preferences.[14] To be able to decide what actions are morally good, one must pay attention to both the number of people having certain preferences and to the strength of these preferences. The majority rule takes care of the number of people. The democratic process also takes some care of the strength of the preferences. Though everyone has one vote and the votes have the same strength, politicians with strong preferences arguably have a relatively greater influence on democratic decision-making than the "silent majority".

Universalisability as a Super-Theory Behind Majority Rule and Its Constraints

Let me say something about preference utilitarianism according to R M Hare. Although Hare's theory is a continuation of a long tradition of British utilitarianism, including such thinkers as Bentham and Mill, it shows a remarkable originality. Hare supports his theory with an analysis of the moral language. He assumes that moral judgements are *i.* overriding, *ii.* universalisable and *iii.* prescriptive.

The requirement of universalisability is interesting in the present context because it brings us an important theoretical hope of being able to justify both the majority rule and its constraints. As stated above, majority rule is an approximation of the calculus of preferences. Constraints on the majority rule are justifiable as making the approximation closer. They are thus justifiable as eliminating the cases in which majority rule contradicts important preferences of people.

According to Hare, moral judgements are universalisable. Any moral judgement follows from a universal principle applicable to all persons, situations, actions etc. of a certain kind. The like ought to be treated alike. If one makes different moral judgements of situations that one admits to be identical in their universal descriptive properties, one contradicts oneself.[15] Hare is thus a rule utilitarianist. He does not hold that one ought to evaluate individual actions directly by reference to their utility. Thus one should not ask oneself whether breaking a particular promise, killing a particular person etc. would have the best consequences. Rather one ought to ask whether a universal rule permitting such actions would do it.[16]

A consequence of the universalisability and prescriptivity of moral judgements is that each person ought to adopt other people's preferences as his own.

> (T)he method of critical thinking which is imposed on us by the logical properties of the moral concepts requires us to pay attention to the satisfaction of the preferences of people (because moral judgements are prescriptive and to have a preference is to accept a prescription), and to pay attention equally to the equal preferences of all those affected (because moral principles have to be universal and therefore cannot pick out individuals).[17]

Furthermore, it follows that one ought to treat others as they want to be treated.

> It follows from universalisability that if I now say that I ought to do a certain thing to a certain person, I am committed to the view that the very same thing ought to be done to me, were I in exactly his situation, including having the same personal characteristics and in particular the same motivational states. But the motivational states he actually now has may run quite counter to my own present ones. For example, he may very much want not to have done to him what I am saying I ought to do with him... But... if I fully represent to myself his situation, including his motivations, I shall myself acquire a corresponding motivation...[18]

In brief, one ought to treat others in accordance with a calculus of preferences, taking account of what they want, how many people have a certain preference, and how strong their preferences are.[19]

One of Hare's original contributions is the following theory of two levels of moral thinking. The critical level includes a complete knowledge of other people's preferences in all thinkable cases, together with the weighing and balancing of these preferences. Only an "archangel" could perform such a task. The opposite of the "archangel", a "parole", lacks the ability to think "critically". He must stay at the intuitive level, *i e* merely follow his own moral intuitions and some established moral principles, for instance that one ought not to live at other persons' expense, lie to one's friends, neglect one's children, torment one's dog etc. The archangel could show that some intuitions and principles more or less correspond to the calculus of the preferences. The parole does not know it but still acts rightly. Ordinary people are neither archangels nor paroles but rather an approximation of both. They have some moral intuitions, follow some principles and have some ability to check whether these correspond to what other people wish.[20]

Both the majority rule and its constraints are thus placed at this intermediate level, between the archangelic preference calculus and a parole's blind obedience to the tradition.

Controversiality of Utilitarianism in General

However, one often criticizes utilitarianism in general and Hare's theory in particular by giving some counter-examples. Assume, for example, that most people show a (consistent and universalisable) system of preferences including a preference to seek happiness in liquors. Ought we then to create a community of alcoholics where spirituous drinks are for free? Assume that such a system includes a preference to exterminate people regarded as endangering the purity of the race. Ought we to kill the "subhumans"?

To answer such objections, Hare simply assumes that most people are neither drunks nor murderers. In this way, his theory comes close to natural-law conceptions, based on assumptions concerning human nature.

Another known objection is that at least some preferences of different persons are incommensurable. One has no right to regard some persons' satisfaction as a sufficient compensation for others' harm. In some cases, the objection is very plausible. One certainly ought not to kill John and transplant his organs to save five other people. In other cases, however, the utilitarian standpoint seems to prevail. It is plausible to assume that one may kill John, if this would prevent a nuclear holocaust with millions of victims. On the other hand, a critic may say that Hare assumes things he cannot know, first that people are good and then that the archangel would be able to correctly weigh the preferences of different persons.

Controversiality of Rule Utilitarianism in Particular

Finally, rule utilitarianism is open to another kind of objection. The rules that Hare's archangel would argue for must be very detailed. For very general rules would certainly leave out some important preferences. Thus, many philosophers feel compelled to reduce rule utilitarianism to act utilitarianism. For example:

> To be sure, we complicate the rule-utilitarian's description still further ...—and assess the utility of the practices of *making-poison-gas-in-order-to-support-one's-family-where-there-is-absolutely-no-other-means-of-acquiring-that-money*. But this is evidently little more than an attempt to dress up act-utilitarianism in rule-utilitarianism's clothes; for the point of making reference to the utility of a practice is progressively lost as that practice is more narrowly defined...
>
> Lyons has suggested that the rule-utilitarian can avoid these absurd conclusions by treating all general rules as having *ceteris paribus* clauses attached to them. Lying is wrong, other things being equal—but other things are not equal if we need to lie in order to save a life. In the same way people are free not to marry, or to grow food, *ceteris paribus*.[21]

This boils down to the view that the deep utilitarian justification can only be provided by act-utilitarianism, and that rule utilitarianism is just an approximation. The only alternative is to add a non-utilitarian constraint to utilitarianism which would mean that the basis of morality would not be utilitarian but hybrid. Needless to say that such hybrids are always open to objection. A philosopher is tempted to search for something deeper behind the hybrid.

On the other hand, the idea of morality as a hybrid between a calculus of preferences and the necessity of rules has an interesting counterpart in the theory of democracy. Majority rule approximates a calculus of human preferences. At the same time, constraints on the majority rule are constitutional rules. As rules, they are plausibly justifiable by a hybrid theory, whereas their justification on a purely utilitarian basis is controversial.

IV. Philosophical Underpinning 2: Justification of Majority Rule Constrained by Rights

Controversiality of Justification of Rights

Passing from the justification of majority rule to the justification of the constraints on it, we face difficult problems, as well. Whatever this justification may be, it appears to be controversial. What reasons compel us to think that all those rights are fundamental enough to work as trumps against the majority rule? To give the rights (some or all or them) the status of trumps, one needs a profound moral theory. But alas, such theories tend to be controversial.[22] No wonder that a relativist made the following emotional statement:

> There is no doubt that the doctrine of human rights belongs within a specific political tradition: the broad European liberal tradition. Human rights have also become a central element, in recent Anglo-American democratic liberalism (the type of political philosophy represented by John Rawls). But the liberal tradition is only one section of European political thought. Not only are human rights not universal, they are not even 'western' or 'European' ... Human rights are not culturally specific, they are politi-

cally specific. The human rights doctrine is a classic political ideology.[23]

This is a problem. We need constraints on the majority rule, yet the constraints are neither precise nor uncontroversially justified.

Deliberative Democracy

An interesting way out is the idea of deliberative democracy. If democracy is to work properly, the majority rule and rights must be completed with a deliberation procedure, allowing for more detailed and historically changeable justifiable standards. This insight gives rise to theories of deliberative democracy.

Deliberation is necessary when there may be reasons for deciding on one course of action but equally compelling reasons for deciding on another. Deliberation leads to an ongoing change of opinions. It is expected to continue into the indefinite future. Deliberation is the most just system for handling differences of opinion since it is based on reasons, not on the status of the participants or on force. Ideal deliberation is free, reasoned and equal, and it aims at consensus.[24]

A clear-cut theory of deliberative democracy would be a procedural one: Whatever results from free, reasoned, equal and consensus-oriented deliberation would then be defined as just and right.

Thus, according to Jürgen Habermas' discourse principle, norms of conduct are valid if and only if those possibly affected by them could accept these norms as participants in an ideal rational discourse. Rational discourse about public matters can only be achieved within the framework of the law. In this framework, the principle of rational discourse becomes the principle of democracy. According to this principle, legal norms may claim legitimate validity only if all legal consociates would accept them in a perfect discursive procedure of law-making.[25] In Habermas' "postmetaphysical thinking"[26], the same applies to basic rights. These are no longer grounded in religion or metaphysics but in the political process as such, and ultimately in rational discourse.[27] Since the agreement of all legal consociates is a "discursively purified" and, therefore, rational act of self-government, no valid norm can violate a basic right.

Habermas thus believes that a perfectly rational procedure of deliberation must render substantively correct results. However, this grand theory is open to objections.

- Cannot the perfect discursive procedure lead to unjust and unreasonable results, for instance because the participants are nasty or stupid? Or can the discourse be so perfect that it automatically corrects the results of nastiness and stupidity? We simply do not know it.
- Moreover, Habermas' procedural theory is "a total idealization."[28] As such, it is almost empty. Even if it could tell us that the results of the perfect discourse must be correct, we do not know—and cannot know—what final content the conclusions of the perfect debate would have.
- Neither can we know whether a result of the perfect discourse is final or not. Nothing precludes the discourse from going on indefinitely. But human beings are neither perfect nor eternal.

In brief, the purely procedural theory of democracy can at best give us an unreachable ideal to approximate, but not a standard to judge actual differences of opinion.

Consequently, Amy Gutmann and Dennis Thompson have developed a theory of deliberative democracy in which procedural principles are supplemented with substantive ones.

> A full theory of deliberative democracy includes both substantive and procedural principles, denies that either are morally neutral, and judges both from the second-order perspective.[29]
> The principles of deliberative democracy are distinctive in two significant respects: they are morally provisional (subject to change through further moral argument), and they are politically provisional (subject to change through further political argument).[30]

All those principles express,

> in various forms, the idea of reciprocity... Reciprocity suggests the aim of seeking agreement on the basis of principles that can be justifiable to others who share the aim of reaching reasonable agreement.[31]

According to their theory,

> reciprocity is not a principle from which justice is derived, but rather one that governs the ongoing process by which the conditions and content of justice are determined in specific cases.[32]

In spite of this substantive addition, this theory resembles Habermas' in an important respect. It is a second-order theory, formulating the ultimate goal of deliberation but being unable to tell us anything theoretically founded about the substantive results of it. Indeed,

> the theory is a second-order theory, because it is "about other theories" in the sense that it refers to first-order principles other theories have developed "without affirming or denying their ultimate validity".[33]

The Weakness of Contractarianism

The idea of reciprocity reminds us of the classical idea of the social contract. Indeed, contractarianism is influential again. The spirit of the philosophy of rights is eminently contractarian. For that reason, let me tell you something about the problems of contractarianism.

Compared with the classical Natural Law, the current contractarianism is more sophisticated, especially in its avoiding the daring philosophical theories of human nature, the objective existence of values etc. Yet, it continues to be controversial.

- One can attempt to base morality on a factual and explicit social contract. But this is a sheer science fiction. There simply never was a time when "everybody" got together and agreed to some set of arrangements.[34]
- A more promising way is to base morality on facts that are evidence of a tacit (implicit) social contract. Alas,

It is not clear what behavioural indications indicate tacit consent to just what arrangements.[35]

- Ideal hypothetical consent theories are more popular. They typically operate with a version of or surrogate for a 'veil of ignorance', behind which objectivity will be assured. Thus, Rawls claims that reason alone would be a sufficient condition for various individuals to unanimously accept certain principles of justice etc, if they were placed behind a "veil of ignorance" (or in "the original position of equality"). Rawls has characterized the "veil of ignorance" as creating a situation in which

> no one knows his place in society, his class position or social status; nor does anyone know his fortune in the dis-

> tribution of natural assets and abilities, his intelligence, strength and the like... This ensures that no one is advantaged or disadvantaged in the choice of principles by the outcome of natural chance or the contingency of social circumstances.[36]

But this is open to the following criticism:

> why should a person who was never actually in the ideal choice situation and never actually agreed to any terms there consider himself bound by what he would have agreed to if he had been there?[37]

In brief, how can a hypothetical contract create an actual obligation?

- One may wonder whether one can make a rational choice between competing versions of the veil of ignorance. How can a contractarianist justify the meta-level propositions about how thick the "veil" should be, that is what knowledge it must exclude and what not—if not by having recourse to the contract behind the very same veil of ignorance? Simply speaking, there is no way to be sure that a rational person behind the veil of ignorance would choose the Rawlsian maximin or Harsanyi's average utilitarianism[38] or even a form of gambling. All depends on the genetic dispositions together with the social roots of the person in question. To be sure, one can *define* the veil of ignorance in a way supporting one philosophy or another, but such definitions are *ad hoc* and hover in the air.[39]

To be sure, contractarianists may have their answers to such criticisms, in increasing complexity. But let us simply state that contractarianism *per se* does not settle the question what rights "exist" and are morally binding.

The Strength of the Weak Contractarianism

To be sure, ideal hypothetical consent theories make an important philosophical point. They elucidate the meaning of the idea of morally right and wrong. Thus, Scanlon's[40] contractarianism, very influential in current moral theory,

> ...holds that an action is wrong if its performance under the circumstances would be disallowed by any set of principles for the general regulation of behaviour that no one could reasonably reject as a basis for informed, unforced general agreement.

This is a very important—and in my opinion correct—observation. Alas, in spite of repeatedly calling his theory "contractarian", Scanlon does not tell us anything more than that about the content of the "contract" behind morality.

Scanlon's theory is philosophically strong only because it is contentually weak.[41] At the end of the day, Scanlon admits that the circumstances of social life may affect the content of morally right and wrong. This comes close to communitarianism and moral relativism. Scanlon describes the difference between his own theory and relativism, as follows[42]:

> I am not claiming that social meanings alone determine what is right and wrong. What I have done is, rather, to explain how these meanings can have moral force by placing them within a larger contractualist moral framework ... The account I have offered ... does this without presenting these judgments as deriving from any substantial universal principle.[43]

And he states the following:[44]

> How many valid moral principles are there, then? An indefinite number, I would say.[45]

This seems to be a much safer position than, for instance, Rawls's derivation of material principles from speculations about the veil of ignorance.

The key concept of Scanlon's theory is "reasonableness".

> Why to speak of "principles which no one could reasonably reject" rather than "principles which no one could rationally reject?"[46] (Whereas) "in recent years 'the (most) rational thing to do' has most commonly been taken to mean 'what most conduces to the fulfilment of the agent's aims'"[47], "reasonable" is a primitive concept, it includes "any consideration"[48] that people "have reason to"[49] regard as "morally significant"[50] and it is "an idea with moral content"[51].

In contrast to utilitarianism and other views which make well-being the only "fundamental moral notion"[52], Scanlon's theory

> can account for the significance of different moral notions, within a unified moral framework, without reducing all of them to a single idea.[53]

It can do this due to the use of the quite open concept of "reasonable".

Applied to rights, Scanlon's theory is a moral-philosophical counterpart of epistemology. It does not answer the questions "what is moral?" and "what rights do we have"? but rather "how is it possible to ultimately justify morality and rights?". Analogously, epistemologists cannot tell what we know, but merely how we can know that we know. It is quite significant that Scanlon builds on the undefinable notion of "reasonable".

Intermediate Conclusions

All right, all these theories are more or less philosophically sophisticated but what do they tell the politicians and constitution drafters? The intermediate conclusions of all this are what follows:

- The majority rule ought to be constrained.
- It can be constrained by a list of constitutionally entrenched rights and principles, but such a list must be both rich in content and justifiable in another way than *ad hoc*.
- Deep theories of democracy help us to understand why the constraints on the majority rule are required but they do not give us much as regards the substantive content of such constraints.

Political theory apparently has to sail between the Scylla of arbitrariness and the Charybdis of emptiness.

V. A New Approach to Deliberative Democracy: A Philosophy for Changeable Constraints

Some Theses to Defend

Yet, there is a hope. The basic insight into the theories of deliberative democracy is right. Let me repeat: If democracy is to work properly, the majority rule and rights must be completed with a deliberation procedure, allowing for more detailed and historically changeable justifiable standards. In particular, I will argue for the following theses:

- It makes sense to constrain the power of majority by such rules as those expressing human and political rights. This is the case despite the fact that those rules are open to limitations. The limitations are merely a special case of general defeasibility of rules. All or almost all rules are defeasible. Defeasibility alone is no argument against rules.
- Neither is the changeability of such rules a good reason against them. Obviously all man-made rules are changeable.

Decisive and Contributing Reasons[54]

To be able to discuss the point and function of flexible and changeable constitutional constraints on majority rule, we must understand the place of legal rules in legal argumentation.

At first, let us make a distinction between decisive and contributing reasons. Decisive reasons determine their conclusions. If a decisive reason for a conclusion obtains, the conclusion must also obtain.

Some decisive reasons determine their conclusion without any possibility of an exception. Other decisive reasons are, however, *defeasible*. Sartor introduces the idea of defeasible reasons as follows:

> Most real-life situations provide grounds for conflicting arguments. In such circumstances, one cannot limit oneself to considering just one argument, since 'the truth depends on a balance to be struck between two sets of conflicting reasons' (Mill...). Therefore both in issues of law and in issues of fact establishing the probative strength of an ar-

> gument requires considering the arguments to the contrary (counterarguments). Has the argument been attacked by any counterarguments? Can it withstand those attacks?
>
> If an argument cannot uphold the attacks we say that it is defeated, *i e*, we cannot accept it as a guide for our judgements and behaviours. Since in the law, and more generally in all practical contexts, the possibility that an argument is defeated cannot be excluded in advance, legal arguments are defeasible.[55]

A decisive reason is defeasible if, and only if

- it is decisive on the basis of the information one possesses, and
- it is possible that the addition of information not previously available converts the reason to a non-decisive one.

In other words, a decisive-and-defeasible reason determines its consequences in normal circumstances, but does not determine its consequences if the circumstances are not normal.

Contributing reasons, on the contrary, do not ever determine their consequences by themselves. There can be contributing reasons that plead for and against a particular conclusion. It is the set of *all* contributing reasons concerning a particular conclusion, both the reasons pro and con, that determine whether the conclusion holds. One can also say that contributing reasons are *pro tanto reasons*.[56]

Thus, there are arguments which are not deductively valid, but which are nevertheless "good" in the sense that their premises provide sufficient support for their conclusions. One can call such arguments valid in a broader sense. Deductively valid arguments are then a subset of the arguments that are valid in this more general sense.[57]

Principles as Contributing Reasons for Legal Conclusions

One may also distinguish between rules and principles.[58] Rules apply in an all-or-nothing fashion, in the sense that if a rule is applied to a case, the conclusion of the rule gives the legal consequence of the case. Principles, on the contrary, only generate reasons that plead for actions that contribute as much as possible to goal states. Once we know that a certain provision is a principle, or that a certain practice or deliberation expresses a principle, we know that it is a contributing reason, not a decisive reason. Principles have a dimension of weight and reasons based on principles need to be weighed against reasons based on colliding principles, if there are any. All use of principles in legal reasoning is for weighing. A lawyer is not supposed to just follow a principle. He is supposed to confront it and to weigh it against other principles relevant to the case. In this sense, the use of principles is never a matter of routine. Principles are always used as defeasible.[59]

The Ideal Theory of Rules: Legal Rules as Decisive Reasons

Reasoning with principles leaves a lot of uncertainty, because of at least two grounds. The first ground is that if there are colliding reasons, it will often be unclear how these reasons are to be balanced. For sure, most persons will be able to cut the knot if necessary, but often it is hard to predict in advance how the relative weight of reasons for and against a conclusion will be. The second ground is that it is often unclear what precisely are the reasons pleading for and against a conclusion in a particular case. Contributing reasons are based on principles, but it is equally well possible to argue that a principle exists because some facts are recognized as reasons, than the other way round.

To restrict the uncertainty, one needs rules. The different logical roles of rules and principles can be accounted for by the assumption that rules *exclude* the application of principles, rather than by saying that rules *outweigh* the principles.[60] Another way to approach the same issue is to state that legal rules generate *decisive reasons* for legal conclusions. Assume now that we know that a certain legal provision is a rule, or that a certain practice expresses a rule. Once we know that it is a rule, we can say that it is a decisive reason, not merely a contributing reason. The facts of a case that make a rule applicable form, if the rule is applied, a decisive reason for the conclusion of the rule. Such a decisive reason need not be balanced against other reasons any more. If there are colliding contributing reasons, the decisive reason wins by definition, so there is no need for weighing.

Exceptions to Rules

Yet, legal rules are *defeasible* reasons for legal conclusions, since they admit exceptions. Exceptions to the rule exclude its application. If there is an exception to a rule in a concrete case, the rule is not applied to that case. There may even be exceptions concerning a class of cases.

The theory that rules generate decisive reasons implies that two rules with inconsistent conclusions cannot both apply. If two rules with logically incompatible conclusions are applicable in the sense that their conditions are satisfied, there must be an exception to at least one of them.

Another reason to make an exception is when there are other reasons not to apply the rule which outweigh the applicability of the rule as a reason for application. In other words, there is a balancing of reasons for and against the application of a rule. If the outcome of this balancing is that the rule must be applied, then the conclusion of the rule follows indefeasibly. However, if the outcome is that the rule ought not to be applied, an exception to the rule is raised, with the effect that its conclusion does not follow.

It should be emphasized, however, that these observations merely sum up the logical possibilities. They do not give directives about what should be done in legal practice. Moreover, the logical distinction between rules and principles does not answer the question whether some rule-like entity in the law is a rule or a principle. The basic idea behind this distinction is that some legal authority has explicitly made rules, and that they summarize and replace the reasons that inspired them. This idea is linked to that of legal certainty and the image of a lawgiver who makes rules and the courts that merely apply them. This picture is, however, an idealization, since the application of legal rules in some cases involves a kind of law-making through interpretation. Moreover, legal certainty may play a role in the case of principles, too. But principles also have a significant substantive weight being independent from the authority of the lawgiver, whereas rules typically derive their weight from authority.

In the real world, the use of legal provisions varies. In most cases, legal provisions are applied if their conditions are satisfied and they generate decisive reasons. With hindsight, such cases may be called routine ones ('easy' ones). Once a case is identified as a routine case, no values and no choices are necessary to solve it. A decision in such a case follows from an established legal rule together with the description of the case.

Sometimes, however, there are major objections against treating legal provisions as 'hard' rules. Then one is prepared to make an exception. Such cases are with hindsight called 'hard' ones. There are also hard cases resulting from interpretation problems.

Thus, the existence of hard cases is due to two factors: the influence of values on the law and the indeterminacy of the language. The use of rules varies between routine cases and "hard" cases. The everyday use of rules is not to weigh them. Weighing rules is not an everyday defeasibility, but a hard-case defeasibility. For a lawyer has a good reason to ask questions about the weight of rules first when these are very objectionable.[61]

The distinction between the two readings of legal provisions is complicated by two circumstances: First, the relevant factors change in the course of time. The lawyers must thus solve cases about which the lawmaker did not think. For that reason, legal provisions that originally almost always were read as rules may increasingly be read as principles. Second, the authority of the law-making agency is not absolute. In some cases, let it be rare ones, a lawyer may have a reason to treat the case in question as hard in spite of the fact that the law-making agency already did consider this kind of cases when making the rule.

Nothing Wrong With Defeasible Constitutional Constraints on Majority Rule

With the theory of defeasibility in mind, let me repeat: It makes sense to constrain the power of majority by such rules as those expressing human and political rights. This is the case despite the fact that those rules are open to limitations. The limitations are merely a special case of the general defeasibility of rules. All or almost all rules are defeasible. Defeasibility alone is no argument against rules. Neither is the changeability of such rules a good reason against them. Obviously, all man-made rules are changeable.

Consequently, it makes sense to impose a high institutional threshold on constitutional change, albeit all rules are defeasible. Defeasibility is one thing, the change of rules is another. Even if the application of a rule constraining the majority power is open to limitations, the rule will still remain a part of the constitution and remain an authority reason for future cases. Only a change (not merely defeasibility) can remove the rule from the constitution, and this change must—for the reasons discussed above—be relatively difficult to make.

However, a major problem is left to discuss. Both the constitutional legislation, creating the constraints on the power of the majority, and the interpretation of such constraints are justifiable by moral or almost moral the unconstrained majority rule, because it is less arbitrary than moral deliberation?

The answer to this question that is defended here is that moral deliberation is much more reliable than the sceptic thinks it is. However, this is the case only if some conditions are fulfilled. One of these conditions is that the persons performing the deliberation intend to keep the moral beliefs as coherent as possible. Another one is that an expertise is possible as regards some fragments of the coherent value system.

VI. The Role of Legal Knowledge in Deliberative Democracy

An Extended Theory of Deliberative Democracy: Procedural Principles, Substantive Moral Principles and Legal Principles

Let me thus draft a constructive solution to the problem of the indeterminacy of the constraints on the majority rule. The starting-point is a theory of deliberative democracy, very much like Gutmann and Thompson's. There are some provisional[62] principles of rational discourse, some provisional principles of democratic procedure and some provisional substantive principles, moral and political. They give us an idea of the goal of the political process but not much information about its correct outcome.

If we wish to have such information, we must rely on the tradition of legal principles, as formulated by the courts and legal research.

Strong Courts and Strong Legal Dogmatics

To facilitate democratic deliberation, we need both strong courts and strong legal dogmatics (in other words, legal doctrine, *scientia juris*).[63] The necessity of strong courts is eminently plausible. In many countries, the courts check and balance the elected legislative through the material review of constitutionality.[64] But why legal dogmatics? Because the courts left alone—without the aid of legal research—would tend to focus on particular cases to be decided. They would have difficulties in reaching the level of abstraction necessary to an optimal coherence of the law. If the limitation and change of the constitutional constraints on majority rule were left to the courts alone, the risk of arbitrariness would not be eliminated. On the other hand, the courts that have access to the *scientia iuris* can base their opinions on a more elaborated value system. With the aid of legal dogmatics, the courts can regard the law as *ratio scripta*, not as a mere product of the will of the politicians. This insight is not new. In Rome, Emperor August gave a few outstanding jurists the authority to answer difficult legal questions, *ius publicae respondendi ex auctoritate principis*. In the Middle Ages, *communis opinio doctorum* was an important source of the law. Most institutions of continental private law have been originally drafted by legal researchers.

What is new is the insight that legal research is necessary in the context of constitutional constraints on the majority rule. For the majority cannot constrain itself. It must be balanced by something else. If this "something else" are the courts, the problem of legitimacy is almost impossible to solve. Surely, the popular majority and its representation have greater legitimacy than the courts. Only if the courts act on the basis of Reason they can be a legitimate counterpart of the majority rule. And Reason cannot be exhausted by a particular decision-making. It also needs a more abstract deliberation, given by expert jurists.

The work of legal dogmatics is almost always value-laden. To be sure, jurists make a distinction between a cognitive inquiry into the law as it is (*de lege lata*), and justified recommendations to the lawgiver, *de lege ferenda*. But as every legal scholar knows, the distinction between *de lege lata* and *de lege ferenda* is not clear-cut. The legal dogmatics is a good example of a practice of argumentation pursuing knowledge of the existing law, yet in many cases leading to a change of the law.[65]

In brief, legal dogmatics has three interesting properties at the same time:

- It works on a high level of abstraction
- It creates a system of beliefs
- It has normative components
- It has a claim to pursue knowledge of the law.

Legal dogmatics may produce exceptions to statutory rules. A more interesting phenomenon is that it may produce "subsidiary" general rules, from which the statutory rules are exceptions. In classical Continental systems, such general rules are often produced by general "theories" such as the previously mentioned theory of adequate causation. But not even Swedish law, programmatically hostile with regard to such theories, can avoid general rules created by legal dogmatics.[66]

The hierarchies of rules and exceptions press down the necessity of weighing. Instead of weighing all the relevant circumstances of the case, one follows the rule and uses the weighing first when in doubt whether there is an exception that should defeat the rule.

Legal dogmatics aims at obtaining a coherent totality.[67] It aims at presenting the law as a net of principles, rules, meta-rules and exceptions, at different levels of abstraction, connected by support relations.[68]

More About Coherence

Back to our main problem. We need a non-arbitrary production, limitation and change of the constitutional constraints on the majority rule. Any substantive theory about what is non-arbitrary in this context is hopelessly controversial. For that reason, let us try a meta-theory. The meta-theory presented here is coherentist.

A non-arbitrary justification is equivalent to a continuous looking for coherence. At a given moment, we have the best constraints on the majority rule, but then the world changes, and we discover a possibility to make another coherent theory, justifying another cluster of constraints.

What is coherence, then? *Jan Wolenski* incorporates the idea of coherence into the so-called classical definition of knowledge.

> According to this definition, knowledge consists in a true justified belief. More explicitly, the phrase '*X* knows that *A* '... is equivalent to the conjunction of the three following condition (a) *X* believes that *A*, (b) *A* is true, and (c) *X's* belief is (correctly) justified ... Where can coherence enter into the classical definition of knowledge? The condition (c) is the only suitable place. Thus, we can combine the classical theory of knowledge with a coherence theory of justification.[69]

The most profound problem of the coherentist justification is its circularity. If nothing is an unshakable foundation of knowledge and everything may be doubted, I need reasons for reasons for reasons ... etc. To avoid an infinite regress, a coherentist must accept circularity. Indeed, a coherent system of acceptances and preferences is like a network of argumentative circles, mostly quite big ones. Metaphorically, a chain of arguments, sooner or later, bites its own tail, and thus may be represented as a circle. In such a chain, p_1 supports p_2, p_2 supports p_3 etc.... and p_n supports p_1. "Support" is only explicable as a reasonable support: p_2 follows from p_1 together with another premise, say r_1. This premise r_1 is reasonable, which implies that it is a member of another such circle.

What is important here is the complexity of the structure of the circle.

> Higher complexity of an appropriate kind gives extra safety, makes the circle more *robust*, less vulnerable to destruction ... To put it metaphorically: nets are safer than chains.[70]

Such a chain of arguments has no obvious end. To be sure, foundationalists claim that all knowledge ultimately rests on evident foundations, such as empirical data. However, foundationalism has been rebutted: the alleged foundations are not certain. The main competitor of it is coherentism. Roughly speaking, whatever is justifiable, is justifiable on the basis of the background system of beliefs (or—in Keith Lehrer's terminology—of acceptances and preferences.[71]

But cannot a coherent system of acceptances and preferences be false, "isolated from the world"? To understand coherentism, one must keep in mind that neither scepticism in general nor this isolation objection in particular has any privileged status, compared with other beliefs. It is merely a competitor of other beliefs. If someone says that my personally justified, coherent system of acceptances and preferences is not "objectively" justified, he has to win the competition with my system.[72] Consequently, if I want to argue that I am justified in accepting or preferring x, I must appeal to my system of acceptances and preferences at that time. And if the sceptic wants to convince me that I am wrong, the appeal to my acceptance system at that time is again all he can make. If what the sceptic accepts is less reasonable than the objection, he loses. The loss means that the acceptance in question is defeated. Lehrer has taken reasonableness as a primitive concept.[73]

Segments of Knowledge and Complexity of Deliberative Democracy

The combination of coherentism and non-reductionism, advocated by the present author[74], can be summarized by the following metaphor. A scientific theory claims to be coherent with a certain branch of science. Legal theories claim to be coherent with the law. Normative political theories claim to be coherent with the basic principles of the political system. Generally, each fragment of knowledge claims to be coherent with a certain branch of knowledge. The branches are like islands, they do not form a single continent. But they are connected with each other. A plausible way of stating this connection is to say that there are bridges between them. The metaphor of bridges echoes "bridging implications"—a term used, among others, by Hector-Neri Castañeda.[75] But a better metaphor is a ferry-boat, not a bridge.[76]

The idea of mutually linked segments of knowledge helps us to understand that deliberative democracy must be a complex process. All deliberation, if reasonable, must approximate coherence, but coherence of what? In some contexts, the law itself—in a more or less positivist sense—must be interpreted as coherently as possible. In those contexts, the deliberation performed by lawyers is superior to a political deliberation by laymen. In other contexts, the best way to deliberate is to participate in the political process. In other words, some normative problems are apt to be reasonably solved on the basis of legal expert knowledge, whereas other normative problems are apt to be reasonably solved on the basis of political debate. In other words, any deliberation is for an audience[77], and different social roles are imposed on different audiences.[78]

In both contexts, the same kind of deliberation, moral or almost moral, justifies introducing (and withdrawing) exceptions to rules and changes of rules. The main differences between introducing defeasible exceptions and changing rules are the following. Only the law-maker can make and change binding rules. On the other hand, legal practice can introduce (and withdraw) exceptions to rules. Such exceptions do not change the authoritative formulations of rules. They only change the interpretation of rules.

Consequences de Constitutia Ferenda

Obviously, a modern constitution cannot include a *jus respondendi* of law professors. Our culture is too democratic for that. But the Constitution can include provisions concerning rights and other rules constraining the majority and it can make the courts guardians of the application of such provisions. The changes of rules constraining majority must pass double-check: they must be acceptable to the majority and they must be reasonable. Reasonableness is a matter of deliberation that is not arbitrary. Such deliberation can be to a great extent articulated by the courts. Whether the courts then would play their role in an optimal manner, depends on the legal culture, not on the constitution alone. And a highly developed legal culture includes a developed legal dogmatics.

Notes

1. *Cf, e g,* Eikema Hommes, 1982, pp 31 ff.
2. Treanor, 2000.
3. The main idea of democracy, the power of the people, is more or less intimately related to each criterion. It has thus a clear conceptual connection with the fact that those in power represent the interests of the citizens, follow the will of the majority and permit the citizens' participation in politics. The connection with freedom of opinion, other basic rights, legal certainty, the division of power and responsibility is less obvious. One may reasonably interpret the concept of democracy in two ways. According to one interpretation, the enforcement of the rights, legal certainty, the division of power etc. merely constitute a causal condition of democracy. According to another interpretation, they constitute a conceptually necessary condition of a fully developed democracy. *Cf* Peczenik, 1989, 36 ff.
4. *Cf* Ross, 1963, pp 92 ff.
5. *Cf* Peczenik, 1989, p 37.
6. Buchanan & Congleton, 1998.
7. Lijphart, recently, 1999.
8. Weiler *et al*, 1995.
9. *Id.*
10. *Cf, e g,* ch 2 of the *Swedish Constitution and the European Convention of Human Rights.*
11. *Cf* Nergelius, 1996 *passim.*
12. According to Kelsen, 1929, p 101, democracy is a consequence of value relativism, though an objectivist can also be a democrat. Generally speaking, majority rule is attractive because it is a procedural idea. Procedural theories are attractive to value relativists. Surely, we cannot agree about substantive values, but we agree about the majoritarian procedure, they would argue.
13. See also Kelsen, 1929, p 3. Taxell, 1987, pp 32 ff, also mentions security.
14. Peczenik, 1989, p 38.
15. Hare, 1981, pp 107 ff.
16. This option allows Hare to avoid two forms of the standard anti-utilitarianist criticism. *i.* First, a critic may point out that a particular action may have the best consequences, yet be morally unjustifiable because a universal practice to perform such actions would not have the best consequences. This criticism is fatal to act-utilitarianism, but not to rule-utilitarianism. *ii* A critic may also ask: Why ought one to concern oneself with the interests of other people at all? Hare could answer: Moral language is such that if I wish to use it, I must respect the interests of others.

17. Hare, 1981, p 91.
18. Hare, 1981, pp 108-109.
19. This formula creates some problems. It "involves putting oneself ... thoroughly into the other person's place, so that one takes on his desires, tastes, preferences, ideals, and values as well as his other qualities... But then it hardly makes sense to talk of putting oneself in his place; hardly any of oneself is retained. Rather, what one is trying to do is to look at things from one's own and from the other person's point of view at once, and to discover action-guiding principles ... which one can accept from both points of view. Or rather, since there is not just one person but infinitely many, from all actual points of view... But... it is doubtful whether any principles will pass so severe a test... We must lower our sights a little, and look not for principles that can be wholeheartedly endorsed from every point of view, but for ones that represent an acceptable compromise between the different actual points of view" (Mackie, 1977, p 93).
20. Hare, 1981, p 44 ff.
21. Scarre, 1996, p 128.
22. A credulous reader may open any text-book in moral theory to check this depressing truth.
23. Treanor, 2000 b.
24. *Cf* Cohen, 1989, pp 146-7.
25. See Habermas, 1992, pp 135 ff. On the criticism of Habermas's principle of democracy see, for example, Alexy, 1994, pp 227-38; *cf* also Peczenik, 1995, pp 69-71, p 523.
26. See Habermas, 1992, pp 83, 87, 127
27. Consequently, in Habermas's catalogue of rights, priority is given to basic political rights (guaranteeing the democratic process), see Habermas, 1992, pp 155, 320, 529.
28. Alexy, 1994.
29. Gutmann & Thompson, 2000, p 163.
30. Gutmann & Thompson, 2000, p 167.
31. Gutmann & Thompson, 2000, p 167.
32. Gutmann & Thompson, 2000, p 167.
33. Gutmann & Thompson, 2000, p 162.
34. Bass, 1999.
35. Bass, 1999.
36. Rawls, 1971, p 12.
37. Bass, 1999. This question has been asked by, among others, Ronald Dworkin.
38. Reidhav, 1999.
39. "(T)he effort to design the ideal choice situation so as to preclude unfair outcomes of bargaining is likely to be question-begging. If we know what a fair outcome is, then, of course, a choice situation can be designed such that rational contractors will choose that outcome. But,

if we know what a fair outcome is, why not implement that fair outcome (or a member of the set of fair outcomes) immediately? There does not appear to be any need to build into the choice situation the conclusions we wish to reach at the end", Bass, 1999.

40. Scanlon, 1998, p 153.
41. He gives some examples of moral principles, such as the Rescue Principle and the Principle of Helpfulness (Scanlon, 1998, p 224) but clearly does not assign a privileged position to them. Neither does he restrict the reasonableness of rejecting a principle to a person's complaint that has to do with its effects on him or her (Scanlon, 1998, p 229). Thus, he does not disregard external preferences (in contrast to Dworkin).
42. Scanlon, 1998, p 342.
43. Consequently, Scanlon (Scanlon, 1998, p 228) restricts the validity of Rawls's principles to a particular context.
44. Scanlon, 1998, p 201.
45. Scanlon's theory is thus very convincing, albeit, in my opinion, it has no satisfactory answer to the question how we can have moral obligations with regard to infants, mentally ill persons or animals. His answer (Scanlon, 1998, p 183) is that "in deciding which principles could not reasonably be rejected we must take into account the objections that could be raised by trustees representing creatures in this group who themselves lack the capacity to assess reasons". The idea of a hypothetical trustee who (Scanlon, 1998, p 184) would object to inflicting pain seems to be *ad hoc*. Another example of an ad hoc point in the theory is this (Scanlon, 1998, p 234): Scanlon's account of the majority principle in contractarian terms is that—hen life is at stake—the members of the smaller group could not reasonably reject the principle that requires one always to save the greater number. Whatever non-contractarian ideas one can conceive, Scanlon would put them into his framework of hypothetical reasonable contract.
46. Scanlon, 1999, p 191.
47. Scanlon, 1999, pp 191-2.
48. Scanlon, 1999, p 217.
49. Scanlon, 1999, p 216.
50. Scanlon, 1999, p 217.
51. Scanlon, 1999, p 194.
52. Scanlon, 1999, p 216.
53. Scanlon, 1999, p 216.
54. Based on Hage & Peczenik, 2000.
55. Sartori, 2000.
56. *Kagan* "distinguishes between *prima facie* reasons (reasons "at first sight") and reasons *pro tanto* ("insofar"). Kagan suggests that certain considerations may appear to be reasons for a decision or a judgement at first sight, so to speak, but then turn out to be irrelevant when

other aspects of the situation have been taken into consideration ... A *prima facie* reason can be *undercut*, so to speak, by other aspects of the situation, and then drop out of sight altogether. It is different with *pro tanto* reasons .... Such reasons are never undercut, even though they may be outweighed in some cases by reasons to the contrary, if the latter are stronger ... The idea of weighing reasons seems natural for the *pro tanto* reasons, but it is not appropriate for the *prima facie* reasons that aren't *pro tanto*" (Rabinowicz, 1998, p 21. *Cf* Kagan, 1989, p 17 and Peczenik, 1998, p 57).

57. One might ask what is the use of defeasible arguments, which may be invalidated by additional information. Some readers may have been raised with the view that there is one way of correct reasoning, and therefore one logic which characterizes this way of correct reasoning. The introduction of defeasible reasoning next to deductively valid reasoning shows that this view is not fully correct, or at least one-sided. Arguments may be evaluated by means of several standards. One standard, that of deductive logic, is very severe. Arguments that satisfy this standard guarantee the truth of their conclusions on the basis of the truth of their premises. However, since the standard of deductive logic is very severe, many real life arguments that are useful do not satisfy it. To be able to distinguish between good and bad arguments outside the range of deductively valid arguments, one can develop other standards, standards for defeasible reasoning.
58. In a way that is closely related to the opinions of both Dworkin (Dworkin, 1978) and Alexy (Alexy, 1978, 1989, 1985 and 2000).
59. The most common form of principles is that of goals, or—in the terminology made famous by Robert Alexy (1978, 1989 and 1985)—*'Optimierungsgebote'*. A goal is a state of affairs that is considered to be favourable. Often it can be realized in varying degrees, as is illustrated by the goal that there is no pollution. If this goal exists in a legal system, the fact that a measure contributes to it is a reason why this measure should be taken. Conversely, if a measure detracts from the goal, that is a reason why this measure should be avoided. The more a measure contributes to a goal, or the more important the goal, the stronger the reason. It should be noted that goals occur in legal systems under different names, such as 'principle', '(human) right', '(legally protected) interest', 'value', etc.
60. *Cf* Raz, 1975, pp 35f.
61. In this context, one may answer the question asked by Wlodek Rabinowicz (Rabinowicz, 1998): "*Can rules be weighed?* According to Peczenik, the process of weighing reasons is central to justification. Ideally, every reason can and should be weighed against other reasons. Applied to law, legal judgments are arrived to by such a process of weighing where what is weighed are not just values and principles but also legal *rules*." He contrasts my position with *Dworkin's*, charac-

terized as follows: "There is no room for weighing a valid rule against other considerations. Certainly, the *interpretation* of a rule might involve some process of weighing... But when a particular interpretation has been determined, there is no room anymore for weighing the rule against other considerations, according to Dworkin. If it is valid, the answer it supplies must be accepted. It would be interesting to know why Peczenik rejects this position".
Now, we do not reject the difference between rules and principles. But we do say that both rules and principles are defeasible, and that the defeat is a result of weighing.

62. (*prima facie, pro tanto*)
63. Peczenik, 2002.
64. Nergelius.
65. Peczenik, 1995, pp 312 ff. *Cf* Savigny, 1993, p 197: Legal dogmatics does not create accomplished rules but a method that continually changes the rules. The very idea of distinguishing between normative and descriptive components of legal dogmatics is contestable, too. *Cf* Eng, 1998, pp 310 ff, on fuzzed statements *de lege lata*.
66. For example, there is a general rule that ideal damage is to be compensated only if there is an explicit statutory rule about it. *Cf* Hellner, *Skadeståndsrätt* (5 ed, and SOU, 1995:33) with references to some legal research. Another example is the unwritten rule that the same activity that invalidates a contract according to 3 Chapter, Contracts Act also leads to liability in torts. A further example is the principle "nemo subrogat contra se" (an information from Jan Hellner).
67. *Cf* Peczenik, 1998, *passim* on epistemological problems concerning coherence in the law.
68. To obtain the goal, legal dogmatics uses such traditional means as an argumentation *per analogiam, e contrario, a fortiori,* an analysis of the purpose of the law together with more modern tools, *e g* "law and economics". The argumentation used in order to achieve coherence involves not only description and logic but also evaluative (normative) steps. For example, arguments based on statutory analogy, argument e contrario, goal reasoning in the law etc. are certainly not purely descriptive. The choice of approach in legal dogmatics is also based on normative standpoints, even if the chosen approach itself claims to be "value-free", evaluations are, for instance, necessary to opt for the law-and-economics approach. The evaluative reasoning steps are justifiable by reasons, ultimately by moral reasons. Thus, the system of law as it is presented in legal dogmatics should not only be internally coherent, but should also be harmonized with its background in the form of morality and (political) philosophy. As a consequence, the description of the law as a coherent whole must be descriptive as far as the conventional and the institutional aspects of the law are concerned, and evaluative where the background of the law in morality

and political philosophy is concerned. To be sure, an analysis of a particular case need not involve philosophical considerations but it must be possible to find intellectual bridges between a lower and a higher level of abstraction.

69. Wolenski, 1998, p 25 and 31. Alexy and Peczenik (Alexy & Peczenik, 1990) have developed a number of criteria of coherence. The more the statements belonging to a given theory approximate a perfect supportive structure, the more coherent the theory. Logical consistency is a necessary condition for perfect coherence at any moment. Logical consistency is, however, no sufficient condition for coherence. There are some additional criteria of coherence. *Ceteris paribus*, the degree of coherence of a theory, depends on such circumstances as how great a number of supported statements belong to it; how long chains of reasons belong to it; how great a number of connections exist between various supportive chains belonging to the theory, such as how many chains of reasons support one and the same conclusion; how many statements belonging to the theory are relevant in the type of reasoning the theory uses; how great a number of universal statements belong to the theory; how great a number of general concepts belong to it; how high the degree of generality of these concepts is; how great a number of cases it covers, and how great a number of fields of life it covers. The degree of coherence is determined by weighing and balancing the criteria.
70. Rabinowicz, 1998, pp 19-20.
71. Lehrer, 1997, p 3.
72. *Cf* Lehrer, 1990, pp 176 ff.
73. *Id*, 1990, p 127.
74. Peczenik, 1998.
75. Castañeda, 1980.
76. I am grateful to Håkan Gustafsson for this profound insight. For a bridge is fixed, it stands where it is. A boat, on the other hand, can find different ways between the islands, depending on the (intellectual) weather. Islands are knowledge, boats are philosophy. Philosophy is not fixed. Philosophy has no paradigms. Yet, philosophy links the part of knowledge into a coherent whole. The merit of reductionism is to look for the links. Its mistake is to look for fixed bridges, instead of using philosophical (metaphysical?) ferry-boats.
77. *Cf* Aarnio, 1987, pp 221 ff.
78. *Cf* Peczenik, 1995, pp 305 ff.

References

Aarnio, Aulis, 1987, *The rational as reasonable*. Dordrecht, Boston, Lancaster & Tokyo: Reidel, 1987.

Alexy, Robert, 1978, *Theorie der juristischen Argumentation*. Frankfurt/M: Suhrkamp, 1978.

—, 1985, *Theorie der Grundrechte*. Baden-Baden: Nomos, 1985; Frankfurt/M: Suhrkamp, 1986.

—, 1989, *Theory of legal argumentation*. Oxford: Clarendon Press, 1989 (translation of Alexy, 1978).

—, 1994, "Basic rights and democracy in Jürgen Habermas' 'Procedural paradigm of the law'", in *Ratio Juris* 7 (1994).

—, 1998, "Coherence and argumentation or the genuine twin criterialess super criterion", in *Coherence in the law (ed* Aarnio, Alexy, Peczenik, Rabinowicz & Wolenski). Lund: Juridiska föreningen, 1998.

—, 2000, "On the structure of legal principles". In press in *Ratio Juris*.

Alexy, Robert & Peczenik, Aleksander, 1990, "The concept of coherence and its significance for discursive rationality", in *Ratio Juris* (vol 3, no 1 *bis*), 1990.

Bass, Robert, 1999, "Pure contractarianism: promise, problems and prospects". http://ernie.bgsu.edu/~roberth/pcn.html. January 1999.

Buchanan, James, M & Congleton, Roger D, 1998, *Politics by principle, not interest : toward nondiscriminatory democracy*. Cambridge: Cambridge University Press, 1998.

Castañeda, Hector-Neri, 1980, *On philosophical method*. Indianapolis: Nous Publications, 1980.

Cohen, Joshua, 1989, "Deliberation and democratic legitimacy", in *Contemporary Political Philosophy (ed* R E Goodin & P Pettit). Cambridge [MA]: Blackwell (Blackwell Philosophy Antologies, 4), 1997 (Originally published in 1989).

Dworkin, Ronald, 1977, *Taking rights seriously*. Oxford: Oxford University Press, 1977.

Eikema Hommes, Hendrik van, 1982, "Rechtsstaat und das Prinzip der Repräsentation", in *Rechtstheorie*.

Eng, Svein, 1998, *U/enighetsanalyse : med saerlig sikte på jus og allmenn rettsteori*. Oslo: Universitetsforlaget, 1998.

Gutmann, Amy & Thompson, Dennis, 2000, "Why deliberative democracy is different?", in *Social Philosophy & Policy* (vol 17, no 1).

Habermas, Jürgen, 1992, *Faktizität und Geltung : Beiträge zur Diskurstheorie des Rechts und des demokratischen Rechtsstaats*. Frankfurt/M: Suhrkamp. (Citation from 4 ed, Darmstadt, Wissenschaftliche Buchgesellschaft, 1994.)

Hage, Jaap & Peczenik, Aleksander, 2000, "Law, morality and defeasibility", in *Ratio Juris (in press)*.

Hare, R M, 1981, *Moral thinking*. Oxford: Oxford University Press, 1981.
Kelsen, Hans, 1929, *Vom Wesen und Wert der Demokratie*. Tübingen, 1929 (2 ed). Reprinted: Aalen: Scientia Verlag, 1981.
Lehrer, Keith, 1990, *Theory of knowledge*. London: Routledge, 1990.
—, 1997, *Self-trust : a study of reason, knowledge, and autonomy*. Oxford: Clarendon Press, 1997.
Lijphart, Arendt, 1999, *Patterns of democracy : government forms and performance in thirty-six countries*. Yale Univ. Press, 1999.
Mackie, John L, 1977, *Ethics. inventing right and wrong*. Harmondsworth: Penguin, 1977.
Nergelius, Joakim, 1996, *Konstitutionellt rättighetsskydd : svensk rätt i ett komparativt perspektiv*. Stockholm, Fritzes, 1996.
Peczenik, Aleksander, 1989, *On law and reason*. Dordrecht, Boston & London: Kluwer, 1989.
—, 1995, *Vad är rätt?* Stockholm: Norstedts, 1995.
—, 1998, "Second thought on coherence and juristic knowledge", in *Coherence theory of law (ed* Aarnio, Alexy, Peczenik, Rabinowicz & Wolenski). Lund: Juristförlaget, 1998.
—, 2002, *Scientia Juris*. Will be published 2002 by Kluwer.
Rabinowicz, Wlodek, 1998, "Peczenik's passionate reason", in *Coherence theory of law (ed* Aarnio, Alexy, Peczenik, Rabinowicz & Wolenski*)*. Lund: Juristförlaget, 1998.
Rawls, John, 1971, *A theory of justice*. Oxford: Oxford University Press, 1971.
Raz, Joseph, 1994, *Ethics in the public domain : essays on the morality of law and politics*. Oxford: Clarendon Press, 1994.
Reidhav, David, 1999, "Utilitas et pactum et industria". Mimeographed. Lund, 1999.
Ross, Alf, 1963, *Varför demokrati?*. Stockholm: Kronos, 1963.
Sartor, Giovanni. 2000, "Argumentation, convention and legal validity". Draft.
Scanlon, T M, 1998, *What we owe to each other*. Cambridge [MA] & London: The Belknap Press of Harvard University Press, 1998.
Scarre, Geoffrey, 1996, *Utilitarianism*. London & New York: Routledge, 1996.
Taxell, Lars Erik, 1987, *Demokrati*. Åbo: Åbo Akademis förlag, 1987.
Treanor, Paul, 2000, http://web.inter.nl.net/users/Paul.Treanor/dem.wrong.html. March 22, 2000.
—, 2000 b, http://web.inter.nl.net/users/Paul.Treanor/human.rights.html. March 22, 2000.
Weiler, J H H, Haltern, Ulrich & Mayer, Franz, 1995, "European democracy and its critics : five uneasy pieces", 1995 Jean Monnet Working Papers, http://www.law.harvard.edu/programs/JeanMonnet/papers/papers95.html

Wolenski, Jan, 1998, "Coherence and knowledge", in *Coherence theory of law (ed* Aarnio, Alexy, Peczenik, Rabinowicz & Wolenski). Lund: Juristförlaget, 1998.

The Moral Standing of Democracy[1]

Mats Lundström

> Democracy as such cannot confer any benefits upon the citizens and should not be expected to do so. In fact democracy can do nothing—only the citizens of the democracy can act ... Democracy provides no more than a framework within which the citizens may act in a more or less organised and coherent way.
> (Karl Popper, 1972, p 350)

Introduction

In our political language the word "democracy" is one of the most positively value-laden. Often it is given the same meaning as the concept of the Good Society. John Dewey once defined democracy as "the truly human way of living" (quoted in Tännsjö, 1992, p 7). Used in this way, the word "democracy" tends to be empty of empirical content, and synonymous with whatever the speaker or writer thinks is the ideal society. It serves a persuasive function, not a descriptive or explanatory function.

This conceptual drift is an obstacle for a rational discussion on the merits and effects of democracy. It is not only a problem for the debate on democracy, but for democracy as a political system. The legitimacy of democracy presupposes a common understanding of the meaning of "democracy". But it does not necessarily presuppose a shared set of values that makes democracy desirable. Political actors may defend democracy for different reasons, but they must know when they defend the same institution and when they do not.

It is often maintained that we live in an era, when democracy has no viable alternative. Democracies are not threatened by any important totalitarian movements. But the political system, which has proven to be the best soil for democratic institutions —the nation-state—, is eroding. Migration, transnational and supranational political structures undermine the nation state as political unit. In search for political institutions for a transnational society, there is a need for a normatively detached perspective on democracy. It cannot be a matter of definition that democracy is *the* good society. The value of democracy must be an open question, decided by empirical and normative analysis. Democracy must be 'secularised'—conceptually and as well as politically.

The normative connotations of the term democracy have, in a historical perspective, been neither neutral nor positive, but negative. The view that prevailed, until the end of the 18th century, was influenced by Aristotle's classification of democracy as one of the "degenerate" forms of government (Aristotle, 1988, p 61).[2] The "ideal" constitutions were supposed to govern the state in accordance with *virtue*, *i e* the teleological morality which Aristotle espoused; under the "degenerate" constitutions, by contrast, the state was an instrument for the realisation of *self-interest* by individuals or groups. Democracy serves, according to Aristotle, the interests of the poor, which conflicts with the principles of virtue and equity. Since the poor are in a majority, however, democracy issues in less mischief that the other two degenerate forms (tyranny and oligarchy). Democracy, then, is the best of the degenerate constitutions. Since all ideal constitutions tend to decay over time into their degenerate form, it was wisest, in Aristotle's view, to choose democracy.

The positive value loading of "democracy" has certainly increased since Aristotle's time, but his negative argument for democracy retains its relevance still. In liberalism democracy has been viewed with scepticism throughout (Bobbio, 1993). It is ascribed no independent moral status, and is accepted primarily for *pragmatic* reasons. A typical exponent of this critical acceptance of democracy is Karl Popper, who regards democracy as way to secure an *Open Society*, which is his label for a *liberal* society (Popper, 1974, p 350).[3] It is the best way to avoid tyranny. Churchill made the same point in his famous comment that "democracy is the worst form of government, except for all the others" (quoted in Ravich, 1992, p 85).

Historically, democracy has proved liberalism's best ally. The liberal acceptance of democratic government appears to rest on a maximin strategy (Hermansson, 1992, p 85). Democracy offers protection against the worst political misfortunes, but it is no guarantee for a good society according to liberal standards. Although democracy implies respect for liberal *political* rights, it does not necessarily entail respect for other liberal rights, which are included in the notion of rule of law; the relationship is empirical rather than logical. It is possible that a society organised on a democratic basis will diverge from liberal ideals in important respects.[4] Regardless of the different conceptions of a just society in the liberal tradition we may conclude that, according to liberal doctrine, democracy has mainly an instrumental value, not an intrincical one.

The notion that democracy has a value in it self is rather rare; it is more common to regard it as an important—but not eternal—institutional tool in the construction of a good society. Democracy enjoys legitimacy because it is thought to aid in the realisation of certain moral values—over the short or the long term (*c f* Nelson, 1980). A review of the history of political ideas, reveals that democratic procedures has been defended on the basis of a great range of ideas (Harrison, 1993): Individual freedom, autonomy, moral development, utility and equality.

The purpose of this essay is to discuss *a*. the nature of an appropriate *definition* of democracy in a political as well as in a scientific discourse and *b*. various *normative principles* that have been suggested in the defence of democratic institutions. I also *c*. examine the relation between democracy and *constitutionalism* in view of different arguments for democracy. Constitutionalism, *i e* different kinds of constraints upon democratic decision making represents the only viable "alternative" to democratic decision making as such. In the dominant liberal strand of thought, democracy and constitutionalism are two sides of a good Polity. But the need for constitutions is based both on a democratic as well as non-democratic principles (Holmes, 1995, Sejersted, 1988). The negative and the positive relationship between democracy and constitutionalism can be equally important.

The analysis is based on a fairly broad classification of different arguments. The discussion is outlined according to four main headings:

I. A naturalistic conception of democracy
II. Normative theories of democracy: three types
III. Democracy and constitutionalism
IV. Concluding remarks

I. A Naturalistic Conception of Democracy

In a discussion of definitions of democracy in a Swedish context, it is difficult not to mention Herbert Tingsten's arguments. The way of defining democracy was a central theme in Herbert Tingsten's discussion on what he called a "democratic super ideology". "You are a democrat, but in addition to that you are a conservative, a liberal or a socialist" (Tingsten, 1945, p 57; my transl). In order to share a common belief in democracy, you must define democracy in a way that is neutral to different ideological positions taken within in a democracy; it must be possible to share a commitment to democracy and at the same time disagree on substantial political matters.

This argument for defining democracy leads to a so-called procedural conception of democracy. According to Nils Elvander, a prominent disciple of Tingsten, the argument for a procedural conception of democracy is *normative*; it is necessary for the acceptance of democratic institutions among the political actors within democratic institutions (Elvander, 1975, p 120). The normativity of this definition lies in its purpose—to create a "democratic super ideology" which is believed to be necessary condition for a stable democracy. On closer examination, this argument for *defining* democracy as a procedure is consequentialistic. The validity of the argument is contingent on the effects of conceptions of democracy on the legitimacy of democracy in certain political context. As a support for a procedural definition this argument is not robust; if another definition were more efficient in the pursuit to create a "democratic super-ideology", you should choose that.

Furthermore, this kind of consequentialist considerations when defining democracy presupposes a goal that is logically independent of democracy. Otherwise the argument is circular. If your goal is to create a stable democracy by means of defining democracy, you must have a notion of what democracy is, regardless of what people think it is or want it to be.

This type of pragmatic strategy for defining democracy is morally dubious, because it is manipulative. Jack Lively makes this point in his critique of a so-called realist notion of democracy, held by Schumpeter and Eckstein. According to Lively they redefine democracy in order to avoid the accusation of defending an undemocratic system, *i e* a rule by elites (Lively, 1975, p 80).

To choose a definition of democracy in order to reach a political goal can be effective, but it creates problems for an open and rational political discussion on the value of democracy. Tingsten's discussion of the definition of democracy was based on a concern for intellectual honesty and terminological clarity, which, indirectly, is a prerequisite for democracy. In the 1960's he strongly criticised the "New Left" for making a "content-oriented" definition of democracy. This kind of definition he regarded as a linguistic trick to make your political opponents appear as "undemocratic". His point was that you cannot stipulate a political content in the notion of democracy, *i e* a socialistic mode of production, which can be, or not be, the result of a democratic decision making. If you follow democratic rules for decision making, it is an open question whether the decision will be for or against socialism (Boström, 1988, ch 1). Democracy does not entail socialist principles, neither as a prerequisite nor as an outcome. The critique of prescribing a "content" in a definition of democracy, does not imply that a proper definition should lack content, but that it should lack *irrelevant* content. The relevant content, according to Tingsten, concerns legal rules that ensure a popular control of the government.

Formally speaking, Tingsten accused the New Left for using a too *narrow* definition of democracy, because it contained redundant conditions. A possible outcome of democracy was made an analytically necessary condition for democracy. One may say the New Left proposed a *persuasive definition* of "democracy".[5] The positive emotive meaning of "democracy" is transferred to "socialism". This is the general function of content-oriented definitions of democracy; a desirable, but controversial, outcome of democracy is defined in terms of "democracy".

Tingsten's definition of democracy is not normative in a political or moral sense, but in an intellectual sense. The content-oriented definition is simply a misuse of language (Boström, 1988, p 162). An effect of this misuse can be a crisis for democracy as political system, because it is not neutral with respect to dominant political ideologies. But political neutrality, in the sense that political actors can (as a matter of fact) accept a definition, is not a condition for choosing a definition of democracy. If that were the case, you should defend any definition that is *comme il faut* in a certain political culture. Historically, collective ownership has been viewed as a necessary element of democracy in many countries (in former communist states). The content-oriented definition proposed by the New Left would be "neutral" in these countries.

Tingsten's concern was *conceptual* neutrality, not political neutrality. The condition of conceptual neutrality must be derived from a theoretical reconstruction of the core meaning of "democracy" in a lexical sense. According to Tingsten, the usual political language suggests that "democracy" means "a specific organisation of governance of the state, an organisation, in which regular and legally independent popular opinions—in practice mainly through elections—are the central political elements" (Tingsten, 1933, p 58; my translation) The same linguistic point is made by Barry , who contends that: "Surely, the normal way of understanding 'democracy' is to suppose that it refers to the internal distribution of power within a political unit" (Barry, 1974 p 493). "Democracy" denotes, in brief, a system which gives a demos power to rule a state. If democracy means "rule of the people", it must be an open question what the people decide when they rule.

It should be noted that the logic of Tingsten's argument against a socialistic "content-oriented" definition of "democracy", applies equally to a liberal "content-oriented" definition. If you include elements of a liberal order, *i e* rule of law, a division of power, liberal virtues etc., in the definition of democracy you commit the same linguistic fallacy as did the "New Left". The fact that liberalism, like the belief in democracy, is very common in Western political culture, is not an argument for including liberal principles in the definition of democracy. Although a liberal doctrine of democracy could be politically neutral, it is not conceptually neutral, which was Tingsten's point in his procedural notion of democracy.

What is then a "true" definition of democracy? Only lexical definitions can be assigned a truth-value, because they supposed to be descriptive statements of linguistic habits. If you have the ambition to describe a use of language or an etymological meaning of a concept, you must investigate how it is used or has been used. Often, several meanings are assigned to a term. Yet, an interpretation of a term and conceptual reconstruction of its meaning can be more or less faithful to ordinary language. The choice of different possible interpretations and conceptual reconstructions can, however, be based on lexical as well as scientific considerations. In fact, lexical and scientific considerations must be combined (Sartori, 1984). If your purpose is to explicate the meaning of "democracy", then a procedural notion (or any other notion you find) should be chosen regardless of its political effects. Furthermore, you can defend a procedural notion, as matter of semantic analysis, without expressing a normative opinion about the moral or political value of procedural democracy.

A definition is normative in the obvious sense that it stipulates a rule of language. This rule can be based on an empirical investigation of how it *is* used and on a methodological consideration of how it *should* be used in order to be a useful tool in a certain discourse (a scientific or political). All definitions are normative in a linguistic sense, whether or not they stipulate a descriptive or normative, *i e* evaluative *use* of the word in question. If a definition stipulates a normative use of a word (*i e* "justice"), it is still a linguistic rule without other normative implications; it simply gives the user of the language an opportunity to express a value judgement. When the definiens (the description of the meaning of a word) contains value-terms, such as "good" or "just", the definition stipulates a judgmental use of the definiendum (the word to be defined).

Definitions that permit normative use of words may be appropriate, depending on the linguistic context. But "democracy" may, in a conceptual reconstruction", be defined in descriptive terms, if you intend to give a name to a political system, which can be evaluated by normative principles. This use of "democracy" is said to be "contested" (Gallie, 1956). But that is no reason to refrain from pursuing a descriptive use of the word.

One must, however, differ between two contestations regarding "democracy": the linguistic and the judgmental. The first concerns the meaning of the word; the second concerns the judgement that a sentence containing "democracy" expresses, given the linguistic rule. You can agree about the meaning of "democracy" is descriptive, but disagree about whether something is a democracy, because the word is *appraisive* (Connolly, 1993, p 22). This is a matter of deciding a zero-point on a scale (Dahl, 1998, p 198.)

If "democracy" has a normative connotation, *i e* if it means "just" or "good" it is, in general, more difficult to reach a judgmental agreement, than if it has a factual connotation. Nevertheless, a factual connotation of a word does not rule out emotive *associations* when using the word. Even though the factual connotation of "democracy" is established, the word can be *value-laden*, not in a semantical sense, but in emotive or psychological sense. Descriptive words, referring to facts, can give rise to bad or good feelings depending on our attitudes towards these facts. The word "Nazism" or "torture", for instance, has a factual meaning, but they are strongly value-laden, because most us dislike the phenomena they denote. The same goes for "democracy", but in the other direction; most of us like the political facts it denotes. The word "democracy" triggers positive associations and feelings. But that is matter of political values and culture; the goodness of "democracy" must not be logically entailed in a definition. If we release "democracy" from normative connotations and emotive associations, our judgement of democracy may be more autonomous.

Of course, there is no objective or eternal definition of "democracy". If we adhere to a nominalistic notion of concepts, a definition is a matter of linguistic convention. But we can deliberate on these conventions in order to clarify the language, and, thereby, clarify our empirical, theoretical and normative reasoning.

If the question of the value of democracy, as political system, is to be meaningful, "democracy" should be defined *naturalistically, i e*, in descriptive and value-neutral terms (Roemer, 1999). Indeed, otherwise it can be rather pointless to investigate whether democracy leads to the realisation of the moral values it denotes—as meaningless as studying whether just institutions are just (Tännsjö, 1992, p 7). It is of course possible to define democracy in terms of one *specific* value, say political fairness, and then analyse its relation to *other* values, say social justice. Yet, the important thing is to know what we are talking about—about an institution or about a normative principle. In the case of "democracy" it is quite obvious that the word can be used as a purely descriptive term *or* as a label for a normative principle. Democracy can, in the same way as the right of private ownership, be studied as a matter of fact *or* as a matter of justice. There is no reason to confuse a pure descriptive analysis of institutions and a plea for the normative principles that are supposed to legitimise them.

One common view among theorists of democracy is that definitions of democracy express an evaluation. Jack Lively, for example, argues that "any attempt to define democracy [...] must involve some commitment to political positions, some positive evaluation of the justifications proffered for different kind of political systems" (Lively, 1975, p 2). According to Lively, democracy means political equality. It is perfectly possible, however, to define democracy in the same manner as does Lively, and yet refrain from embracing the *principle* of political equality.

Political equality can be regarded as a state of affairs *or* as a normative principle. One can investigate whether or not, as an empirical matter, political equality actually prevails. One can also debate whether or not such a state of affairs is morally desirable. The principle of political equality can, of course, serve as an argument in this debate. In an analogous way, one can distinguish between democracy as an empirical state of affairs and democratic values as a set of normative principles; democratic normative principles can be used as arguments for democratic institutions.

A meaningful definition of democracy should enable us to measure the degree of democracy empirically. According to Norberto Bobbio, the concept of democracy has retained its descriptive content ever since antiquity (Bobbio, 1993, p 17). "Democracy" means "rule of the people". The vagueness of this definition does not change the fact that is descriptive.

What has changed over the course of history is not the concept of democracy, but the various *doctrines* about democracy, *i e*, the views concerning democracy's advantages and drawbacks (Bobbio, 1993, p 17).[6] The institutional recommendations how to implement democracy has also changed. The idea of direct democracy in the Athenian era has been replaced by the idea of representative government. But this modification has also a descriptive element, independent of the normative ideas behind it. Robert Dahl coined the term "polyarchy" to describe the indirect, representative democracy (Dahl, 1979). Thereby he tried to save the original descriptive content of 'democracy'. A naturalistic conception of democracy does not, of course, imply that democracy exists in the real world.[7]

Joseph Schumpeter chose another strategy than Dahl, to reconcile democracy with reality. He revised the classical conception of democracy in terms of a "competitive struggle for people's vote's" (Schumpeter, 1979, p 269). His "revisionism" was motivated by a normative theory called "realism". But he did not change the descriptive character of "democracy". His revision of the classical conception of democracy, may have had a normative purpose, but his conception of democracy is still descriptive. Any definition can, of course, be motivated by normative considerations, whether or not it stipulates a normative or descriptive use of the word.

According do the dominant descriptive use of "democracy" the word denotes a system of political and legal institutions. The concept of democracy can be positive, *i e* factual, in the same way as the concept of law (Hart, 1961). It was this descriptive view that led Tingsten to define democracy in terms of a procedure for political decision making. Many political scientists have pursued the procedural definition after Tingsten. The best known is Robert Dahl, who we turn to in the next section.

A Procedural Definition of Democracy

Using Athenian democracy as his model (*cf* Bobbio, 1993, p 17), Dahl identifies five criteria for democracy (Dahl, 1989, p 222).

1. Voting equality at the decisive stage
2. Effective participation
3. Enlightened understanding
4. Final control of the agenda
5. Inclusiveness

Full procedural democracy obtains, according to Dahl, when these conditions are fulfilled (Dahl, 1979). The five criteria constitute an *ideal-type* of procedural democracy, which in practice are impossible to realise. It is a theoretical purification of the meaning of procedural democracy. The five conditions are not supposed to classify *existing* political systems as democracies or non-democracies. Each of the conditions can, however, be operationalised in terms of actually existing political rights and institutions in a society. The criteria of procedural democracy require, Dahl avers, that the following rights and institutions apply: *1*. Elected officials (Dahl, 1989, p 222). *2*. Free and fair elections. *3*. Inclusive suffrage. *4*. Right to run for office. *5*. Freedom of expression. *6*. Alternative information. *7*. Associational autonomy. The result, when these rights and institutions are upheld by an existing system of law, is "polyarchy". By using the term "polyarchy" Dahl wants to avoid any illusion that classical democracy is possible in large political units (Dahl, 1979). The seven criteria for polyarchy delineate the set of political systems where the idea of procedural democracy is put into practice in modern states.

It bears noting that Dahl's definition of procedural democracy has the following characteristics: *i*. It is naturalistic. *ii*. The concept of democracy is an ideal type, which is supposed to realise a maximum of political equality and popular sovereignty. (The third statement should not be conflated with a *normative* principle of political equality.) Moreover, Dahl's definition is supposed to be *precise*, *i e* complete and exhaustive: no requirement is missing and no requirement should be added.

In the a report from *The Democratic Audit of Sweden* (DAS henceforth) it is maintained they adhere to a procedural definition (Petersson *et al*, 1996, p 13). The problem is, however, that they, in their definition of democracy, *add* requirements to Dahl's conditions for procedural democracy, which put substantial restrictions on outcomes of democratic procedures.

According to DAS, democracy should meet three requirements: rule by the citizens, the rule of law, and system capacity. From this they seem to draw the mistaken conclusion that democracy must be *defined* in terms of *all* these requirements (Rothstein, 1995, p 122).[8] It must be important, however, not to mix analytical requirements of democracy and political requirements that may be sound, but are external to democracy as such. The first requirement, rule by the citizens, corresponds to Dahl's definition of procedural democracy. But the second and the third condition are neither contained nor implied. On the contrary, they can conflict with Dahl's five conditions of procedural democracy. Nevertheless, they could be used as criteria of evaluation of democracy, without being elements of the definition of democracy. In fact, the evaluation would be more informative regarding the normative status of democracy, if democracy is defined independently of rule of law and ability of action. "The more we postulate in the definition, the less there is to study", as Hadenius puts it (Hadenius, 1992, p 8).

In particular, the inclusion of the rule of law (in which the separation of powers and respect for liberal rights are comprehended) in the notion of democracy is controversial.[9] DAS include the rule of law in an additive index assumed to measure the degree of democracy in Sweden (Rothstein, 1995, p 131). The reason given for this is that democratic governments which do not respect the rule of law "has been revealed by experience to be self-dissolving" (Rothstein, 1995, p 11). To this one may ask how it is possible to know "by experience" whether disrespect for rule of law *leads* to the dissolution of democracy, if the condition of rule of law is postulated in the definition of democracy. The common methodological rule is that an empirical relation is not reason for a definitional relation (Hadenius, 1992, p 8).

However, the real reason why DAS incorporate the rule of law into their concept of democracy seems to be that they, referring to Montesquieu (Rothstein, 1995, p 93), consider the rule of law to be *desirable* in its own right, because it safeguards individual liberties *against* democratic rule. They appear to take the view that the conflict between popular governance and the rule of law is an "inherent dilemma of democracy" (Rothstein, 1995, p 11). One could as well see the conflict between democracy and the rule of law as a conflict between *different* ideals—that of democracy and that of the rule of law (Sejersted, 1988). The "inherent dilemma" may be said to characterise political systems where democracy is combined with liberal constitutionalism —but not democracy as such. In the Swedish political system, where the ideal of popular sovereignty is more important than the rule of law, this dilemma is not "inherent" in the same way as in other, more liberal political systems like that of the United States (Holmström, 1996). But one can, of course, maintain that democracy in Sweden *should* be balanced by the rule of law. The normative argument for this requirement should, however, be stated in political principles, rather than as a definition of democracy.

The conflict between the notion of rule of law (and other normative principles) and procedural democracy is pointed out by Brian Barry. His account of democracy is close to Tingsten's and Dahl's: "By democratic procedure I mean a method of determining the content of laws (and other legally binding decisions) such as that the preferences of the citizens have some formal connection with the outcome in which each counts equally." (Barry, 1991, p 25). The theoretical and conceptual implication of this definition is clearly stated by Barry:

> That is to say, I reject the notion that one should build into 'democracy' any constraints on the content of the outcomes produced, such as *substantive equality, respect for human rights, concern for the general welfare, personal liberty, or the rule of law* (Barry, 1991, p 25; my italics).

This was about the same point as made by Tingsten in his critique of "content-oriented" definitions of democracy. From a logical point of view it is difficult to modify a procedural definition by adding other conditions than the formal requirements of the procedure. By adding further requirements as the rule of law, you restrict the range of possible outcomes of the procedure.

According to Sejersted "the rule of law and democracy correspond to two different concepts of liberty, the negative which makes liberty dependent on curbing authority, and positive which makes it dependent on existing authority" (Sejersted, 1988, p 131). The fact that democratic rule must be subject to the principle of legality does not imply "rule of law" as this expression is normally used (Elster, 1988, p 3). Rule of law implies normative requirements on political power, which are not contained in the principle of legality. That's the reason why rule of law can conflict with democracy.[10] Whether democracy should be maximised is a normative issue, to which we turn in the next section.

II. Normative Theories of Democracy: Three Types

Procedural Theories

A normative theory of democracy should, as has been emphasised, be distinguished from a definition of "democracy". The former states an evaluation of, or an argument for democracy; the latter states a rule of language. A procedural definition of democracy does not entail any kind of normative theory of democracy, not even the theory that is called "procedural".

A procedural theory of democracy holds that democracy is justified in terms of the conditions of participation in political decision making. The fairness of political participation is a fundamental rather then a derived principle (Beitz, 1989, p 23). Democratic institutions are justified because they treat citizens as equals in terms of political agency and power over decisions and actions of the state. Political fairness does not, according to this type of theory, necessarily mean equality regarding the outcome in terms of welfare or interests. Only the fair treatment of each citizen as agents in the decision procedure is relevant.

Dahl describes his theory of democracy as *procedural* (Dahl, 1979). His fundamental argument for democracy has to do with political equality in terms of power. However, as will be discussed below, Dahl's proceduralism is linked to a notion of best result. He combines a principle of fair political participation with an idea of just outcomes of the political process. His basic principle is the so-called "Strong Principle of Equality". This consists of two parts: "the Principle of Equal Consideration of Interests" and "the Presumption of Personal Autonomy" (Dahl, 1989, p 105). Dahl justifies democracy by an egalitarian liberalism, close to Rawls and Dworkin, which is based on equal concern for autonomy both in terms of political procedures and of political outcomes.[11]

The principle of political equality can also, according to Beitz (Beitz, 1989, p 20f), justify democracy from two other normative theories: those arguing that democracy yields the *best result,* and those stressing the capacity of democracy to realise the *popular will.*

Best Result Theories

Utilitarianism is the most typical example of a result-oriented theory of democracy. The value of democracy lies in its ability to maximise utility. James Mill and Jeremy Bentham have formulated theories of this type. Such theories presuppose that different social states can be ordered according to a *social welfare function* based on an impersonal principle. Democratic procedures are assumed to maximise utility according to a normative principle that applies independently of the preferences of individuals. This does not mean that the principle cannot be want regarding (Barry, 1965, p 38). The crucial point is that the want-regarding principle applies independently of people's preferences for a political decision. Anthony Downs "economic theory of democracy", can be interpretated as a want regarding, *i e* preference utilitarian, best outcome theory of democracy (Downs, 1957).

Theories that evaluate democracy in terms of *moral excellence*, are also examples of a "best result theory". In view of J S Mill, democracy has a value as an instrument for moral progress towards autonomy. Autonomy as a perfectionist idea should be distinguished from freedom or want satisfaction. The principle of autonomy, as a yardstick for political state of affairs, is ideal regarding (Barry, 1965, p 43).[12]

Theories arguing that democracy should lead to *social justice—e g*, Rawls' theory of justice—also legitimise democracy in terms of the best outcome. The principle of social justice serves as social welfare function that ranks social outcomes independently of individuals' preferences (Beitz, 1989, p 20). One can also interpret theories of participatory democracy (Pateman, 1970) and theories of discursive democracy (Elster, 1998) as emphasising the importance of the outcomes resulting from democratic procedures. Exponents of participatory democracy look to the moral development of the individual, while adherents of discursive or "epistemic" democracy focus on the moral or epistemological value of the of the decisions and insights reached (Dryzek, 1994).

A related normative theory of democracy is proposed by William Nelson (Nelson, 1980), who regards democracy as the best way to find out what justice is, and reach just decisions, or at least to prevent us from unjust decisions.

Popular Will Theories

Theories, which view democracy as a method for realising the popular, *will* focus also on the outcome of democracy. But it does not measure the outcome according to an abstract moral principle. They are based on the notion that democratic institutions should produce decisions in accordance with citizens' preferences whatever they are. Political fairness means equality regarding weights of preferences. These types of normative democratic theories are very much influenced by neo-classical economic theory. The citizen is granted the same sovereignty in politics as the consumer in the market (Elster, 1986). The difference is that democracy gives every citizen an equal opportunity to influence the outcome.

Popular will theories of democracy is a branch of theories on *social choice,* which focus on the relationship between individual preferences and social, *i e* collective decisions. The value of a social decision procedure (*e g* democracy) lies in its ability to aggregate individual choices. Kenneth Arrow's so called impossibility theorem proceeds from a normative theory which can be regarded as typical popular will theory, in which the rank ordering of political outcomes is determined by the preferences of individuals (Arrow, 1963). This type of normative theory of democracy is *morally empty,* in the sense that it prescribes no moral evaluation of democratic decisions and consequent policies. The basic norm is instead *collective rationality,* which is assumed to be derived from individual rationality. Like individual rationality, collective rationality can be seen as a rank ordering of outcomes. This collective rank ordering should fulfil a number of conditions, *e g,* transitivity, completeness and Pareto optimality (Elster, 1986). According to social-choice theory, the value of democracy is purely extrinsic—it derives from individual's utility functions.

The difference between "best result theories" and "popular will theories" is that the former rank political outcomes according to a normative principle which is *independent* of individual preferences, but dependent on a universal moral principle, while the latter rank political outcomes *dependent* on individuals' preferences, but independent of universal normative principles (Beitz, 1989, p 22).

Political Fairness

All three types of normative theories proceeds from a common assumption of political fairness: all citizens should be treated as equals—either in the procedure, the outcome or the collective decision. The difference between the three theories regarding their conception of political fairness can be explained by means of John Rawls' classification of different principles of procedural justice (Rawls, 1971, p 85). Rawls divides just procedures into two categories: those, which are not assessed against an independent criterion (*pure procedural justice*), and those, which are so assessed (*impure procedural justice*). He then divides procedures of the latter sort are into two further categories: *perfect* procedures, which always satisfy the independent criterion; and imperfect procedures, which sometimes "miss" the independent criterion.[13]

The procedural theory of democracy views political fairness in terms of pure procedural justice, whereas the other two advocates democracy in terms of impure procedural justice. While democracy hardly can guarantee the optimal outcome, neither in terms of the *best result* nor in terms of the *popular will*, the democratic procedures must be regarded as a case of imperfect procedural justice. The important point to make is that if you regard democracy as a case of impure procedural justice, it is a matter of contingent facts whether you actually should defend democracy in terms of a just procedure. If democracy fails to meet the independent criterion of justice, you should try other political institutions. Which system you choose depends on your theory of justice and your empirical assumptions on the effects of democracy. The constitutional choice, whether it leads to restrictions on democratic procedures or not, cannot be justified by a democratic decision, although politically legitimised by such a decision.

Dahl's Combination

The definition of democracy is, as stated above, logically independent of which normative theory of democracy one embraces. There is no necessary connection between Dahl's definition of democracy and his normative theory of democracy. But, on the other hand, his political preference to introduce democratic institutions, following from a definition of democracy, is naturally dependent on which normative theory of democracy one embraces. (It could be the case that Dahl prefers and proposes his definition of democracy, *because* he thinks it accords with his normative democratic theory. *Cf* Dahl, 1989, pp 108-118). But that is a motivational matter, which does affect the normative neutrality of his definition. Dahl believes that his definition is descriptive. It is an "ideal type", *i e* a analytical purification of the Athenian conception of democracy.)

The three types of normative theories, described above, do not exclude each other. Robert Dahl may be interpreted as combining the procedural theory with a best result theory. He contends that the value of democracy consists in its process *and* substance (Dahl, 1989, ch 12). "The strong principle of equality" is a norm for political and social justice; all citizens have the right to an equal control over their own lives (autonomy). The value of democracy consists in the fact that it furnishes both a just procedure (in which citizens can *actively* exercise political autonomy) and political outcomes, which maximise citizens' personal autonomy. A crucial premise in Dahl's defence of democracy is that actors participating in a democratic decision-making process embrace "the strong principle of equality" and therefore never decide to introduce measures which violate citizens' autonomy. The political and moral *convictions* of democratic actors serve as a moral barrier against the tyranny of the majority, Dahl believes. If the criterion of enlightened understanding is fulfilled, it will lead to "the best substantive outcomes" (Dahl,

1989, p 168). He therefore thinks that constitutional obstacles to popular sovereignty are in principle superfluous. Dahl's opposition to constitutionalism is not absolute; it is based, rather, on an *empirical* hypothesis about the moral conceptions guiding political decisions in a democracy. The fact that his defence of democracy contains a result-oriented component opens the way, however, to constitutional limitations on democracy.

Inspired by John Rawls, Dahl describes his normative theory of democracy as a theory of "imperfect procedural justice" (Dahl, 1989, p 165). Like Rawls, he argues that societal institutions—democratic procedures included—can be assessed against an *independent* criterion. For Rawls, these criteria are stated in his two principles of justice: the Equal-liberty-for-all principle and the Difference principle (Rawls, 1971, p 60). For Dahl, the independent criterion is the somewhat vaguer "strong principle of equality." Dahl's defence of democracy is similar to that offered by Rawls. Both build on an egalitarian liberalism devoted to the equal rights and resources of all persons to pursue their conception of the good. Dahl appears, however, to ascribe a greater intrinsic value to democratic procedures than does Rawls.

Dahl seems to defend democracy for two reasons: political equality in terms of pure procedural justice and fair outcomes in terms of social and economic equality (Dahl, 1989, pp 167-8). These two arguments go together with an empirical hypothesis about the social and economic conditions for a democratic process. Democracy is, and must be, egalitarian both in terms of procedures and outcomes. The procedural rights that are integral to the democratic process (*i e* conceptually linked to democracy) presuppose the fulfilment of rights that are external to the democratic process (*i e* empirically necessary rights for the democratic process). Freedom of expression, which is an integral right, presupposes a social right in terms of the satisfaction of certain basic needs (people must not starve and must be able to read). Generally speaking, Dahl thinks that democracy will and should maximise the overall autonomy of people. An important part of his conception of autonomy is equal responsibility for societal changes, which implies equal political power. The equally shared political power should be used to support autonomy in the private sphere as well. Political and private autonomy of the citizens goes together in Dahl's optimistic vision of democracy. The former is a procedural value, while the latter is an outcome-oriented value.

Other Variants

It is also possible, of course, to defend democracy on the basis of principles expressing a minimal pragmatism having nothing to do with political fairness. Schumpeter's (Schumpeter197,9) and Riker's (Riker, 1982) pessimistic theories of democracy, according to which democracy is unable to fulfil any substantive principle of political justice, may be interpreted in that direction. Both authors take the view that the concept of 'the common good' meaningless.

The public-choice theory of democracy (Buchanan & Tullock, 1969), can be regarded as kind of "exchange theory" (Beitz, 1989, p 24). Democratic institutions are judged on a principle comparable to principle of "mutual advantage". This is a Hobbesian account of democracy (*c f* Gauthier, 1987). The arguments for (or against) democracy is based on a rational calculation of the benefits you will gain, regardless of any notion of fairness. In general, public choice-theorists argues in favour of the unanimity-rule, against the majority rule. They regard the political arena as a market, where you exchange goods according to the principle of free contract between sovereign individuals. Public choice-theory is not a popular will-theory of democracy (as described above), because it has no account of fairness in terms of equal consideration of *political* preferences. On the other hand, public choice theory may qualify as a kind of best result theory, if one regard efficiency in terms of Pareto improvements as a *morally* desirable result (because no one has interest to object to Pareto improvements. Beitz, 1989, p 26).

Libertarians, if they defend democracy, may be said to defend democracy in view of a best result theory. The independent criterion of justice is deontological liberalism (Nozick, 1974). Democracy is (morally) legitimate if it, compared to all other political systems, is the best way of protecting just procedures for the acquisition of private property.

F A Hayek's defence of democracy is often interpreted in the same way. In fact, however, his view of democracy is consequentialistic and utilitarian. Hayek does not share Nozick's concern for deontological liberalism. His basic arguments for democracy exhibit similarities with that of J S Mill. He believes that a limited democracy, together with the market, is the best "mechanism of discovery" in a process of social evolution the ultimate goal of which is the self-realisation of individuals (Hayek, 1979, p xiii). Yet, his positive argument for democracy is not as important as the negative, *i e* to safeguard "rules of just conduct" , which, in their turn, are defended in terms of a kind of probabilistic, preference based utilitarianism (Gray, 1984, p 79).

Best result theories can justify democracy, then, as a way of maximising a value or of minimising risks. Liberals have emphasised, as mentioned, the latter type of democratic outcome. Since they see democracy as morally unreliable, they have often called for constitutional restrictions on the exercise of democratic power. But constitutional restrictions can also be justified on the grounds that they increase the efficiency of democracy—in terms of deliberation, decision-making and political actions (Holmes, 1995, p 7). I turn to these questions in the following section.

III. Democracy and Constitutionalism

In rough terms, the three normative theories of democracy under consideration offer the following arguments on behalf of democratic institutions: 1. They embody to just political procedures. 2. They lead to results satisfactory from the standpoint of a universal theory of justice. 3. They issue in collective rationality. Let us assume, for the sake of argument, that representatives for these three different theories *a.* accept Dahl's procedural definition of democracy, and *b.* accept his proposals for institutionalising it in the form of representative democracy (polyarchy). In that case we can put the following two questions: *i.* What constitutional restrictions on democracy would each of these theories recommend? *ii.* Why would they recommend such constitutional restrictions?

To be able to answer these questions, we need a common conception of what a constitution is. Formally speaking, a constitution is a collection of "meta-rules," *i e,* rules about other rules (Elster, 1988). A political constitution often takes the form of written statues, decided by a political body. Unwritten constitutions which are not deliberately designed can, however, perform the same function to regulate the manner in which decisions are made to change the rules governing the making of decisions.

Like democracy, constitutions can be given a *naturalistic* definition in terms of an existing system of law. Whether or not a constitution exists is determined, ultimately, by whether or not it is observed. And like democracy, constitutions can be justified in terms of a normative theory. In the history of Western political ideas, "constitutionalism" refers to a normative theory, which calls for political power to be limited and exercised under laws. Constitutionalism is often defended from the idea of rule of law.

The concept of constitutional government is, however, broader than the concept of rule of law. A constitution restricts on how to *change* laws (including the constitution), but it need not limit the powers of the state in other respects. A constitution can perfectly well allow for the extensive exercise of political powers; the critical thing is that certain principles be followed. A state may be constitutionally bound and yet be charged with the performance of extensive duties covering a broad field of society. The exercise of political power in illiberal societies can be regulated in a constitutional manner, *i e* according to the principle of legality—*i e* as in a communist society or in a theocratic, Islamic republic.

What is the relation of democracy to constitutional government and the rule of law? Let us examine the relation between constitutional rules and the three normative theories of democracy more closely.

The Procedural Theory of Democracy

According to Beitz' definition, the procedural theory of democracy calls for fairness vis-à-vis citizens seen as political actors. It exhibits, moreover, structural similarities with the principle of legality (or formal justice) contained in the idea of constitutional rule. Both focus on the equality of all citizens before a system of rules. The principle of legality emphasises juridical processes, while the procedural theory of democracy stresses political processes. The former concerns the output of political power, whereas the latter concerns the input. The basic principle common to both is the equal status of all citizens in respect to the procedures regulating the exercise of power. The *effects* of this exercise of power, on the other hand, are a secondary consideration.

The procedural theory of democracy can, as mentioned earlier, prescribe rules that uphold democracy, *i e*, so-called democratic rights and freedoms. It can be legitimate, therefore, to institute a legal order which prevents the abolition of democracy, or at any rate makes it harder. This argument for a constitution is based on the principle of self-binding. A metaphor for this type of measure is the order Ulysses gave to his crew to bind him to the mast, in order that his ship could sail past the isle of the sirens safely. The purpose of such self-binding is to remove one's own weakness of will (akrasia) as an obstacle to goal-fulfilment (Elster, 1984, p 39). It is ultimately an empirical question, however, whether or not self-binding is an adequate measure. It is a method for maximising expected utility by means of a sort of strategic rationality. An actor binds himself in order to optimise the outcome of a conflict within himself. A demos is not, however, an actor in sense of being a person. Members of a demos dies or emigrate; new members acquire political rights by birth or by immigration. Thus, self-binding by a demos, implies infringements of the political power of future members of the demos.

A constitution as a way of self-binding, may have an instrumental value as a safeguard for democracy's survival. This is a conceivable argument, from the standpoint of a procedural theory of democracy, for a constitution. It may be worth noting that, in such a case, the constitutional framework has no procedural value, but is rather justified by the result it produces—namely, the protection of democratic procedures. This argument for a constitution is consequentialist, in contrast to the argument for democracy, which is of a proceduralist character.

The procedural theory of democracy can also call for constitutional provisions, which go beyond the direct protection of democracy, *e g*, safeguards for the rights of private ownership. Empirical hypotheses concerning the significance of private ownership for democracy's legitimacy may be thought to justify constitutional safeguards for private ownership. If democracy is unstable and under threat by "the propertied," restrictions on the exercise of democratic power may be viewed as a tactical retreat enhancing the chances of democracy's survival (Elster, 1988 and Przeworski, 1988). Generally speaking, the procedural theory of democracy can accept constitutions as a method to safeguard or improve procedural democracy. The purpose can be to improve democratic procedures in terms or effectiveness and rationality, or to protect them from non-democratic forces. In both cases, self-binding, can be an appropriate tactical measure. But the democratic procedure must, at least in principle, have priority over self-binding constitutions. Constitutions can be possible *outcomes* of democratic procedures, not normative prerequisites for democratic procedures.

Constitutional restrictions aimed at increasing the efficiency and rationality of democratic decisions are in principle unproblematic, as long as such restrictions have been adopted in good democratic order, and as long as they are reversible (so that future generations can revoke such provisions if they wish).

The procedural theory of democracy recognises, in principle, the role for a constitutional protection of democratic procedures. Such limitations can, however, come into conflict with the theory's fundamental value—the right of citizens to exercise political power . There is a tension between consequentialism and deontology in the procedural theory of democracy: by restricting democracy, the procedural values of democracy can be upheld. A "strong" version of democratic proceduralism would, however, be indifferent to the outcomes of democratic decisions. It would allow for undemocratic outcomes. A "weak" version of democratic proceduralism would be consequence-sensitive with respect to democracy it self.[14]

A short digression: Constitutions and rationality

A limitation of the sphere of democratic decision-making can increase the ability of political bodies to function effectively, not only in terms of preserving democracy. Constitutional rules can be a way of warding off "weakness of will" concerning long-term objectives within the framework of democratic decision-making (Holmes, 1995, ch 5). In respect to economic policy especially, several scholars have averred that self-binding is needed for this reason. The demand for a constitutional prohibition against state budget deficits is a well-known example, as is the demand for constitutionally independent central bank.

This type of self-binding is not justified by reference primarily to democracy, but rather on grounds of rationality. The purpose is to maximise expected utility, assuming a certain utility function. All rational political actors, whether they are democratically elected or not, can benefit from self-binding (Elster, 1984, ch 2). Self-binding can be strategically rational for solving internal conflicts within a political actor (individual or collective), or for solving conflicts with other political actors. Constitutional restrictions on freedom of action can, for instance, enhance the prospects of success during negotiations, *e g*, with other states (see Schelling, 1980).

If we hold to the original metaphor for self-binding—Ulysses bound to the mast—we may say that this is a question of making decisions under *risk* (Hansson, 1991). The actor is assumed to be capable of assessing the probability that the various options will lead to certain outcomes. Self-binding is, in short, a way of maximising expected utility. It does not represent an act of omission; it is, rather, a positive action in its own right—and one justified by "cost-benefit" analysis (Elster, 1984, p 44). Self-binding in the Ulyssean sense is thus *not* a method for handling an information problem.

When F A Hayek, for his part, argues for far-reaching constitutional limitations on the exercise of democratic power, his purpose is to solve a completely different problem than that faced by Ulysses. For Hayek, constitutionalism is justified by reference to a fundamental information problem, which he considers to beset all discretionary political measures: their effects cannot be foreseen. The space for direct goal-oriented decisions should therefore be minimised. The foremost task of state authority is to uphold the "rule of law" (Hayek, 1979). The binding to rules is a way of tackling the problem of decision-making *under conditions of uncertainty.* It is meaningless, when the probability that a given action will result in a certain outcome cannot be calculated, to try to maximise expected utility. The "ends-means rationality" associated with the idea of "economic man" is based on an overestimation of human rationality and an underestimation of the information problem, according to Hayek.[15]

The type of constitutionalism represented by Hayek is akin to the concept of "bounded rationality" developed by the Herbert Simon and James March (Simon & March, 1958). Laws and "rules of just conduct" are "rules of thumb" that develop in an evolutionary manner, without rational considerations on the part of political actors (Lundström, 1993, p 72). There is a functionalistic tendency in Hayek's constitutionalism (Udehn, 1987, p 208; Hayek, 1967 ch 4). It is therefore a dubious conclusion that Hayek is a champion of the *Ulyssean* notion of self-binding. Stephen Holmes thus, in my view, misinterprets Hayek in ascribing to him the following view: "A constitution is the institutionalised cure for chronic myopia; it disempowers short-sighted majorities in the name of binding norms" (Holmes, 1995, p 135). The main problem Hayek wishes to solve is not "myopia" but ignorance.

Instituting barriers to majority decisions in the area of state expenditures can be a way of avoiding a political business cycle within a democratic decision-making framework. Economists of the public-choice school advocate democracy's "self-binding" for this reason (Buchanan & Tullock, 1969, Myrhman 1984). Their rationalistic argument for a constitution, however, is foreign to Hayek. An evolutionary game-theoretical interpretation—one stressing value of survival rather than utility value—is more in line with Hayek's case for a constitution (Sugden, 1986, pp 9-31, Lundström, 1993, pp 86-101).

Best Result Theories

What distinguishes best result theories from procedural theories is that they do not have the protection of democratic procedures as a *goal*. A best result theory can recommend a limitation on democracy on the grounds that this is legitimate in the light of a universal normative principle. The same principle can legitimise *both* democracy and the constitutional restrictions on democracy. The conditional liberal defence (in various versions) of democracy, for its part, allows for limitations on democracy for moral reasons that are referred to in the *defence* of democracy as well. Contrary to the procedural theory of democracy, the liberal best result theory does not derive the justification of constitutions from democratic decisions, but from fundamental principles of individual rights that are prior to democratic rights.

Constitutional restrictions finding their justification in the self-binding argument (in its Ulyssean variant) are supported differently in the best result theory from in the procedural theory. The decisive thing is what goals are sought. According to the procedural theory, the democratic procedures have an intrinsic value. According to the best result theory, however, the increased power following from strategic self-binding is only acceptable if it maximises the value sought in the theory, *e g*, welfare, social justice or moral development.

A hard-boiled best result theory—*e g*, "Government House Utilitarianism", associated with Sidgwick (Sidgwick, 1981)—ascribes a purely instrumental value to *conceptions* of democracy as well. It can be appropriate to advocate a (false) procedural theory in order to secure democracy's legitimacy. It can even be necessary to keep the best result theory of democracy in secret, in order to induce a right based justification of democracy (if that proves to be the most effective way of preserving democracy).

Mistaken notions about the moral status of democracy may be a precondition for maintaining the legitimacy of democratic procedures, and thus for obtaining the results in which democracy's value consists. Jon Elster contends, for example, that J S Mill and Alexis de Tocqueville see the value of democracy as lying in its "essentially by-products" (Elster, 1986). Each stresses democracy's value as a learning process—both morally and intellectually. If the actors in the democratic system are guided by these goals, however, they are not reached. A characteristic feature of essentially by-products is that they cannot be pursued consciously. Therefore, Elster claims, normative theories, which see an intrinsic value in essentially by-products are "self-defeating." If an actor is guided in his actions by such a theory, the effects that are sought cannot be achieved. But the problem of "self-defeat" concerns the relation between action and motivation in a democracy, not the relation between democracy and the justification of democracy (Copp, 1993, p 113). Elster's discussion of essentially by-products would gain in clarity had he distinguished between normative *conceptions* and normative *theories*. Striving for essentially by-products need not be irrational. Elster points out a practical problem of motivational psychology—which is not impossible to solve. In principle, two solutions are thinkable: first, that democracy's ultimate value is concealed from the citizens; and second, that citizens are guided by different motives in a "context of regulation" and in a "context of action" (Riker & Ordeshook, 1973 p 276). You can "forget" to the ultimate principles or motives that guides you in the constitutional choice, when you act within the constitution.

The problem with the first solution is that it violates the autonomy of citizens. However, consequentialist theories, which distinguish between criteria decision and criteria of rightness of moral action (Sidgwick, 1981, p 413), discern no intrinsic value in the moral autonomy of persons. David Hume held such an instrumental view of political norms and institutions, which has since been passed down to F A Hayek, whose indirect utilitarianism renders him indifferent to the veracity of political ideas. In terms similar to Burke, Hayek defends prejudice and superstition if "useful" traditions are sustained with their aid (Hayek, 1989, p 157). Since notions of natural rights can also be "useful," constitutional restrictions on democracy may be defended on the basis of a best result theory.

Liberal best result theories that place a value on the autonomy and rationality, however, cannot "pull the wool over people's eyes" when defending democratic institutions. The moral status of democracy and the possible need for constitutional limitations must therefore be discussed and accepted in public. Political institutions must be "transparent" (Waldron, 1987). Congruence must obtain between the "real" and the "imagined" legitimacy of democratic institutions.

The problem of constitutions' binding future generations does not, however, have the same moral weight for best result theories as for procedural theories. It can be legitimate to use coercion against future generations if good consequences result. In contrast to procedural theories, there is no tension between deontology and consequentialism in the defence of democracy.

Popular Will Theories

Popular will theories locate political sovereignty in people's preferences; there is no higher moral authority than people's interests or preferences (Beitz, 1989, p 50). The popular will is defined independently of the procedures employed for making collectively binding decisions, *e g*, democratic procedures. A given procedure for making decisions—the majority principle, for example—acquires its value from the fact that decisions made in accordance with it are congruent with the popular will (Beitz, 1989, p 52). The converse, however, does not obtain (that the popular will is legitimate because it is the result of a democratic decision).

One may say that the popular will is a criterion of rightness against which all procedures for social decision-making can be tested. Like the best result theory, the popular will theory focus on democracy's capacity to achieve a certain result. The paradoxical thing about popular will theories is that they disregard the autonomy of individuals in their capacity as political *actors,* while at the same time proceeding from individual autonomy in the formation of preferences. In contrast to procedural theories, popular will theories do not stress the value of *agency* in the making of political decisions (although its instrumental value may be recognised). Citizens are the *recipients* of a policy according to a notion of the common good.

Rousseau, who is an exponent of a kind of perfectionist popular will theory, emphasises popular participation in political decisions in order to ensure the general will. John Plamenatz (Plamenatz, 1992, p 176) notes, however, that Rousseau does not explain the relation between popular participation and the general will. It is not self-evident people must take part in making the laws that make them "free". The popular will, interpreted in a rationalistic as well as in a "moralistic" way, can be realised if the laws are in accordance with the general will, regardless of who has the *political* power or right to make them.

Popular will theories face difficulties when it comes to protecting both democratic rights and rights which are not necessary to democratic procedure itself, *e g*, rights of private ownership. As Amartya Sen has shown, a minimal private sphere—into which the collective and social decision procedures does not reach—is incompatible with Pareto optimality and thus with collective rationality (Sen, 1982). One possible solution to this problem is provided by Dworkin (Dworkin, 1979, p 234), when he makes a distinction between internal and external preferences. The former are preferences about your own life; the latter are preferences about others way of life. Only internal preferences should be counted in a social decision procedure. Otherwise some preferences are "double-counted". Dworkin's distinction between legitimate and illegitimate preferences can be used to defend constitutional limitations on democratic decisions. But then you introduce a normative principle that is not contained in the popular will theory of democracy

In the view of popular will theories constitutional limitations on democratic decisions are defended by the same standards as democracy is, to maximise collective rationality. But it should be noted that preferences *about* constitutions (and political institutions in general) should not be taken into account in the social choice function. The desirability of all types of constitutions is decided by the popular will theory, not by people's preferences.[16]

IV. Concluding Remarks

A normative assessment of democracy as political system—whether in terms of morality or of rationality—is helped by a naturalistic definition of democracy. Democracy should be defined descriptively, *i e* as a structure of power upheld by legal and political norms. According to the procedural definition of democracy, it is political system that provides a procedure for political decision making. A definition has no other normative function than being a linguistic rule. It does not answer the question of the moral standing of democracy or questions of what outcomes are morally desirable or forbidden.

The puzzling problem of whether democracy allows for its own abolition proves less insoluble if we hold three types of problems apart from one another: the conceptual, the normative and the legal. These three problems correspond to three different questions, which are often conflated: 1. Is the statement—"It is permitted in a democracy to abolish democracy"—contradictory? 2. Does a democratic constitution permit democracy's abolition? 3. Does a normative theory of democracy permit democracy's abolition? The first question is a matter of linguistic convention According to the definition of democracy used by Dahl, the answer is no.

According to Barry (Barry, 1991, p 25) it is however contradictory. In view of his procedural definition of democracy, all outcomes that overrule the legal prerequisites for the democratic procedure are forbidden. But this restriction is, in my view, logically redundant. What follows from the procedural notion of democracy, is that the procedure pay due respect to all democratic rights in the decision process, not in the outcome of the decision, even if the decision is to abolish democracy. One must distinguish between *un*democratic decisions and *non*-democratic decisions. The former refers to the content or outcome of the decision, the latter to the process of the decision. In the same way as it is possible to restrict the range of democratic decisions by democratic decisions, it is possible for a demos to give up the right to make democratic decision. If a demos decides to dissolve itself as a political subject, *i e* by integrating it self to another demos, this means that democracy within the first demos is abolished. But the decision may very well be democratic. The same applies to a democratic decision to give the power to a monarch—it is undemocratic, but not non-democratic.

The answer to the second question is found in the existing system of law, *i e*, the institutions on which the governmental form is founded. Dahl's proposed democratic institutions, neither in the ideal-type definition nor in the pragmatic operationalisation of this (polyarchy), do forbid democracy's abolition. Nor does the constitution of Sweden; on the contrary, it lays down a procedure for how this can be accomplished according to the principle of legality. The German constitution, on the other hand, states an eternal rule of law that forbids any infringements on democratic rights by constitutional change.

The third question, which is the morally interesting one, is answered differently by different normative theories of democracy. Of the three normative theories of democracy discussed, it is the procedural theory that offers the strongest argument against democracy's abolition. Its conception of justice is tied *logically* to the existence of democratic procedures. The crucial question is whether political justice, according to this theory, contains self-referential restrictions. A strong version of a procedural theory would allow for the elimination of democracy—as matter of procedural right. A weak version would not—as matter of protecting procedural rights.

The other two theories base their defence of democracy on the thesis of a *contingent* connection between democracy and other values. The best result theory assumes that democracy assists in the realisation of principles of justice; the popular will theory presumes that democracy will realise the popular will. The values espoused by these theories are not conceptually linked to democracy; consequently, a defence of democracy founded on these theories is instrumental. The abolition of democracy is not in principle wrong.

The three normative theories of democracy can all recommend constitutional limitations on democratic decision-making—but for varying reasons, since each type of constitutional limitation can have either a positive or a negative effect on the values espoused by the theory (procedures, results or preference aggregation). The effects of such measures are determined in large part by empirical circumstances. Three reasons to introduce such restrictions may be distinguished:

1. To protect institutions which are constitutive of democracy from the deleterious decisions of democratic authorities.

2. To protect institutions which are not constitutive of democracy from the deleterious decisions of democratic authorities.

3. To enhance, by means of "self-binding," the rationality and efficiency of the democratic exercise of power. Three different subpurposes may be discerned here: *a.* To counteract weakness of will (akrasia) on the part of democratic actors. *b.* To counteract an information problem through limited rationality. *c.* To increase autonomy in the formation of preferences by forcefully injecting an element of "reflection" into the decision-making process.

The procedural theory can call for constitutional restrictions of all three types. The purpose with the second type of restriction, however, is to increase, by means of a strategic concession, the chances of democracy's survival. The results-oriented theory adopts an instrumental perspective to constitutional restrictions of all kinds. If constitutional restrictions increase the likelihood of justice, then limiting democracy's domain may be regarded as unproblematic. Since this theory ascribes no intrinsic value to the democratic exercise of power, it supplies a weaker foundation for the Odyssean motive for self-binding. The popular will theory, finally, extends conditional support to all constitutions, which facilitate collective rationality. As Sen has shown, liberal rights aimed at removing issues from the democratic agenda present a problem for popular will theories—Pareto optimality cannot be reached. A popular will theory can, however, be subordinated to a liberalism, which stresses other values.

The three theories I have examined are neither exhaustive nor exclusive among the possible defences for democracy. They are based on principles of justice, which can be combined and mixed, as well as assigned varying weight in the different social spheres (*c f* Walzer, 1983). Democracy need not be defended on the basis of a monistic theory of political fairness. All three types of theories can be combined, perhaps in a lexicographic order.

Which of the three kind of values, defended by three normative theories should we place at the top in a lexicographic order?

All three theories satisfy a basic demand for universalism: they treat all citizens as equals—but in different ways. The procedural theory is universalistic regarding political procedures; the popular will is universalistic regarding preferences; and the best result theory is universalistic regarding the outcome.

The procedural and the popular will theory are, in principle, indifferent to the moral value of the outcome of democracy. If we believe that democratic decisions should lead to the fulfilment of some moral standards, we must give priority to the best result theory.

Placing democratic procedures at the top of the hierarchy of principles would seem unreasonable. The Kantian principle "fiat justitia pereat mundus" (May justice prevail even if the world perish), does not seem sensible, applied to democratic procedures. The popular will theory can be questioned for the same reason: the realisation of the will of the people cannot be permitted unconditionally, regardless of the outcome.

In his interesting article "The Moral Standing of the Market", Amartya Sen (Sen, 1985) argues for an instrumental view of the market economy. In contrast to Nozick, he does not believe that justice is a matter of just entitlement of goods. The defence of the rights that uphold the market system must be "consequence sensitive", according to Sen. The same perspective can applied in answering the question of "the moral standing of democracy". Neither the free market nor democracy can be defended solely in terms of pure procedural justice. Their moral standing must be viewed also in terms of their consequences.

In this paper I will not elaborate on *which* outcome that justifies democracy. But I think both democratic procedures and outcomes of democracy must be defended from a second order universalism, *i e* principles "that no one has a reasonable argument to reject" (Barry, 1995, ch 4). If we don't know which these principles are, we can include the finding of these principles in the desired outcome of democracy (Nelson, 1980). Democracy can be defended both as method for public moral deliberation and as a method for public moral action. If democratic procedures fail in this respect, they should not be defended unconditionally.

Notes

1. A previous version of this paper has been presented at *The Swedish collegium for advanced studies in the social sciences* (Scasss), Uppsala University in November 1998. I am grateful to John Broome, Sven Danielsson and Howard Sobel for useful comments.
2. Aristotle divided the forms of government into six types—three ideal types and three degenerate forms. Their rank ordering is such that the best ideal type is paired with the worst degenerate form: *i*. monarchy-tyranny; *ii*. aristocracy-oligarchy; *iii*. politeia-democracy (Aristotle, 1988).
3. The notion of an Open Society is close to Hayek's idea of "The Great Society" (Hayek, 1969, p 163). According to Roger Scruton (Scruton, 1989, p 334) "Open Society" have the following meaning: "In short, it is a society which is as free from the state as possible, while maintaining good order, cohesion and constitutional politics".
4. According to Hayek (Hayek, 1969, p 161) the difference between liberalism and democracy becomes clear if you consider their opposites: "the opposite of liberalism is totalitarianism, while the opposite of democracy is authoritarianism." See also Bobbio (Bobbio, 1993).
5. Charles Stevenson (Stevenson, 1969, p 210) describes the general feature of a "persuasive definition" as follows: "In any 'persuasive definition' the term defined is a familiar one, whose meaning is both descriptive and strongly emotive. The purport of the definition is to alter the descriptive meaning of the term, usually by giving it greater precision within the boundaries of its customary vagueness; but the definition does *not* make any change in the term's emotive meaning. And the definition is used, consciously or unconsciously, in an effort to secure, by this interplay between emotive and descriptive meaning, a redirection of people's attitudes.
6. This is, perhaps, an exaggeration of the permanence of the meaning of "democracy". In the era of Tocqueville "democracy" meant social equality in terms of equality of status in contrast to aristocracy (Sartori, 1987, p 8). But this use of the word is quite rare nowadays.
7. Often there is a demand for "realism" in the definition of democracy (Hadenius, 1992, p 7). This must not mean that you accommodate your definition to what actually exists or can exist. You must start from a definition in order to investigate whether the phenomenon of interest exists can exist. A definition of anarchy, for instance, cannot

be dependent on whether it exists or not, nor on the possibility to realise it. But the definition of anarchy can be naturalistic and descriptive in the sense that it denotes factual circumstances (which rarely exists). A demand for "realism" concerns the empirical relevance of *study* of a phenomenon, not the definition of it.

8. In the 1996 report of DAS, the expression "democratic ideal" is often used to describe these requirements. The relation between a definition of democracy and "democratic ideal" is not explained. Their purpose is said to construct a number of criteria for a "good system of government" (p 11). These criteria form an "ideal-type" which can be used to measure the "democratic quality" of an existing political order. But if "democratic quality" means *degree* of democracy, and if democracy is a procedure, then it is difficult to understand why they include other requirements than the fulfilment of the procedure. A more plausible interpretation of their criteria, is that they measure the quality of Swedish democracy according to a "democratic ideal" which consist of something more than democratic procedures. But then there is a discrepancy between the procedural definition and the ideal-type of democracy, which is difficult to cope with (if you buy Dahls definition, which is an ideal-type). One possible solution to these theoretical problems is to evaluate democratic procedures according to a *political* ideal, which emphasises rule of law and ability of action. (Some of these points are made by Boström (Boström, 1995.)
9. Even the inclusion of government performance in a definition of democracy can be questioned. Effectiveness in terms of goal-fulfilment is external to democracy in a procedural account. It must be permitted make mistakes in a democracy, *i e* to take "wrong" decisions and implement "wrong" policies in view of desired aims. The decisions that lead to the financial problems, may very well be the result of decisions that are highly democratic in terms of procedural criteria. Even the effects of the financial deficit, in terms of dependence on the international capital market, do not lead to a lower degree of democracy in Sweden. The poorer a country is, the less democratic it is. seems to be the logic of DAS (Rothstein, 1995, p 129). But the crucial point is not power in terms of maximising utility or welfare by means of public policy, but power in terms of popular control over political decisions and measures in Sweden (internal efficiency) regardless of economic restrictions on possible outcomes. The lack of economic resources to use state power to implement desired goals, does not lower the degree of democracy in a procedural sense. See Barry 1974 for a discussion.
10. According to Elster (Elster, 1988, p 3) the principle of legality forbids retroactive legislation and arbitrary punishment, whereas the rule of law requires stability and predictability of the legal system. The requirement of predictability is also stipulated by the principle of legality, but in a different sense. It requires predictability of *the legal*

consequences of your actions when you *undertake* them. Rule of law requires predictability of the legal consequences of your actions in the future. Sartori (Sartori, 1989, p 324) use the phrase "guarantisme" to explain the principle of rule of law. In his classic study *Law of the Constitution,* Dicey (Dicey, 1915, p 191) argues that rule of law, in the English judicial system, means that the legal source of citizen's rights are to be found in common laws. While common laws are not changed by political commands, but in courts, they protect citizens from political power. In German jurisprudence a distinction is made between *materieller Rechtstaat* and *formeller Rechtstaat*. According to Hayek (Hayek, 1969, p 165) the former corresponds to rule of law, and the latter to what we call "principle of legality".

11. A similar "complex proceduralism" is suggested by Charles Beitz (Bietiz, 1989, p 100). He argues that the terms of democratic participation are fair when they are acceptable from the point of view of each citizen. No one should have a "good" argument for refusing the terms of participation. A "good" argument for refusing to accept democracy is that it fails to meet one of three 'regulative' interests: recognition, equitable treatment and deliberative responsibility. These three interests are not indifferent to the outcome of the procedure, but they do not define a *specific* desired outcome. Rather, they define criteria that can be used to evaluate a procedural arrangement from a plurality of regulative interests.
12. A modern version of a perfectionist doctrine of autonomy is proposed by Joseph Raz (Raz, 1989).
13. Nozick's (Nozick, 1974) theory of just entitlement provides an example of pure procedural justice. A legal process in a court is an example of imperfect procedural justice; sometimes an innocent person is convicted by mistake. A division of a cake between several people, where the person who divides the cake gets the last part of it, is an example of perfect procedural justice, according to Rawls (Rawls, 1971, p 85) assuming that the independent criterion is equality.
14. This problem of "self referential" proceduralism is analogous to the problem of being free to sell oneself as a slave. Nozick who takes a pure deontological view on the problem, has problems not to accept self-chosen slavery, whereas J S Mill explicitly reject this right (on utilitarian grounds). See Lewin (Lewin, 1990, p 177) for a discussion.
15. Hayek argues for a limited state in terms of a "probabilistic utilitaranism." The scientific arguments he adduces are in line with the rationalist Enlightenment tradition, but his anti-rationalism can be interpreted as an ideology propagated for rationalist reasons (Lundström, 1992).
16. This can be a problem similar to the problem discussed by Sen (Sen, 1986); there can be an impossibility of a Paretian democrat, according

to the popular will theory, for the same reason that a Paretian liberal is impossible.

References

Aristotle, 1988, *The politics.* Cambridge: Cambridge University Press, 1988.
Arrow, K, 1963, *Social choice and individual values.* New York: Wiley, 1963.
Barry, B, 1965, *Political argument.* London: Routledge & Kegan Paul, 1965.
—, 1974, "Size and democracy", in *Government and Opposition,* vol 9, no 4, pp 492-503, 1974.
—, 1991, *Democracy and power.* Oxford: Clarendon Press, 1991.
—, 1995, *Justice as impartiality.* Oxford: Oxford University Press, 1995.
Beitz, C, 1989, *Political equality.* Princeton [NJ]: Princeton University Press, 1989.
Boström, B-O, 1988, *Samtal om demokrati.* Stockholm: Doxa, 1988.
—, 1995, "Demokrati är inte alltid bäst" in *Dagens Nyheter* June 1, 1995.
Bobbio, N, 1993, *Liberalism och demokrati.* Stockholm: Daidalos, 1993.
Brennan, G & Buchanan, J, 1985, *The reason for rules.* Cambridge: Cambridge University Press, 1985.
Buchanan, J, 1988, *Maktens gränser.* Stockholm: Timbro, 1988.
Buchanan, J & Tullock, G, 1969, *The calculus of consent.* Ann Arbor: The University of Michigan Press, 1969.
Connolly, W E, 1993, *The terms of political discource.* Oxford: Blackwell, 1993.
Copp, D, 1995, "Could political truth be a hazard for democracy?", in Copp, Hampton & Roemer, 1995.
Copp, D, Hampton, J & Roemer, J E (eds), 1995, *The idea of democracy.* Cambridge: Cambridge: University Press, 1995.
Dahl, R, 1971, *Polyarchy.* New Haven: Yale University Press, 1971.
—, 1979, "Procedural democracy," in *Philosophy, Politics and Society,* 5th Series (*eds* Laslett & Fishkin), New Haven: Yale University Press, 1979.
—, 1982, *Dilemmas of pluralist democracy.* New Haven: Yale University Press, 1982.
—, 1989, *Democracy and its critics.* New Haven: Yale University Press.
—, 1998, *On democracy.* New Haven: Yale University Press, 1998.
Dicey, K, C, 1915, *Law of the constitution.* London: MacMillan, 1915.
Downs, A, 1957, *An economic theory of democracy.* New York: Harper & Row, 1957.
Dryzek, J S, 1994, *Discursive democracy.* Cambridge: Cambridge University Press, 1994.

Dworkin, R, 1979, *Taking rights seriously.* Cambridge [MA]: Harvard University Press, 1979.
Elster, J, 1984, *Ulysses and the sirens.* Cambridge: Cambridge University Press, 1984.
—, 1986, "The market and the forum : three varieties of political theory," in Elster & Hylland, 1986.
—, 1988, "Introduction", in Elster & Slagstad, 1988.
— (ed), 1998, *Deliberative democracy.* Cambridge: Cambridge University Press, 1998.
Elster, J & Hylland, A (eds) 1986, *Foundations of social choice theory.* Cambridge: Cambridge University Press, 1986.
Elster, J & Slagstad, R (*eds*), 1988, *Constitutionalism and democracy.* Cambridge: Cambridge University Press, 1988.
Elvander, N, (ed), 1975, *Demokrati och socialism.* Stockholm: Rabén & Sjögren, 1975.
—, 1975 a, "Vänstern vacklar i synen på demokrati", in Elvander, 1975.
—, 1975 b, "Demokrati och socialism", in Elvander,1975.
Gallie, W B, 1956, "Essentially contested concepts", in *Proceedings of the Aristotelian Society.* vol 56, 1956.
Gray, J, 1984, *Hayek on liberty*, Oxford: Basil Blackwell, 1984.
Habermas, J, 1988, *Kommunikativt handlande.* Göteborg: Daidalos, 1988.
Hadenius, A, 1992. *Democracy and development.* Cambridge: Cambridge University Press, 1992.
Hansson. S-O, 1991, *An overview of decision theory.* Stockholm: Statens Kärnbränsle Nämnd (SKN Report 41), 1991.
Hansson, S-O & Hermansson, J, 1992, *Idéer om demokrati.* Stockholm: Tiden, 1992.
Hart, H L A, 1961, *The concept of law.* Oxford: Clarendon Press, 1961.
Hayek, F A, 1969, *Studies in philosophy, politics and economics.* New York: Simon and Schuster, 1969.
—, 1979, *Law, legislation and liberty.* Chicago: The University of Chicago Press, 1979.
—, 1988, *The fatal conceit.* London: Routledge, 1988.
Hedenius, I, 1963. *Rätt och moral.* Stockholm: Wahlström & Widstrands förlag, 1963.
Hermansson, J, 1986, "Demokrati i västerländsk mening," in *Statsvetenskaplig tidskrift,* 4, pp 253-264.
—, 1992, "Introduktion till 'Varför demokrati?'" in Hansson & Hermansson, 1992.
—, 1994, "Hur kan demokratin rättfärdigas?" i Sannerstedt & Jerneck, 1994.
—, 1996, *Om möjligheten att demokratiskt rättfärdiga den ekonomiska och monetära unionen.* Uppsala universitet, Statsvetenskapliga institutionen (Uppsats för EMU-utredningen), 1996.

Holmes, S, 1995, *Passions & constraints.* Chicago: The University of Chicago Press, 1995.
Holmström, B, 1996, *Domstolar och demokrati.* Uppsala University, Department of Government, 1996.
Lively, J, 1975, *Democracy.* Oxford: Basil Blackwell, 1975.
Lundström, M, 1991, "Maktutredningens 'vetenskapliga' liberalism", in *Statsvetenskaplig Tidskrift*, 94, pp 161-169.
—, 1992, "Is anti-rationalism rational? : the case of F A Hayek", in *Scandinavian Political Studies,* Vol. 15, pp 235-248.
—, 1993, *Politikens moraliska rum : en studie i F A Hayeks politiska filosofi.* Stockholm: Almqvist & Wiksell International, 1993.
—, 1996, "Varför bör demokratin fördjupas?", in *Svensk Tidskrift*, vol 83, no 2, 1996.
March, J & Simon, A H, 1958, *Organisations.* New York: John Wiley & Sons, 1958.
Nelson, W, 1980, *On justifying democracy.* London: Routledge & Kegan Paul, 1980.
Nozick, R, 1974, *Anarchy, state and utopia.* Oxford: Basil Blackwell, 1974.
Pateman, C, 1970, *Participation and democratic theory.* Cambridge: Cambridge University Press, 1970.
Paul, E F & Miller, J (eds), 1985, *Ethics and economics.* Oxford: Blackwell, 1985.
Petersson, O, 1989, *Makt i det öppna samhället.* Stockholm: Carlssons, 1989.
—, 1993, *Svensk politik.* Stockholm: Publica, 1993.
—, 1996, *Rättsstaten.* Stockholm: Publica, 1996.
Petrén, G, & Ragnemalm, H, 1980, *Sveriges grundlagar.* Stockholm: Publica, 1980.
Plamenatz, J, 1992, *Man and society* (vol II). London: Longman, 1992 (second edition).
Popper, K R, 1972, *Conjectures and refutations.* London: Routledge & Kegan Paul, 1972.
Przeworski, A, 1988, "Democracy as a contingent outcome of conflicts", in Elster & Slagstad, 1988.
Ravich, D (ed), 1992, *The democracy reader.* New York: Harper Perennial, 1992.
Rawls, J, 1971, *A theory of justice.* Cambridge [MA]: Harvard University Press, 1971.
Raz, J, 1986, *The morality of freedom.* Oxford: Clarendon Press, 1986.
Regeringsformen (The Swedish constitution). *Sveriges grundlagar* 1989.
Riker, W H, 1982, *Liberalism against populism.* San Francisco: W H Freeman, 1982.
Riker, W H & Ordeshook, P, C, 1973, *An introduction to positive political theory.* Engelwoods Cliffs [N J]: Prentice-Hall, 1973.

Roemer, J, 1999. "Does democracy engender justice?", in Schapiro & Hacker-Cordón, 1999.
Ross, A, 1963 (1946), *Varför demokrati?* Stockholm: Tidens Förlag, 1963.
Ross, H, 1993, *Democracy*. London: Routledge, 1993.
Rothstein, B (ed), 1995, *Demokrati som dialog.* Stockholm: SNS Förlag, 1995.
Sartori, G, 1974, "Guidelines for concept analysis", in Sartori, 1974.
— (ed), 1974 a, *Social science concepts.* Beverly Hills: Sage Publications, 1974.
—, 1987, *The theory of democracy revisited* (vol. 1-2). Chatham: Chatham House Publ, 1987.
Sannerstedt, A & Jerneck, M (eds), 1994, *Den moderna demokratins problem*. Lund: Studentlitteratur, 1994.
Schapiro, I & Hacker-Cordón, C (ed), 1999, *Democracy's value.* Cambridge: Cambridge University Press, 1999.
Schumpeter, J, 1979 (1942), *Capitalism, socialism and democracy.* London: Allen & Unwin, 1979.
Scruton, R, 1983, *A dictionary of political thought*. London: Pan Books, 1983.
Sejersted. F, 1985, *Demokrati og rettsstat.* Oslo: Universitetsforlaget, 1985.
—, 1988, "Democracy and the rule of law : some historical experiences of contradictions in the striving for good government", in Elster, 1988.
Sen, A, 1979, "Utilitarianism and welfareism", in *Journal of Philosophy*, vol 78, p 463.
—, 1982, "The Impossibility of a paretian liberal," in *Choice, welfare and measurement.* Oxford: Basil Blackwell, 1982.
—, 1985, "The moral standing of the market", in Paul & Miller, 1985.
Sen, A & Williams, B, 1982, "Introduction" in Sen & Williams, 1982 a.
— *(eds)*, 1982 a, *Utilitarianism and beyond.* Cambridge: Cambridge University Press, 1982.
Sidgwick, H, 1981 (1907), *The methods of ethics.* Indianapolis: Hackett Publishing Co, 1981.
Simmonds, N E, 1989, *Juridiska principfrågor*. Stockholm: Norstedts, 1989.
Stevenson, C, 1969 (1944), *Ethics and language.* New Haven: Yale University Press, 1969.
Sugden, R, 1986, *The economics of rights, co-operation & welfare.* Oxford: Oxford University Press, 1986.
Tingsten, H, 1945, *Demokratiens problem*. Stockholm: Norstedts, 1945.
Tännsjö, T, 1992, *Populist democracy : a defence.* London: Routledge & Kegan Paul, 1992.
Waldron, J, 1987, "Theoretical foundations of liberalism", in *The Philosophical Quarterly*, 37, pp 128-150.
Walzer, M, 1983, *Spheres of justice.* New York: Basic Books, 1983.

Parliamentary Supremacy Under Attack: The British Constitution Revisited

Joakim Nergelius

This article may from certain points of view be seen as a kind of "case-study", since it deals with and illustrates the perils and the one-sidedness of unlimited parliamentary supremacy, which in the end has led even the motherland of parliamentarism and parliamentary democracy, the United Kingdom, to modify those ancient and very established principles. This was done mainly by means of the enactment of the Human Rights Act 1998, which also changed the position of the courts. Despite some resistance, both in political circles and in the legal doctrine, those changes have been brought about in a remarkably smooth manner. It is my opinion, therefore, that the development in the United Kingdom may serve to illustrate tendencies of general interest in the contemporary constitutional development (and in today's constitutional law). Not least, it may be of particular interest to other democracies heavily dominated by a majoritarian paradigm, like the Nordic countries.

I. Introduction and Background: Basic and Characteristic Traits of the British Constitution

Unwritten Constitution

The two most characteristic traits of the British constitution, which give it a very peculiar character, are of course the absence of a written constitution or Bill of Rights or any other constitutional text and the unlimited parliamentary supremacy, which should be understood together with the absence of judicial review in the traditional sense of the word, *i e* consisting of the right of the courts to review the compatibility of a law (Act of Parliament) with some other, legal document of a higher status. (In fact, when the term judicial review is used in British law, it refers to the review in the courts of decisions made by administrative agencies, which is a totally different meaning of the term compared with, *e g*, the one used in the USA.)

Since Israel is now in the process of adopting a formal constitution, the United Kingdom is probably the only Western democracy without a written constitutional document, which has a superior status in relation to ordinary laws. This means then, among other things, that the highest organs of the state and the political process are to a large extent ruled by customs, case-law and common law in the constitutional field, traditions and what is normally referred to as *constitutional conventions*. Certain written laws which regulate constitutional issues exist, like the Royal Assent Act from 1967 dealing with how a royal assent to a new law should be given, but those laws do not have a higher status than other laws. This means, among other things, that the British constitution is from a certain point of view flexible and easy to adapt to new conditions, *e g* by new legislation. On the other hand, it means that this constitution consists of a mixture of rules of different kinds—written and unwritten, old and new and so forth. Still, it must be borne in mind that this constitution has worked reasonably well for several hundred years and obviously provided the United Kingdom with favourable conditions for a vital democracy. Any discussions concerning constitutional reforms must be seen against that background.

Parliamentary Supremacy

Although there is a clear relation between the two factors, the idea of parliamentary supremacy is from many points of view more important for today's discussion than the fact that the British constitution is unwritten as such. This has to do with the fact that parliamentary supremacy in the British model means unlimited popular sovereignty and thus an unlimited competence to legislate on any matter at any time. The parliament may thus be seen as omnicompetent or even omnipotent, legally speaking. No formal guarantees exist for basic individual rights and individual liberties, although those are generally acknowledged *as such*, not least in common law. According to the very influential constitutional lawyer and theorist A V Dicey, parliamentary supremacy means that the Parliament has, "under the English constitution, the right to make or unmake any law whatever; and further that no person or body is recognised by the law of England as having a right to override or set aside the legislation of Parliament".[1] Although Dicey wrote this in the 19th century, more than a hundred years ago, the concept itself has not changed much since then.

What does this mean, then, except from the above-mentioned fact that courts are not allowed to set Acts of Parliament aside? The impact of the principle has changed a lot in the last fifty years or so and should perhaps be seen in the light of the general development of the British legal system during this time. In particular, it must be observed that legislation—*statute law*—is no longer, as it used to be, an exception or an "abnormal" source of law in relation to the dominating common law. Historically speaking, British law was to a large extent developed by the courts via cases, which formed the core, in most legal areas, of what is generally known as *common law*. During the 20th century, legislation has grown enormously, from purely quantitative points of view, and thus turned into a much more important source of law than before—in particular given that there is no other source of law which may be considered as higher and which would in case of conflict prevail over a law enacted by Parliament. Parliamentary supremacy does of course also mean that Parliament has a right to enact laws which overrule certain findings in common law.[3]

The idea of parliamentary supremacy was established after the Glorious Revolution in 1688-89. Ever since that event, political power and constitutional supremacy has been located in and even centralised to the British Parliament. Basically, parliamentary supremacy means—in line with the outcome of the revolution—that Parliament was superior to any other body of the state, including the King. Gradually, it also came to mean that an Act of Parliament is, consequently, the highest source of law, a development which stressed popular sovereignty but on the other hand marked the end of older tendencies in common law that had pointed towards the existence of judicial review in the traditional meaning of the word (*e g* in the reasoning of Chief Justice Coke in the well-known Dr Bonham's case from 1610)[4]. In other words, the revolution meant not only that all ideas about the Monarch ruling with some kind of Divine authorisation were swept away; all ideas about human rights as part of some kind of natural law disappeared simultaneously.

Apart from the Glorious Revolution, however, the great *continuity* in British history is perhaps the most striking feature of the constitutional development; that's the reason why so many old traditions have continued to exist, forming, together with the principle of parliamentary supremacy, what is today the British constitution. Finally, the influence of theorists and constitutional lawyers like Bentham and Dicey, arguing against the existence of natural rights and defending parliamentary supremacy, must be stressed in order to explain why this principle was not questioned until fairly recently.

However, there are at least two exceptions from or modifications of the principle. First of all, no Parliament has a right to bind future parliaments, which is perhaps only a logical consequence of the principle. Any law may thus be repealed by a new Act of Parliament.[5] More problematic is probably the relation to EC law, with its claims for supremacy over national laws in all the Member States. From a domestic point of view, this issue has been regulated by the European Communities Act of 1972, which gives direct effect to EC law—already in itself an important limitation of the traditional supremacy—and obliges British courts to interpret any kind of domestic law in the light of the relevant EC law. Still, this Act may be repealed by a new parliament in the same way as any other Act of Parliament.[6] But furthermore, the Act does not regulate what would actually happen if Parliament deliberately legislated contrary to EC law (which has not yet happened). The prevailing opinion of the doctrine is that the courts would then have to apply the domestic law, since doing otherwise would mean violating parliamentary supremacy, which is still the pre-eminent constitutional principle. However, the outcome in the well-known Factortame case from 1990, where the European Court of Justice (ECJ) prevented the British courts from applying an Act of Parliament while its compatibility with the EC Treaty was reviewed by the ECJ (which in the end found it to be contrary to art. 6 (now 12) of the Treaty, forbidding discriminations between nationals[7]) meant a serious blow to this conception of unlimited parliamentary supremacy.[8] The House of Lords, who had asked for this preliminary ruling from the ECJ, complied with the ruling, which in reality meant that a British court refused, for the first time ever, to apply an

Act of Parliament.[9] Although the scope of the judgement may be subject to discussion, it certainly shows that the British courts must normally give priority to EC law before domestic laws in cases of conflict, at least as long as Parliament has not expressly declared that it wishes to act contrary to EC law.[10] Thus, parliamentary supremacy is now somewhat more limited than before.

Still, the long history of this principle and its crucial, even dominant role in the British constitutional development makes it easier to appreciate the importance of the constitutional reforms that have taken place in recent years and which will be dealt with in the next section. Notably, perhaps, this is the case as concerns the devolution project, which may even be seen as a small step towards federalism in a traditionally very centralised state, and the incorporation of the Human Rights Act, which is probably, despite the big impact of EC law, the most serious challenge to the idea of parliamentary supremacy *so far*. In order to fully understand why such radical reforms have been considered necessary to introduce, however, some words should be said about the development, in particular concerning human rights, that the unlimited parliamentary supremacy and the lack of any formal guarantees for individual rights eventually brought about (or, rather, proved itself unable to prevent).

The Development in the 1980's and 90's

The above-mentioned characteristics of the British constitutional system may from a contemporary comparative constitutional perspective seem so odd and peculiar that it may seem justified to ask if this system is at all fit for today's realities, given that modern society is more complicated than the world of yesterday. In other words, even if we assume that the British constitution has worked fairly well until recently, also from the perspective of the citizens (otherwise, it would hardly have survived until now), we may still ask if it is adopted to protect the citizens in today's UK, where written legislation—just like in most western societies—is becoming a main source of law and where the needs of the state to regulate new areas of societal life may put the interests of the individual in jeopardy more often than before. Having this general societal tendency in mind, it is not surprising that an in fact very vivid and intense debate on the lack of protection of individual rights (and some other flaws) in the British constitution started in the late 1970's and gradually gained considerable attention.[11]

This debate, which may also have gathered steam from the quite numerous cases where the United Kingdom was found by the Strasbourg court to have violated the European Convention on Human Rights (ECHR), focused on the impossibility to challenge legislation, or the lack of remedies for individuals to invoke against the Acts of Parliament. It should be seen in the light of a number of disputed cases and events where rights like freedom of speech or freedom of association had been restricted or even violated, like the *Spycatcher* affair concerning the publication of a book and *the Broadcasting Ban*, where certain opinions concerning the situation in Northern Ireland were simply not allowed to be expressed on TV and the radio.[12] Those and other affairs led many scholars to consider the situation of human rights as critical[13], an opinion which may be based either on the concrete, specific situation of various human rights at a particular moment or on the fact that parliamentary supremacy in itself and the very absence of mechanisms protecting the individual against the legislator may cause a permanent risk for violations of basic rights. Logically enough, influential pressure groups like Charter 88, arguing for a written constitution and/or Bill of Rights, were also formed during this period. The core of the problem may thus be described as the alleged need of formal guarantees for basic human rights in a modern democracy, where the citizens, in the absence of such guarantees, would have to settle with the scope of freedom that remains once all legislative enactments have been made. Why should this ”good chaps theory of government”, as it is sometimes called, work more satisfactorily in the UK than in other countries?

At least since the early 1970’s, this debate has been growing and gaining ever more attention in political and academic circles. Various—failed—attempts have been made to interest Parliament in the incorporation of the ECHR, but the two leading political parties remained hostile until some years ago, the Tory Party mainly because of considerations that such reforms could undermine parliamentary supremacy and national sovereignty and the Labour Pary partly because of hostility and suspicions towards the courts and the judges, perceived in general to be reactionary or at least conservative.[14] Apart from such arguments, however, both parties seemed until 1997 to oppose constitutional reforms in general, at least when they were in power, since that would mean handing over or sharing an otherwise unrestricted power to other bodies.[15]

In the debate, various arguments were heard concerning the incorporation of the ECHR or the elaboration of an entirely new constitution or Bill of Rights, and what the respective measures would mean to the idea of parliamentary supremacy, as well as to the relations between the courts and Parliament. A rather striking feature of the debate was that almost all participants focused on what was going to happen if Parliament deliberately decided to legislate contrary to the superior constitutional document, while the debate which merits attention in most other countries (on which normal limitations of the basic human rights that are possible to decide through legislation) has not gained much attention. Also some rather strange suggestions were launched, like enacting a Bill of Rights but not giving it supremacy over other, ordinary Acts of Parliament until after a generous transitional period of 20-30 years![16] During this period, the text was mainly intended to have a pedagogic effect. Anyway, the debate finally led the Labour Party to change its position and propose important constitutional changes in the electoral campaign in 1997, after which the reforms discussed below were initiated. The importance of the debate must therefore not be underestimated, although some of its features may have been a bit peculiar (and in fact impossible to understand outside the British legal context).

Another factor which could be mentioned here is the question if the ancient mechanisms for protection of individual rights that exist in common law may be used even today, in order to correct errors that may occur in the legislative process or to fill the gaps in this protection that will most likely exist in a country like the UK. Traditionally speaking, this has been perhaps the most important area where the courts have been able to protect and enforce human rights.[17] During the twentieth century, though, the importance of this kind of protection diminished, as indicated above, due to the increased scope of legislation. What is however interesting, nevertheless, is that the House of Lords showed an interest in renewing this mechanism of protection of the human rights in the 1990's, shortly after having declared that the ECHR was not a part of British domestic law.[18] In two cases in 1992 and 1993 subsequently, which both concerned issues that were not regulated by law, the House of Lords stated that if it was possible to protect certain rights by means of principles derived from common law, it was simply unnecessary for the courts to investigate too deeply into what the ECHR might or might not admit.[19] In the latter case, a judgement from the Strasbourg court was even said not to be binding for the British courts although it "reinforce(d(a conclusion that we have arrived at in the light of the principles of our domestic jurisprudence".[20] This method of going around the obstacle that the lack of incorporation of the ECHR created was applauded in parts of the doctrine[21], but at the same time it is fairly easy to show the weakness of a protection of human rights that can *only* rely on rather vague principles of this kind. First of all, it offers, as indicated above, no protection at all against the legislator, if he decides to restrict a certain right. Secondly, it is dependant on the attitudes of the individual judge(s) deciding in a particular case.[22] Therefore, it seems from many points of view to be a rather weak alternative to legislative protection like *e g* the one offered by the Human Rights Act.

II. The Constitutional Reforms Initiated since 1997—A Survey

Already in the election campaign of 1997, the constitutional issues became a hot political topic in a way which is not very usual in political campaigns in today's western democracies. Briefly speaking, this was due to the fact that the Labour Party had a few years earlier joined the Liberal Party in urging for constitutional reforms in a number of areas, including the incorporation of the ECHR[23], while the ruling Tory Party opposed this.

Very shortly, then, after the landslide victory in the election on 1 May 1997, the new Government launched an ambitious programme for constitutional reforms. Already in the Queen's Speech on May 14th that year, constitutional bills (constitutional, that is, although formally not different from other laws) were promised in a number of areas, such as referendums on the devolution in Scotland and Wales, with the ambition of establishing local assemblies there, to incorporate the ECHR into national law, to implement the Amsterdam Treaty (which was incredibly much smoother than the implementation of the Maastricht Treaty had been in 1993), and to initiate a thorough parliamentary reform. As far as the latter issue is concerned, the House of Lords Act, cutting the number of hereditary peers to 92 and reducing the life peers to 527 (with an additional 26 bishops and 27 current and former law lords), was passed in November 1999.[24] A proportional mode of electing the MEP's was used for the first time in the election to the European Parliament in June 1999, but apart from that, no electoral reform looks likely to occur before the next parliamentary election. Neither has any other reform concerning the House of Commons been proposed.

Apart from that, however, almost the entire reform programme has already been carried through, which is somewhat impressive in itself.[25] A devolution, for instance, has already taken place, which is a significant development in the UK, traditionally a very centralised state (also the Northern Ireland Act from 1998 could be mentioned in this context). An important Freedom of Information Bill, replacing the strict Official Secrets Act from 1989, has been proposed in 1999. Of particular interest here, however, from legal and theoretical points of view, is the incorporation of the ECHR via the Human Rights Act of 1998.[26]

Although enacted in 1998, the law will in fact not enter into force until 2 October 2000, due to the fact that extensive preparations for the courts and the Government, in order for them to be able to live with and adapt to the new law, have been considered to be necessary. This shows to some extent the importance and significance of the new law. But the question still is if the content of the law does in fact correspond to or justify the fuss which it has already caused.

The Act turns the ECHR into British national law, with the exception of two of the most important or crucial rules of the Convention, namely art. 1 and 13. Article 1 provides for the State to secure for everyone within its jurisdiction the rights and freedoms mentioned in articles 2-18 of the ECHR, while article 13 provides that everyone whose Convention rights and freedoms are violated shall have an effective remedy against the alleged violation. The opinion of the Government here was that the Act itself meant the fulfilment of article 1 and that adequate remedies were also provided by the Act (section 8); it also stated that additional remedies may exist under common law, which should in that case not be encroached upon.[27] The first statement may seem logical enough, but it is, after all, perhaps not entirely clear that domestic remedies correspond to the ones referred to in the ECHR.[28] Even more striking or alarming, though, is the fact that the Government refused to bind the domestic courts to the jurisprudence of the Strasbourg court, the ECtHR. Section 2(1) of the Act now only requires the courts to "take into account" the jurisprudence of the Strasbourg organs. The Lord Chancellor[29] here made it clear during the enactment procedures in Parliament that the courts were in fact free to depart from this jurisprudence where it was found to be appropriate, *e g* when there was no clear ruling on an issue from the court to be found and a decision from the Commission in the same area might seem outdated.[30]

However, the model of incorporation now used basically means that legislation should always be read and given effect, as far as possible, in a manner that makes it compatible with the convention rights (clause 3(1). Where this is not possible, though, the courts are not empowered to strike down the law, a fact that serves, it seems, as a kind of preservation of the parliamentary sovereignty. In the words of Parliament itself, the duty of construction which follows from *sect* 3, and which is imposed on all British courts, does not "affect the validity, continuing operation or enforcement of any incompatible primary legislation". Instead, section 4 of the Act introduces an entirely new mechanism, through which the courts can signal to the Government that a provision of legislation is in their view incompatible with the ECHR. The actions then to be taken by the Government[31] will be discussed below, but one point may be made already here about the constitutional significance of the reform. The method of obliging the courts to interpret laws in accordance with another set of norms is familiar from the European Communities Act of 1972 (*sect* 2). Still, what is entirely new here is the possibility for the courts to signal to the Government that the ECHR is, according to their opinion, being violated by a certain law.[32] It should, however, be observed that this possibility is not open to all the courts; only the House of Lords, the Privy Council and the Courts-Martial Appeal Court may make use of it, together with the Court of Appeal and the High Court in England and Wales and the Court of Session or the High Court of Justiciary in Scotland. This limitation may of course be criticised, but might also reflect the risk, real or not, that Parliament would otherwise more or less drown in such declarations. Furthermore, the Government or indeed Parliament will not be obliged to take action once such a signal has been sent, but as the Home Secretary has made clear in parliamentary discussions concerning the topic, it seems likely that they would, in most cases, "wish to respond to such a situation and would do so rapidly".[33] Still, such a declaration of incompatibility has no operative or coercive effect and does not effect the validity, continuing operation or enforcement of the law in question.[34]

One thing that must be observed, however, is that the courts may under section 3(2) c of the new act strike down *secondary legislation*[35], as well as the Acts of the new Scottish Parliament and the Northern Ireland Assembly, which are here defined as subordinate legislation, and the rules from the Welsh Assembly, which have the formal status of secondary legislation (*sect* 21).[36] Thus, the parliamentary supremacy of the British Parliament and the House of Commons itself is somehow put in a "preferred position".

Furthermore, section 6 of the Human Rights Act forbids all public authorities to act in a way that is incompatible with a convention right, unless they are required to do so in order to give effect to primary legislation. Here, once again thus, the preserving, at least on a theoretical level, of the model of parliamentary supremacy may be observed (this issue will be further discussed in the next chapter).

An intense discussion, which cannot be recaptured here, has taken place as to what is to be counted as a "public authority" under this section.[37] Suffice it to say that all state authorities and the courts are included and that the court have the possibility of giving effect to the ECHR also in conflicts between private parties, although they are not forced to do so. A certain horizontal effect of the ECHR may thus take place. Individuals who feel that their rights under the convention have been violated may, according to article 7, invoke this as a legal argument in any kind of proceedings, but it is also possible to initiate proceedings solely on the ground that such a violation has taken place. However, the failure of Parliament to legislate on a certain matter may never be counted as a breach of the law (*sect* 6(6), which seems logical considering what was said above about the attempts to preserve the parliamentary supremacy.

Should a court find that a violation committed by a public authority has actually taken place, it may grant whatever remedy available that seems just and appropriate to the suffering part. Thus, also financial compensation may be a result.

The remaining point of interest then, from a constitutional point of view, are the reactions of the Government and Parliament once the court has signalled under section 4 that a certain law does in fact violate the ECHR. Of course, the assumption is that those two bodies act and intend to act in a way that is compatible with the Convention, and this does indeed characterise the whole construction of the Act[38]. However, the question as to what will happen if a violation should after all take place is for many reasons more interesting, not least from a principled point of view.

The Home Secretary made an interesting remark in this context concerning the right of the Government to ignore such a warning from the courts, should it touch upon certain important and politically sensitive issues like *e g* abortion.[39] The example may be good or not (many experts and commentators, including myself, would say that other examples of judicial review from recent years, notably in Germany, have concerned issues like foreign policy, which the courts are more genuinely unfit to deal with than they are with abortion)[40], but that is strictly speaking beside the point here. What is important is that the Government preserves the "right" to ignore such a warning or signal from the courts. What would remain for the alleged violated party, then, would be to complain to the Convention organs (a procedure which may, as we know, take a certain time). This would amount to a new and unprecedented situation in the history of the jurisprudence of those organs and how they would handle the situation would of course depend on the situation. Anyway, the Home Secretary has also declared that the Government (and thus Parliament, presumably) would in the end follow such a judgement from the ECtHR.

Quite apart from that rather bizarre situation, there is according to section 10 of the new Act a possibility for the Government, in response to a declaration of incompatibility from the higher courts (and after the appeal process is exhausted in a given case), to issue a so-called "remedial order", empowering the courts to set the legal provision in question aside (a possibility which some critics have referred to as an "Henry VIII power", since no scrutiny by the Parliament is foreseen to take place[41]). This opportunity also exists if and when a new judgement passed by the ECtHR makes a provision of a law incompatible with the Convention. As far as subordinate legislation is concerned, it is there whenever a Minister considers it to be incompatible with the ECHR. Moreover, this rather interesting new construction will probably tend to make the courts more independent in relation to Parliament, a fact that will be further discussed in the next chapter.

Finally, it should be noted that section 19 of the Human Rights Act introduces an entirely new requirement on government Ministers, when introducing legislation in Parliament, to make a written statement either that the provisions of the legislation are compatible with the ECHR or that they cannot make such a statement but nevertheless wish Parliament to proceed in considering the Bill. If this kind of statement cannot be made, the parliamentary scrutiny of the Bill is of course likely to be intense[42], but apart from that the statement as such does not seem to have any legal effect.

III. The Constitutional Impact of the New Reforms, Particularly of the New Human Rights Act

It should perhaps be stressed at once that the very fact that so many important constitutional changes have occurred in such a relatively short time is of course of particular importance in a country with a legal system like the UK, where the unwritten constitution is largely based on ancient principles, which have existed in most cases for 300 years or even more. In this context, and focusing on the rule and legitimacy of judicial review in relation to majority rule, popular sovereignty and parliamentary supremacy—prevailing ideals in the UK like in Sweden—it can hardly be doubted that the new Human Rights Act does in fact mean quite a lot in terms of new ideas, new legal rules and institutions in British constitutional law, despite the fact that the Act does formally leave parliamentary sovereignty unrestrained (if not unchanged). Quite how far this change goes must however be analysed a bit further.

In order to grasp the importance of these changes, some words must first be said about the position of the courts. In the doctrine, different opinions (which may to a certain extent reflect the opinions of the various writers themselves) have been expressed as to the significance of the reforms in recent years and the enactment of the Human Rights Act in particular, stretching from the opinion that parliamentary supremacy remains intact[43], to the opposite idea that already the unlimited capacity of the courts to interpret laws in relation to the ECHR under *sect* 3 and 4 of the Act is so unclear and imprecise that it might undermine the supremacy as it has hitherto been known.[44] In this respect, it may be noted that the Lord Chancellor, when presenting the Bill to Parliament, described its purpose as giving the courts "as much space as possible to protect human rights, short of a power to set aside or ignore Acts of Parliament"[45], a description which is rather bold, having the constitutional history of the UK in mind. An important further point has here been made in an article by the Lord Chancellor himself, who has underlined the new possibility under the Act for the British courts to adjust the violations of the ECHR themselves, instead of having to wait for a reaction from Strasbourg.[46] This could even, as he stresses, have a "spill-over-effect" into other areas of law.[47] Although parliamentary supremacy is formally upheld, in the words of Ewing, "(T)his is not to deny that the Human Rights Act confers a significant political power on the courts, or indeed that it enables the courts formally to set the agenda on human rights questions". Ewing, who is not known as a proponent of handing over political power to the courts, continues:

> Nor is it to deny that in the 'overwhelming majority of cases', a declaration of incompatibility will be accepted by the Government and Parliament of the day, thereby ensuring that the elected branch will in practice defer to the unelected branch.[48]

Thus, it seems impossible to deny that the new Act in itself means a strengthening of the position of the courts, a development which may also be marked by events like the well- known Pinochet case[49], where it became clear to everyone that the courts possessed hitherto unknown powers (due mainly to developments in international law) in relation to former heads of state. Also the strengthening of the protection of basic rights in common law which took place in the middle of the 1990's contributed to this situation[50], together with a general development of what is known as judicial review in British law, which however mainly refers to the (in latter years increased) authority of the courts to strike down an illegal administrative action by the public authorities[51], which may now increase even more due to the new Human Rights Act and the obligations it puts on all public authorities.[52] Certain important things have therefore undoubtedly been changed in British law, for better or for worse but anyway for ever, as it seems now.

What, then, does this new development mean to the very concept of parliamentary supremacy and sovereignty as such? In relation to EC law, we have already seen that parliamentary supremacy as such is left untouched, since it is assumed that British courts must uphold the legislation which is enacted though being recognised as contrary to EC law (something which has not yet happened) and Parliament may at any time by express enactment repeal the European Communities Act of 1972, just like it may do with any other law. The outcome in the Factortame case[53] has challenged this notion as far as the duty to await the judgements of the ECJ on the validity and interpretation of EC law is concerned, but it is still valid as such, thus turning the limitation on parliamentary supremacy that EC law entails into a temporary and reversible one.[54]

Still, the impact of what has taken place in recent years (including the devolution and the commenced reform of Parliament) is striking, not least in a historical perspective. This development may of course be seen in the light of a general development in international public law, where much more emphasis is today put on human rights (and, consequently, less on state sovereignty) than fifty years ago and where a large corpus of law, recognising fundamental freedoms, now exists.[55] Certainly, this development contributes to a change of values also in national law, not least in states where an emphasis has traditionally been put on sovereignty. The real capacity of the Parliament, or other authorities, to act in a way that would violate the ECHR is of course immensely smaller than it was, say, ten years ago.

Nevertheless, it is a fact that the incorporation of the ECHR has been secured in a manner which, in the words of Ewing, "subordinates Convention rights to constitutional principle and democratic tradition".[56] The Human Rights Act does in fact not give the courts the power to strike down legislation and may therefore, after all, not be the big breakthrough for the ideas of the separation of powers or constitutionalism in the traditional sense that could mean the undermining or final reformulation of the idea of unlimited parliamentary supremacy. On the other hand, as may be illustrated in the doctrine, the attempts to show that parliamentary supremacy still exists in an unchanged form tend to be rather theoretical.[57] There seems to be no doubt, after all, that the enactment of the Human Rights Act of 1998, together with the developments that have already taken place in recent years within EC law (such as the Factortame case and the development of judicial protection and the right to a legal remedy in general), common law and in the area of—British—judicial review, have had a huge impact on the British constitution, changing once and for all the relations between the courts and the Parliament/Government and largely weakening, if not entirely destroying, the concept of unlimited parliamentary sovereignty. Nowhere is this easier to see than in the constitutional debate on these issues, for instance in the legal periodicals. Ten years ago, this debate focused almost entirely on a crisis in the British constitutional system, with alleged frequent violations of basic rights (as described above in chapter 1) and an absence of remedies or formal guarantees against those violations. Today, the debate concerns the extent of the undermining of parliamentary supremacy that the recent developments have brought about. Feldman, for instance, is of the opinion that the capacity of the courts, or some of them, to grant a declaration of incompatibility "subtly alters the allocation of powers", since, for the first time, Parliament has invited the judges to tell it that it has acted wrongly by legislating incompatibly with a Convention right.[58] Even though Parliament will not have to obey such a remark from a court, it seems correct to talk, as Leigh and Lustgarten do, of "an authoritative repudiation of the Diceyian heritage".[59]

Even if this development follows its own paths, respecting the British legal traditions (which is the reason why it can only be fully understood in the light of those traditions), it must be seen as yet another example of what is internationally most often called *the judicialisation of politics* and which seems to be more or less a world-wide phenomenon, strengthening the position of the courts and other legal bodies in modern democracies.[60] Even the UK, the motherland of parliamentary democracy, is thus not immune against this development.

IV. A theoretical Analysis and Concluding Remarks

Finally, a few theoretical aspects of this development should be observed. One aspect of this very interesting development is of course, as underlined most sharply by Jowell[61], that an unwritten and thus "open" constitution like the British is open to changes, which makes it logical, then, that it will adapt to the changing conditions of society. Still, we are talking here of legal traditions which have existed (and functioned) for more than 300 years and which must thus be described as solid. This situation could even, to put it in philosophical terms, be described as a triumph for what John Rawls refers to as "the idea of public reason" in a constitutional democracy, since it means adapting the democracy to new conditions in order to make it function better without necessarily changing the constitutional institutions.[62] Still, the fact that the changes in recent years have been described in the doctrine as perhaps the most important ones since 1688[63] (since they represent the most dramatic challenge to the idea of parliamentary supremacy, the very landmark of the Glorious Revolution, witnessed since that date), must be underlined. What we are discussing here is in other words not everyday business, to put it bluntly. It should also be underlined that less than ten years ago, the very *inability* for a hange in the British constitution was in the focus of the debate, as mentioned above.

From a constitutional, theoretical and perhaps also ideological perspective, two points are especially striking. From a purely theoretical point of view, it should be observed that the Human Rights Act means an important change of the very concept of a basic right in British law, since this will no longer be classified as a *residual liberty*, consisting of the freedom that remains in a particular area once all the restrictions that follow from the applicable legislation have been taken into account, but rather as a right against the public authorities, which always exists and which those authorities have to respect.[64] This will of course also affect the reasoning of the courts, since their decisions will often have to be based on a more principled, and perhaps moral, basis than before.[65]

Ideologically, the fundamental shift in the position of the Labour Party is particularly interesting. In the early 90's, this party was still deeply suspicious about the contribution of judges to civil liberties and even more suspicious of letting courts handle controversial political issues. In the procedure of enactment of the Human Rights Act, the Home Secretary has described the law as nothing less than "a key component in our drive to modernise our society and refresh our democracy ... to bring about a better balance between rights and responsibilities, between the powers of the state and the freedom of the individual".[66] Some years ago, this could have been described as "constitutional newspeak", coming from a member of the current government, but in fact the Lord Chancellor has been even more outspoken in this respect, describing the Act as a demonstration of the Government's view that the most serious threat to liberty in a modern society is an absence of written guarantees of freedom. "The Human Rights Bill is our bulwark against this danger. The traditional freedom of the individual under an unwritten constitution to do himself that which is not prohibited by laws gives no protection from a misuse of power by the State, nor any protections from acts or omissions by public bodies which harm individuals in a way that is incompatible with their human rights under the Convention."[67] This echoes of the criticism that so many scholars and independent organisations raised against the Government some ten years ago, but is in fact most contrary to traditional views in British constitutional law as taught *e g* by Dicey. The Lord Chancellor especially underlines the lack of protection against the state itself which is inherent in the traditional British conception of a right and the traditional view on unlimited parliamentary supremacy. Here, it could be justified to talk of a real breakthrough in the political environment, of great interest also to other countries.[68]

Generally speaking, the debate on the enactment of the Human Rights Act has been most revealing in terms of showing the emergence of a new constitutional landscape. It has also stressed the importance of legal discussions in contemporary society.[69] Thus, it marks a very important constitutional change, with global implications. Still, it could be remembered that the fact that the change has come about so relatively quickly and undramatically is partly due to the parliamentary supremacy itself and the effect and huge impact of the great victory of the Labour Party in 1997—which is of course one of life's many paradoxes.

Notes

1. See Dicey, 1950, pp 19-20.
2. *Cf* David, 1985, p 361: "...in the eyes of an English jurist, law which is legislative in origin—statute law—has traditionally appeared as somewhat abnormal in character."
3. *Cf* Feldman, 2000, p 166.
4. *77 English Reports*, p 646.
5. See in detail: Allan, 1985, p 627.
6. It could also be mentioned that a referendum concerning continued membership in the European Communities did in fact take place in 1975.
7. C-221/89, ECR I 1991, p 3905.
8. C-213/89, ECR 1990 I, p 2433.
9. *Regina versus Secretary of State for Transport*, ex parte Factortame Ltd, (1990) 2 A C 85.
10. *Cf* Bamforth, , 1998, p 572. As to the general effects of EC law or European law in general, including ECHR, see also Jacobs, 1999, p 232-245, and Hammond, 1998, p 34-43.
11. The debate as such is treated (in Swedish) by Nergelius (Nergelius, 1996, pp 343 ff). Maybe the best overview of the legal position of the basic individual rights in British law before the reforms initiated in 1997 is provided by David Feldman in the huge study Feldman, 1993.
12. Other well-known cases regarding limitations of basic rights during this period concerned Clive Ponting, a civil servant who informed a Labour MP about certain defence matters related to the Falklands war and was subsequently prosecuted (an affair which preceded the controversial Official Secrets Act of 1989, now to be replaced by a new Freedom of Information Act) and a prohibition for staff in civil intelligence (Government Communications Headquarters in Cheltenham) to organise themselves in trade unions. It seems in fact to be a very general and broadly accepted opinion that the *standard of human rights* in the UK, *i e* the level of their protection and the degree to which they were respected by the Parliament and Government, deteriorated during the 1980's; see *e g* Dworkin, 1990, and in "Devaluing liberty", in *Index on Censorship* 8/1988.
13. See *e g* Robertson, 1989, p 390.
14. Some ideological arguments of this kind were presented by John Griffith in Griffith, 1977.
15. *Cf* Wright, 1981, p 320: "However, I suspect that the main obstacle in the British Parliament is not handing over power to judges in particular, but handing over power at all...We must remember that, in Britain, the ruling political party controls both the executive and legislative branches."

16. See Feldman, 1993, p 87.
17. See *e g* the well-known case Entick versus Carrington from 1765 (1765, 19 State Trials 1030), where a house search was considered to be "subversive of all the comforts of society".
18. A conclusion which was reached in a case concerning the Broadcasting Ban, Regina versus Secretary of State for the Home Department, ex parte Brind (1991) 1 A C 696. See also the case Regina versus Secretary of State for Defence, ex parte Smith, (1996) Q B 517.
19. Derbyshire County Council versus Times Newspapers Ltd., (1993) 2 Weekly Law Reports 449, 456 and Regina versus Secretary of State for the Home Department, ex parte Leech, (1993) 4 *All England Law Reports*, 539.
20. Ibidem (Leech), p 555.
21. See in particular two articles by Laws, 1993, p 59-79 and 1994, p 213-27.
22. This could be illustrated by a recent case, Regina versus Secretary of State for the Home Department, ex parte Simms, judgment 8 July 1999 (www.parliament.uk/house_of_lords/judgments), concerning the right for prisoners who claimed that they were innocent though serving life sentences, to give oral interviews to journalists. The Court of Appeal found that this right was not covered by the freedom of speech in common law, whereas the House of Lords reached a different conclusion.
23. Traditionally, the Labour Party adhered to the idea of parliamentary supremacy and opposed reform ideas of this kind; see Nergelius, 1996., p 348 ff. A historical survey of the development within the Labour Party is provided by K D Ewing, (Ewing, 1999, p 80-82). See also Feldman, 1998, p 169 and Marquand, 1999.
24. A second step of this reform expected to include a final decision on the number of members that the House of Lords was going to have and the installation of special committees to appoint those members was announced and generally supposed to take place in the next few years, though probably not until after the next parliamentary election.
25. For an overview of what has taken place, see Hazell, 1999, p 84-103
26. In fact, in the doctrine there has already been some discussion as to whether a true incorporation of the Convention will actually take place through the enactment of this law (see *e g* Ewing, 1999, p 84). That this is the purpose and the real legal effect, with some exceptions to be discussed below, seems however to be reasonably clear; see *e g* Francesca Klug, The Human Rights Act 1998, *Pepperversus Hart* and all that, PL 1999, p 246. This is also clear from certain statements made by the Minister of Justice, The Lord Chancellor, when the law was enacted, which are also referred to by Klug, 1999.
27. It is of course possible that the protection of a right under common law could in a particular case go further than the same protection

under the ECHR, notably in regard of the rather dynamic development of the protection of basic rights in common law that has in fact taken place in recent years; see *e g* Fenwick, 1999, p 503 and Laws, 1998 pp 254 ff. As Laws rightly points out, it is also a fact that the rather broad and general language of the ECHR does in fact correspond more to the development of general principles within common law than with the construction of statutory provisions. Still, the Lord Chancellor was careful, when presenting the new Bill to Parliament, to warn the courts from "legislating" via common law in such cases or even generally to do so, where a convention right would be infringed by incompatible legislation (or even, theoretically, by the very absence of legislation): "In my view, the courts may not act as legislators and grant new remedies for infringement of convention rights unless the common law itself enables them to develop new rights or remedies." (583 H L 783, November 24, 1997.)

28. *Cf* Ewing, 1999, p 85 and 90.
29. Who may be described as the Minister of Justice but also has certain other tasks; for a recent survey of his various competencies, see Woodhouse, 1998, p 617-32.
30. See Klug, 1999.
31. *Cf* Ewing, 1999, p 88.
32. *Cf* Feldman, 2000, p 165: "The Act initiates a fundamental constitutional change by introducing new values and an altered frame for reference to UK public law. These, and the mechanisms which the Act introduces for protecting human rights, will significantly affect the operation of traditional constitutional principles." See also, p 180.
33. 306 H C 780 (February 16, 1998).
34. Certain theoretical aspects as to whether such a situation could amount to what is generally known as *implied repeal* of the questioned law (which does in fact not seem to be the case) are treated by Bamforth, 1998, p 573 ff.
35. Here, a comparison with Swedish conditions is of particular interest. The so-called manifest rule (*"uppenbarhetskravet"*) in chapter 11, article 14 of the Swedish constitution applies to laws enacted by parliament as well as to secondary legislation issued by the Government, a fact that may be seriously questioned. For a definition of primary legislation, see Feldman 2000, p 181.
36. See here, concerning the relation to the Devolution project, Craig & Walters, 1999, p 274-303.
37. See, among others, Klug, 1999, and Ewing1999, p 89.
38. See generally Steyn, 1997 p 85.
39. 317 H.C. 1301 (October 21, 1998).
40. See in particular two cases from Bundesverfassungsgericht, the German Constitutional Court, from 1993-94, concerning the possibility

for German troops to take part in international military actions, Entscheidungen des Bundesverfassungsgerichts 89, 38 and 90, 286.

41. *E g* Klug, 1999, p 264, and Feldman, 2000, p 187 s.
42. Although the importance of this scrutiny in a situation of that kind may of course be questioned, given the tight grip that governments now tend to have on Parliament; *cf* Ewing, 1999, p 96 f.
43. *Cf* Steyn, 1997.
44. *E g* Marshall, 1998, p 167-70. See also Ewing, 1999, p 86 f.
45. 582 H L 1228 (November 3, 1997).
46. Irvine, 1998, p 225.
47. Irvine, 1998, p 230.
48. Op.cit., p 99.
49. (1999) 1 All E.R. 577.
50. See *e g* the case Regina versus Home Secretary, ex parte Fire Brigades Union (1995) 2 A C 513, where a Law Lord who insisted that it was " the task of Parliament and the executive in tandem, not of the courts, to govern the country" and that the courts should observe the boundaries which had existed for more than 300 years (p 567-68) found himself dissenting from the majority.
51. A rather heated discussion has here taken place in recent years as to whether this kind of control over the administration is restricted to a control of whether its actions are *ultra vires* or not, *i e* whether it is limited to a control of whether there was any kind of implied or express legal support for its actions, or if it may also amount to a more general control of the legality of administrative action. A leading proponent of the first view is Mark Elliott (see Elliott, 1999, p 119-37, but this view has been questioned and criticised, among others by A H Hammond (Hammond, 1998, p 42), Jeffrey Jowell (Jowell, 1999, p 448-60) and Paul Craig, (Craig, 1999, p 428-442) all stressing, among other things, the importance of the development that has taken place within common law. Although the issue is sensitive and has an obvious relation to the discussion on the role of the courts and parliamentary supremacy, since the ultra vires doctrine is traditionally seen as the consequence of this principle and the proper justification for judicial review may therefore indicate the limits of judicial power, it can not be developed further here, due above all to lack of space.
52. See Leigh & Lustgarten, 1999, p 518 and in detail pp 522 ff.
53. Regina versus Secretary of State, ex parte Factortame (No 2) (1991) 1 A.C. 603.
54. *Cf* Elliott, 1999, p 128. For an argument to the contrary, claiming that Factortame has in fact undermined the idea of parliamentary supremacy in relation to EC law once and for all (which seems in fact exaggerated), see Bamforth, 1998, p 578 f.
55. *Cf* Irvine, 1998, p 221.
56. Ewing, 1999, p 98.

57. See *e g* Elliott, himself claiming (Elliott, 1999, pp 133 f) that the adversaries of unlimited parliamentary supremacy tend to point to theoretical and unlikely examples like massive violations of human rights (which may, however, have important practical implications) in order to show that the supremacy has its limits. See also Bamforth (himself an adversary, as it seems, of unlimited supremacy; Bamforth, 1998), who goes to lengths in order to mobilise an imagined defence of a still existing unlimited supremacy.
58. Op.cit., p187.
59. Leigh & Lustgarten, 1999, p 509.
60. *E g* Ewing (Ewing, 1999, p 79) has described the Human Rights Act as representing "an unprecedented transfer of political power from the executive and legislature to the judiciary, and a fundamental restructuring of our 'political constitution'." He then continues: "As such it is unquestionably the most significant formal redistribution of political power in this country since 1911 and perhaps since 1688".
61. Op.cit, p 458 and in particular, p 460. It may be noted here that Jowell in fact criticised, in 1989, the inability for change in the British constitution; see "The constitution : decline and renewal", in Jowell & Oliver, 1989, p 368: "The peculiar genius of the British constitution is supposed to consist in its flexibility and capacity for evolutionary change. But the most striking characteristic of our constitution has been its failure to adapt to the changed needs of the nation." Obviously, the events of the last few years have led him to a different conclusion.
62. See Rawls' essay "The idea of public reason revisited", in Rawls, 1999, pp 131-80 (where Rawls this time abstains from defining what a constitutional regime means in institutional terms and just talks about public reason in collective, democratic decision-making).
63. Ewing, 1999.
64. See *e g* Irvine, 1998, p224, who talks of a shift from negative rights to "a positive entitlement expressed in clear and positive terms". See also Feldman, 2000, p166 and 204: "Human rights and fundamental freedoms are becoming part of the legal scenery in the United Kingdom for the first time."
65. Feldman, 2000, p 229: "In reaching its judgment, therefore, the Court will need to expand and explain its own view of whether the conduct is legitimate. It will produce in short a decision on the *morality* of the conduct and not simply its compliance with the bare letter of the law." See also Feldman, 2000, p 235, as far as judicial review of administrative decisions is concerned, as well as Feldman, 2000, p 193 and Leigh & Lustgarten, 1999, p 538 f.
66. 306 H C 769 (February 16, 1998).
67. Op cit 224 f.
68. See further Marquand, 1999.

69. Ewing, 1999, p 79, illustrates this by a quotation from a debate in the House of Lords, where one lord protested against "these esoteric lectures on law at this time of night", having "never heard anything like this after dinner" in the 18 years he had been in the Lords (HL Deb vol 583 col 829, 24 November 1997). Ewing continues: "He had better get used to it: the law and the lawyers are about to dominate all the debates, at all times of the day and night, before and after every mealtime." This may be exaggerated, but the tendency as such seems to be clear enough.

References

Allan, T R S, 1985, "The limits of parliamentary soverignity", in *Public law*. 1985, p 614-636.

Bamforth, Nicholas, 1998, "Parliamentary sovereignty and the Human Rights Act 1998", in *Public Law* 1998, pp 571-82.

Craig, P, 1999, "Competing models of judicial review", *Public Law*, pp 428-447.

Craig, P & Walters, M, 1999, "The courts, devolution and judicial review", in *Public Law* 1999, p 274-303.

David, R, 1985, *Major legal systems in the world today*. London: Stevens, 1985 (3rd ed, English translation by J E C Brierley of *Les grands systèmes de droit contemporains*. Paris: Dalloz.

Dicey, A V, 1950, *Introduction to the study of the law of the constitution*. London: Macmillan, St.Martin's Press, 1950 (9th ed).

Dworkin, Ronald, 1990, *A Bill of rights for Britain*. London: Chatto & Windus (Chatto CounterBlasts, 16), 1990.

"Devaluing Liberty", in *Index on Censorship* nr 8/1988, p 7 ff.

Elliott, Mark, 1999, "The demise of parliamentary sovereignty? : the implications for justifying judicial review", in *Law Quarterly Review*, 1999, pp 119-37.

Ewing, K D, 1999, "The human rights and parliamentary democracy", in *Modern Law Review* 1999, pp 79-99.

Feldman, David, 1993, *Civil liberties and human rights in England and Wales*. Oxford: Clarendon Press, 1993 -

—, 2000, "The Human Rights Act 1998 and constitutional principles", in *Legal Studies*, 2000, pp 165-206.

Fenwick, Helen, 1999, "The right to protest, the Human Rights Act and the margin of appreciation", in *Modern Law Review*, 1999, pp 491-514

Griffith, John, 1977, *The politics of the judiciary*. London: Fontana, 1977.

Hammond, A H, 1998, "Judicial review : the continuing interplay between law and policy", in *Public Law*, 1998, pp 34-43.

Hazell, Robert, 1999, "Reinventing the constitution : can the state survive?" in *Public Law*, 1999, pp 84-103.

Irvine, L (Baron Irvine of Lairg), 1998, "The development of human rights in Britain under an incorporated Convention on Human Rights", in *Public Law*, 1998, pp 221-236.

Jacobs, Francis G, 1999, "Public law : the impact of Europe", in *Public Law,* 1999, p 232-245.

Jowell, Jeffrey, 1999, "Of vires and vacuums : the constitutional context of judicial review", in *Public Law,* 1999, pp 448-460.

Jowell, J & Oliver, D (*eds*), 1989, "The constitution: decline and renewal", in *The changing constitution*. Oxford: Clarendon Press, 1989.

Klug, Francesca, 1999, "The Human Rights Act 1998 : *Pepper v Hart* and all that", in *Public Law,* 1999, pp 246-273.

Laws, Sir John, 1993, "Is the high court the guardian of fundamental constitutional rights?" in *Public Law,* 1993, pp 59-79.

—, 1994, "Judicial remedies and the constitution", in *Modern Law Review,* 1994, pp 213-227.

—, 1998, "The limitations of human rights", in *Public Law,* 1998, pp 254-265.

Leigh, I & Lustgarten, L, 1999, "Making rights real : the courts, remedies and the Human Rights Act", in *Cambridge Law Journal*, 1999, pp 509-45.

Marquand, David, 1999, "Populism or pluralism? : New Labour and the Constitution" (paper). London (School of Public Policy, The Constitution Unit), 1999.

Marshall, Geoffrey, 1998, "Interpreting interpretation in the Human Rights Bill", in *Public Law* 1998, p167-70.

Nergelius, Joakim, 1996, *Konstitutionellt rättighetsskydd : svensk rätt i ett komparativt perspektiv* (diss). Stockholm: Fritzes, 1996.

Rawls, John, 1999, *The law of peoples.* Cambridge [MA] & London: Harvard University Press, 1999.

Robertson, Geoffrey, 1989, *Freedom, the individual and the law.* Harmondsworth: Penguin, 1989 (6th ed).

Steyn, J (Lord Steyn), 1997, "The weakest and least dangerous department of government", in *Public Law,* 1997, pp 84-95.

Woodhouse, Diana, "The office of Lord Chancellor", in *Public Law,* 1998, pp 617-32.

Wright, J Skelly, 1981, "The Bill of Rights in Britain and America : a not quite full circle", in *Tulane Law Review*, 1981, pp 291-325.

Arbitrary Democracy

Sverker Härd

I. Democracy and Collective Decisions

The central tenet in most conceptions of democracy is that power must be derived from the people and that democracy realises the popular will. Various constitutional mechanisms contribute to representing the citizens' opinions in order to define a democratic choice or decision. This study raises questions about the effects of constitutions and different constitutional solutions. Do constitutions matter? This study discusses electoral systems, one of the most important instruments in the constitutional toolbox of democratic institutions. Do different electoral systems have an effect on the distribution of seats in parliament and political power, and if so, in what ways? Is it possible to define the popular will and form a representative parliament? Should it have been different if Sweden had chosen another electoral system than the proportional plurality rule? These are the questions that are central to this study.

The Debate on Electoral Systems In Sweden

This analysis has an empirical and a theoretical point of reference. Our empirical context is the debate on constitutional issues in Sweden. The Swedish political and economic development in the 1980's and 90's has warranted stronger governments with more political influence and efficiency. One argument is that the budget deficit and the downscaling of public welfare schemes have diminished the room for political manoeuvre. Another is that the same period has seen an increasing fragmentation of the party system, resulting in decreasing co-operation between parliamentarians and parties.

The debate has therefore centred on the perceived failure of the existing electoral system in producing strong governments with clear parliamentary majorities. The suggested rectification for an impotent government has been to infuse features into the electoral system that would strengthen the majority by the over-representation of larger parties. The British majoritarian electoral system has been suggested as an attractive model to replace the systems of proportional representation. However, the opposite argument—that electoral systems should primarily produce representative political assemblies—has not been argued with equal fervour. Proportionality has taken a back seat to efficiency; fair representation is subordinate to power.

A related observation of the constitutional debate concerns the political parties' arguments and positioning. Reference is often made to justice and equality in the party political debate on issues relating to the electoral system, but the arguments are clearly also informed by strategic calculations in the aspiration for power. The principle of justice usually denotes procedural justice, while just representation and proportionality are seldom discussed. The positions the parties have taken in the debates on legislative assemblies, electoral systems and the use of referendums have been determined by the parties' influence in parliament—at the expense of a fair representation. One argument in this study is that a fair representation should be the superior criterion. But, as we shall see, proportionality and fair representation are ambiguous concepts.

Social-choice Theory

The thesis also makes an argument in relation to the scholarly debate on the theories of collective decision-making, a debate that is generally lacking in empirical context and testing. The theories on collective decision-making explore the preconditions and methods to produce the winning alternative. Many fruitful analytical frameworks and concepts have been generated in this research. Our ability to understand the importance, possibilities and delimitation of various forms of preference aggregation in order to elicit the popular will has greatly improved since this research really gained momentum in the early 1970's. Several theoretical problems and paradoxes have been made explicit; some of which have posed serious challenges to previous assumptions of how democracies can take decisions on the basis of the will of the people.

The theoretical debate has, however, been biased in favour of abstract reasoning to a degree that, with a few exceptions, has left its relevance to actual politics unexplored. Scholars have preferred constructed theoretical models, with adjusted examples of preference structures, to more cumbersome empirical data. The empirical relevance of the theories of collective decision-making has therefore seldom been tested. This study aims at making a contribution to the scholarly debate by combining theories on collective decision-making with empirical data from opinion surveys.

Democratic Decision Rules and Election Systems

Collective decisions, rankings and distribution of seats in a parliament are strategies for identifying the popular will and the social-choice theory offers various methods for doing this. Naturally we are only interested in decision methods that satisfy the fundamental criterion of democracy. In this analysis three criteria determine if a collective-decision method should be regarded as democratic. First, the method should satisfy the *equality* or *anonymity* criterion. This means that all votes should be of equal value.[1] Second, the collective-decision method should be *neutral*. This implies that nothing but votes should effect the collective choice. The decision method should not favour or discriminate one or more of the alternatives in any way.[2] A third criterion is *monotonicity*. Democracy demands a connection between citizens' preferences and society's collective decision. The monotonicity criterion could be defined in a more or less demanding way, but the gentlest variant demands that an alternative should never be disadvantaged by an increased support among the voters.[3] The democracy criterion thus demands that the voters should be equal, no alternative should be privileged, and an alternative should never be disadvantaged as a consequence of an increased voters' support.

One fundamental difference between the various collective-decision methods is how much information on individual preferences is included in the aggregation process. One additional decision method is included in this study for the purpose of exploring the effects of an increased use of information about individual preferences.

Following the criteria of anonymity, neutrality, monotonicity and a more ambitious use of preference information, different methods or principles for collective decisions could be defined. The analysis will include four alternative methods for the distribution of seats in parliament:

- Plurality rule
- Approval voting
- Borda count
- Standardised utility method[4]

Plurality Rule

The plurality rule gives the voters one vote each and defines the alternative which gets most votes as the winning alternative. It is easy to apply the method for the distribution of seats in a parliament. These are distributed to the parties proportionally to the number of votes that each party obtains. This is called the proportional plurality rule. The parties could also be ranked based on the number of their votes.

Approval Voting

Approval voting is a newcomer among the collective-decision methods.[5] The plurality rule implies that the voters give the most preferred alternative one vote. Approval voting allows the voter to vote on all alternatives he or she agrees with or approves of. This implies that the voter can vote on more than one alternative, but it is only allowed to give each alternative one vote. The alternative which gets most votes is the winning alternative.

National election systems based upon the idea of approval voting do not exist in practice, but it is unproblematic to construct such an approval election system. In this study, parliamentary seats are allocated according to approval voting in the following way. Each party's approval votes are counted and related to the total number of approval votes. Each party's share of seats in parliament is equivalent to the party's share of the total number of approval votes. The parties could also be ranked with regard to the number of approval votes.

Borda Count

The French mathematician Jean Charles Borda developed a decision rule, which takes into account all positional or ordinal information on individual preference orders. The voters are asked to rank all alternatives and the Borda count method gives each alternative points according to the positions of the alternatives in the voters' ranking orders. If there are k alternatives, a first place in the voter's preference order gives the alternative k-1 point; a second place gives k-2 points etc. The alternative which is regarded as the worst, receives no point at all. The alternative with the highest total points is the winner and the collective choice. An election system according to the Borda count is designed by relating each party's Borda points to the total amount of Borda points. A party's proportion of the parliamentary seats is the same as the party's proportion of the total amount of Borda points. The Borda points also define the collective ranking of the parties.

Utilitarian Method

The utilitarian method is built upon the idea that the individuals, in addition to ordinal information, also can connect each alternative with a subjective cardinal utility value. This value could be looked upon as a measure of the intensity of the individual preferences. By summing the individual utility values it is possible to define a winning alternative.

The utility method implies that votes are not only *counted* but also *weighted*. This means that the utility method does not satisfy the basic democracy criterion of anonymity or equality. The criterion of equality disqualifies voting methods based upon cardinal information about individual preferences, because cardinal values and preference intensity are inconsistent with the idea of "one man, one vote".

A second problem concerns the measuring and comparing of individual preference intensities. Interpersonal comparisons require comparable utility scales with starting levels which are equal to all individuals. Such a scale does not exist and interpersonal comparisons and aggregation are therefore meaningless.[6] On top of this the utility method is vulnerable to strategic voting.

Utility methods violate fundamental democracy criteria, and there are considerable methodological problems associated with those methods. The utility method used in this analysis is called the standardised utility method, and the fundamental idea is to let individuals place the parties on standardised scales or sympathy thermometers. If the individual has intensive preferences for a certain party, the latter is placed close to the maximum value of the scale. If the preferences are not so intense the party is placed closer to the minimum value of the scale. Each party's total intensity points are calculated and the party with the highest total intensity points is defined as the winner. The parliamentary seats are distributed proportionally to the parties' intensity points. The parties could be ranked according to each party's total utility points.

II. The Effect of the Choice of Decision Methods

The Arbitrariness of Collective-decision Methods

A big supply of alternative, democratic, collective-decision methods, one could argue, does not have to be a problem. What is important is that the alternative is chosen which best reflects the voters' preferences or the popular will. The choice of decision method is irrelevant provided that the basic criteria of democracy are satisfied.

However, the dilemma is that the choice of a collective-decision method could be crucial to the voting outcome. Different democratic collective-decision methods define different winning alternatives, although the preferences of the electorate remain the same.[7] This has implications for the idea of democratic self-governance and democracy as a realisation of the popular will. Before this argument is taken further, we will briefly study the "arbitrariness" of democratic decision and ranking methods.

This example is based on a small society with eleven individuals who have to make a collective choice from five different alternatives. Individual preference orders are displayed in *figure 6.1.*[8]

No of voters	4	2	1	1	1	1	1
1st choice	c	a	a	e	b	e	e
2nd choice	d	e	b	a	c	a	d
3rd choice	b	d	c	d	a	b	a
4th choice	e	b	d	b	d	c	b
5th choice	a	c	e	c	e	d	c

Figure 6.1. Eleven voters and five alternatives. Approved alternatives are underlined.

The plurality rule defines alternative *c* as the collective choice since *c* has more first rankings (4) than any of the other alternatives. Alternative *a* gets 2 votes and *b*, *d* and *e* one vote each. In order to define the approval voting winner we have to count the underlined alternatives. Alternative *b* wins with *6* votes, *d* gets *5* votes, *c* gets 4, *e* gets 3 and alternative *a* receives 2 votes. If the Borda count is used alternative *d* is defined as the winner. The Borda count gives the alternatives *d* 23 points, *a* 22 points, *c* 22 points, *e* 22 point and *b* 21 points.

In this example five different collective-decision rules have been used in order to define the collective democratic choices. The plurality rule, the approval voting and the Borda count are all satisfying the three fundamental democracy criteria, but they define the different winning alternatives, although the voters' preferences remain the same.

The Arbitrariness of Electoral Systems

Are election systems just as imprecise as decision methods? In the following example (*figure 6.2*) 110 voters will define a parliament representing the electorate.

No of voters	40	20	10	10	10	10	10
1st choice	c	a	a	e	b	e	e
2nd choice	d	e	b	a	c	a	d
3rd choice	b	d	c	d	a	b	a
4th choice	e	b	d	b	d	c	b
5th choice	a	c	e	c	e	d	c

Figure 6.2 110 voters and five parties.
Approved alternatives are underlined.

The distribution of seats according to the proportional plurality rule, the Borda count and the approval voting are displayed in *figure 6.3* (next page).
It is obvious that the choice of election system effects the distribution of seats. The proportional plurality rule generates one large party (*c*) with more than 35 per cent of the votes and two medium-sized parties with 25 per cent each of the seats. The support for the other parties is 8 and 0 per cent. The Borda count generates a totally different situation with equal-sized parties. Finally, the approval voting leads to yet another party structure with different support for the parties.

Social-choice Theory and Democracy

The theories of collective decision-making offer several ways to reach collective decisions and there are various ways of distributing seats in parliament. These alternative decision methods and electoral systems are equally democratic. The theories of col-

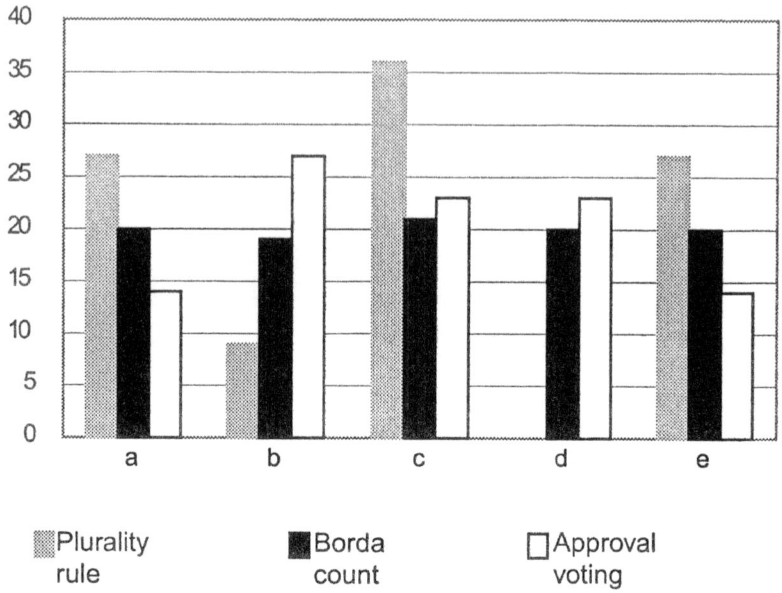

Figure 6.3. Relative distribution of seats according to proportional plurality rule, Borda count and approval voting.

lective decisions emphasise the arbitrary nature of the decision methods, which means that the democratic decision methods all fall short of clearly naming a winning alternative. When these decision methods are transferred to electoral systems it can be shown that the election results and the allocation of parliamentary seats are equally arbitrary. Different electoral systems will distribute parliamentary seats differently, although the preferences of the electorate remain the same.

The social-choice theory implies that we can never know for sure that a collective decision is a fair representation of the voters' preferences. William Riker takes this argument further and clarifies the consequences the social-choice theory has for the idea that democracy means that power must be derived from the people and that democracy realises the popular will.[9] Riker's conclusion is that the social-choice theory rejects the populist interpretation of voting, that is a conception of democracy—originating from the work of Rousseau—which regards democracy as a method to determine the General Will and thereby a means for self-government. Riker argues that:

> The essence of populism is this pair of propositions: 1. What the people, as a corporate entity, wants ought to be social policy. 2. The people are free when their wishes are law. ... But if the notion of popular will is itself unclear, then what the people want cannot be social policy simply because we do not and cannot know what the people want. An election tells us mostly which alternative wins; it does not tell us that the winner would also have been chosen over another feasible alternative that might itself have a better claim to be the social choice. Hence falls proposition 1. And if we do not know the people's wishes, we cannot make them free by enacting their wishes. Thus falls proposition 2. Populism as a moral imperative depends on the existence of a popular will discovered by voting. But if the voting does not discover or revel a will, the moral imperative evaporates because there is nothing to be commanded. If the people speak in meaningless, they cannot utter the law that make them free. Populism fails, therefore, not because it is morally wrong, but merely because it is empty.[10]

Riker's arguments are convincing. If we do not know the people's will we cannot know if people govern. In the light of the social-choice theory the populist interpretation of democracy becomes unclear. But what is the empirical relevance of Riker's arguments?

III. Questions and Study Design

Theoretical Curiosities or Empirical Relevance?

The results of the social-choice theory challenge the central tenet in democracy theory. Riker claims that the idea of realising the popular will is not realistic. If we do not know the people's will, we cannot know if they govern. Is there any reason for democrats to be seriously concerned by Riker's conclusions? Is the arbitrary problem only theoretical curiosities or is it empirically relevant?

Should it be Different?

In Sweden the parliamentary seats are distributed according to the proportional plurality rule. There are several modifications and variations of the proportional method but the fundamental principle is always that the distribution of seats should be proportional to the distribution of votes. There are several variants of the proportional plurality rule. The applications are different with regard to the number of seats, the number of constituencies, equalisation seats, barriers against small parties etc, but the fundamental idea is always that the seats are distributed proportionally to the number of votes that each party obtains. Would modern Swedish political history have been different if another democratic electoral system had been used?[11]

Design and Disposition

The empirical analysis of the social-choice theories has primarily focused on the paradox of voting.[12] More comprehensive empirical studies of social-choice decision methods do not exist and the main reason for this is the lack of useful empirical data.[13] In order to test the empirical relevance of the social-choice arbitrary dilemma we need complete data about the voters' preference orders. Election data cannot help us since they only give information about the first preferences. This study uses data from Swedish electorate surveys.[14] The electorate surveys include so called "dislike-like-scales". The individuals are asked to place each party on a scale varying from –5 to 5. The value –5 means "strongly dislike" and value 5 represents "strongly like". By comparing the respective scales of each party it is possible to reconstruct the individuals' complete preference orders. It is also possible to use the scales as a base for distributing seats according to the approval voting and standardised utility method.[15]

In our analysis we will try to rewrite Swedish modern political history. We will allow the voters to return to the ballot boxes, and count the votes according to different electoral systems. This will be done, practically, by conducting several analyses of the material in electorate surveys.[16] We will take the election year 1982 as a starting-point and focus on four related concepts or components of the political configuration or conflict structure.[17] 1982 is an interesting election year in Swedish politics. After six years with non-socialist governments, the Social Democratic party is allowed to form a minority government. The party remains in government until 1991, and during this period two additional parties enter the parliament. The strategy of the analysis is illustrated in *figure 6.4* (next page).

The main question is what effects alternative election systems have on the distribution of seats in parliament. Based on these distributions we will study the parliamentary fragmentation, the effects on political alliances, the effects on the distribution of parliamentary voting power and collective preference orders. Before we can perform this analysis we shall explain central concepts and instruments.

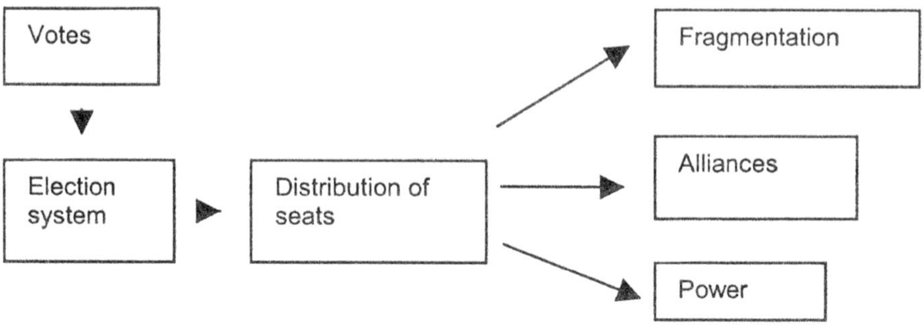

Figure 6.4. Analysis strategy

Differences in the Distribution of Seats in Parliament

In this study the proportional plurality rule, the approval voting, the Borda count and the standardised utility method will be applied as for the distribution of seats. These methods are equally democratic (except for the standardised utility method) but they are different with regard to how much information about individual preferences they take into account. Sweden is regarded as one constituency and the study includes the Left Party (V), the Green Party (Mp) the Social Democrats (S), the Centre Party (C) the Liberal Party (Fp), the Christian Democrats (Kd) and the Conservative Party (M).

Fragmentation and Strong Government

Different methods and techniques are available when studying the political configuration on a parliamentary level. One possibility is to study the degree of party division or fragmentation in parliament. This is of special interest since parliamentary fragmentation is connected to the debate on strong governance. The argument is that a fragmented parliament lacks decision capability. In this study we will use Herfindahl's and Hirschman's concentration index (HH) as a measure of parliamentary fragmentation. HH is calculated by adding the parties' squared shares of the parliamentary seats.[18] This gives us indices that vary between 0 and 1. Value 1 means that one party dominates the parliament and value 0 means that the parliament is totally fragmented.[19] In terms of weakness and strength value 0 indicates a weak parliament and value 1 is an expression of political strength and parliamentary decision capability.

Party Alliances

An objection to measuring political parliamentary configuration by fragmentation and concentration techniques is that this strategy disregards the ‚political parties' ability and willingness to form coalitions or alliances. Swedish politics is characterised and described in terms of two or three major party alliances. The socialistic party alliance consists of the Left Party and the Social Democratic Party. This alliance has dominated Swedish modern political history. The non-socialist alliance includes the Centre Party, the Liberals, the Christian Democrats and the Conservative Party. In practice the size of the two alliances has decided the formation of the government. In addition to these two alliances we will also study the Social Democratic Party's and the Centre Party's total share of the seats in parliament. The reason is that these two parties have co-operated on several occasions during the second half of the 20th century.

Distribution of Power

The distribution of seats is not identical with the distribution of power. Small parties can be more powerful than their share of seats indicates. The concept of power is one of the most disputed concepts in political science. Lane and Stenlund separate two groups of definitions of power. The first group is based on power as a causal model. The second group focuses on decision situations in which actors or groups of actors could decide the collective choice by voting for or against it.[20] In a study of the distribution of seats and power in parliament it is relevant to discuss power in terms of formal decision power in voting situations.

Power in voting situations is usually calculated according to Banzhaf's or Shapley-Shubik's techniques.[21] Shapley-Shubik's index of power builds upon the idea that the actors could be ordered sequentially and that all sequences are of equal probability. The index is calculated by adding the probabilities for coalitions in which a party is pivotal or decisive. Banzhaf's index of power has a slightly different and for this study more relevant starting-point. An actor's power in voting situations is based on the assumption that all coalitions are of equal probability. The index is calculated by adding the probabilities for the coalitions in which the actor is decisive. An actor is decisive in a coalition if the coalition transforms from a winning majority coalition to a losing minority coalition when the actor abandons the coalition. Banzhaf's index of power is not standardised, *i. e*, the total power could exceed 1. However, it is unproblematic to standardise the index, and in this study Banzhaf's index will vary between the minimum value 0 and the maximum value 100.[22]

IV. Effects of electoral systems

Distribution of Seats

We will first look at the distribution of seats in the parliament. *Figure 6.5* displays the parties' support in the electorate and shares of seats in 1982 according to different election systems.

The distribution according to the proportional plurality rule is not identical with the real voting results. This can probably be explained by strategic voting and by the difference between answering in an electoral survey, on one hand, and voting in practice on the other.

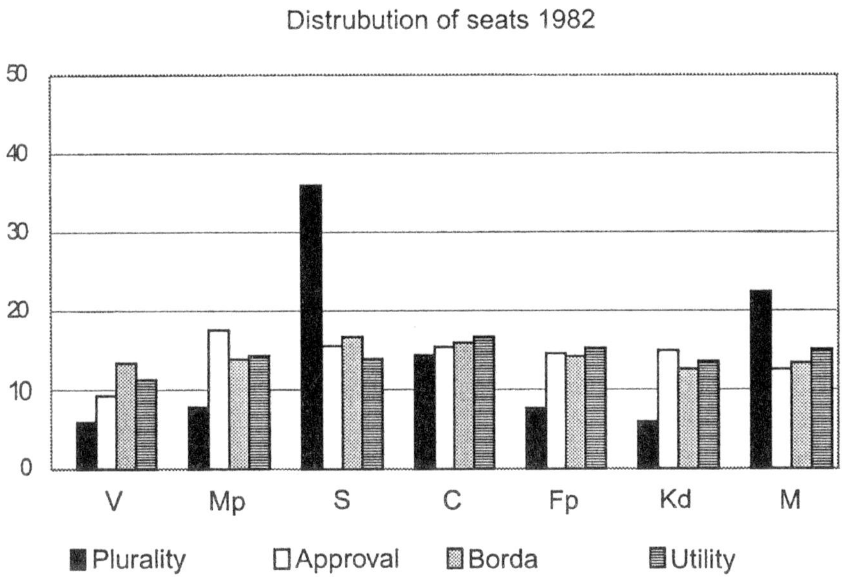

Figure 6.5. Distribution of seats in Parliament according to proportional plurality, approval voting, the Borda count and the standardised utility method 1982.

The analysis of data from the electorate survey proves that the choice of election system is decisive for the distribution of seats. According to the proportional plurality rule there are two dominating parties in Swedish politics.[23] The Social Democratic Party's share of the seats is 36 per cent and the Conservatives' share is between 22 and 23 per cent. The Centre Party receives 14 per cent of the seats and The Liberals' and the Green Party's shares are between 7 and 8 per cent. The other parties' shares are less than 6 per cent.

According to the approval voting the voters should be represented differently. The dominance of the Social Democratic and the Conservative Parties disappears and all the other parties increase their shares of the seats in parliament. The change related to the Social Democratic Party is remarkable. If all ordinal information about voters' preferences is added to the election process this does not change the approval voting situation very much. The difference compared with the proportional plurality method remains. The Borda count improves the situation of the Left Party, the Green Party, the Centre Party, the Liberals and the Christian Democrats while the Social Democrats and the Conservatives come out worse. The utility method gives the same overall pictures as do the Borda count and the approval voting, and in addition to that the method indicates that some parties, the Conservatives and the Liberals, have intense preferences. The main conclusion, however, is that it could have been different.

Fragmentation and Strong Government

Parliamentary fragmentation is related to parliamentary action capability or a strong government.[24] As a measure of this aspect of conflict structure or political configuration we use Herfindahl's and Hirschman's concentration index. The results are displayed in *table 6.1* on next page.

The proportional plurality rule generates a less fragmented parliament compared to the other election systems. The approval voting, the Borda count and the utility method result in a more fragmented parliament with small equal-sized parties, and this could decrease the parliament's decisiveness and capability for strong action. The conclusion is that election systems affect the preconditions for strong political action capability.

	Plurality rule	Approval voting	Borda count	Utility method
HH	0,22	0,15	0,14	0,14

Table 6.1. Fragmentation of Swedish parliament 1982 according to different election systems. Herfindahls and Hirschmans concentrations index.

Party Alliances

An objection to the fragmentation analysis is that this technique disregards ideological patterns of co-operation between parties. Swedish politics is often discussed in terms of party groups and common values as well as ideology cement alliances and these constellations. There are two major alliances in Swedish politics: the socialist alliance and the non-socialist alliance. A third, looser alliance is the co-operation between the Social Democratic Party and the Centre Party. The sizes of these alliances or groups decide the formation of the government. The traditional division of the parties in two groups has been challenged by the Green Party and several political issues such as the European Union membership, but it is still relevant to characterise Swedish politics in terms of two dominant party groups.

This is the reason why we study the effects of the election system on the sizes of the party alliances. *Figure 6.6* displays the voters' support for the socialist and non-socialist alliances according to the proportional plurality rule, the approval voting, the Borda count and the standardised utility method.

Approval voting, the Borda count and the utility method describe the non-socialist alliance as bigger than the socialist alliance. The difference compared with the size of the alliance according to the plurality rule is quite remarkable. Approval voting, the Borda count and the utility method give the non-socialist alliance a clear majority in parliament. The Centre Party and the Social Democratic Party would probably not have been a major force in Swedish politics under alternative electoral systems.

The analysis of the sizes of the party alliances gives unambiguous indications. The relative sizes of the alliances and, as a consequence, the preconditions for coalitions and parliamentary interaction, would have been different if the proportional plurality rule had been replaced by another electoral system (see *figure 6.6* on next page).

Power

The distribution of the parliamentary seats is of course the base for the parties' influence or power, especially in voting situations. But the distribution of seats is not identical with the distribution of power. A party with five per cent of the seats does not automatically dispose of five per cent of the parliamentary power. Several factors affect the distribution of power. The parliamentary decision rule and the parties' relative sizes are two important factors (see *table 6.2* on page 159).

Banzhaf's index of power focuses on the parties' formal role or decisiveness in voting situations. An objection to this is that the technique is "ideology blind". In practice, not all coalitions are of equal probability, but this aspect is partly covered by the analysis of the party alliances.

The Banzhaf index of power for each party is the sum of the probabilities of coalitions in which the party is decisive. The party is decisive if a winning coalition transforms to a losing coalition when the party abandons the coalition. In this study the index is standardised and varies between 0 and 100.[25] *Table 6.2* shows the parties' parliamentary power when alternative electoral systems are applied. The situation changes dramatically if the proportional plurality rule is replaced by approval

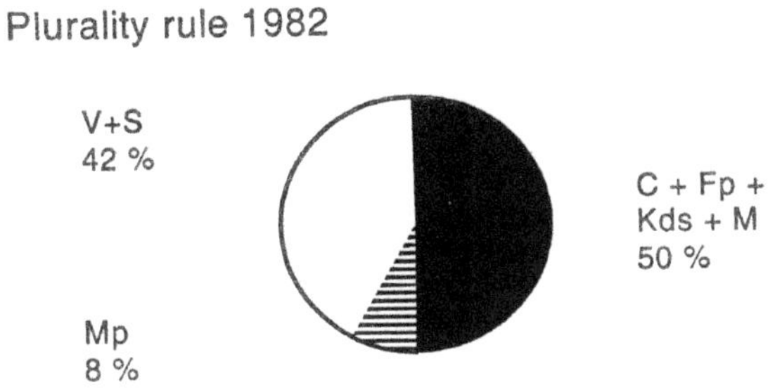

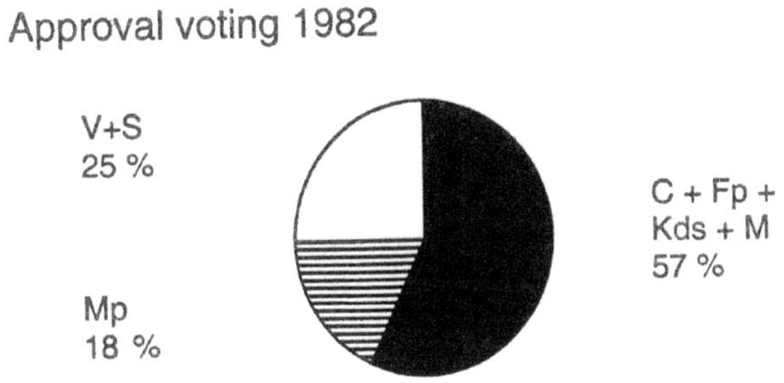

Figure 6.6. Party alliances (and the Green Party) sizes according to proportional
(continued on next page)

voting, the Borda count or the utility method. The Social Democratic Party's index depreciates considerably from around 40 according to the plurality rule to around 14, according to the approval voting, the Borda count and the standardised utility method.

Borda count 1982

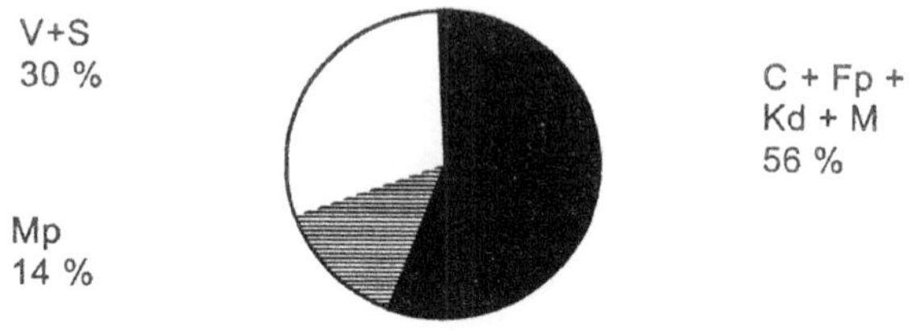

Utility method 1982

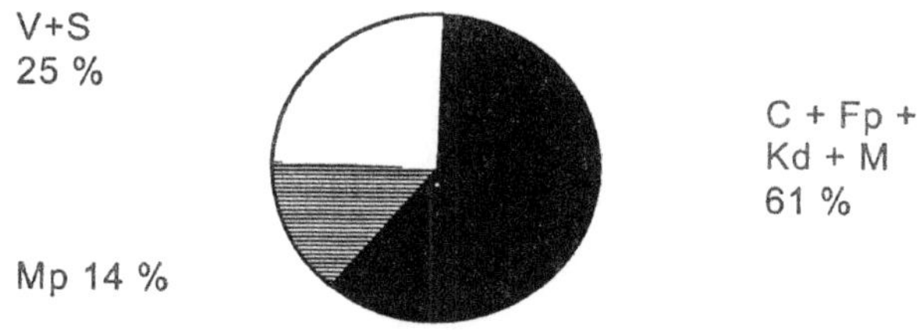

plurality rule, approval voting, Borda count and standardised utility method 1982.

It is obvious that the distribution of power becomes more even, if more information about the voters' preferences is included when the votes are counted and aggregated. The distribution of power according to the standardised utility method indicates that if cardinal information about preferences is used, the distribution of power becomes equal among the parties. This

	Plurality rule	Approval voting	Borda count	Utility method
V	3,76	13,93	14,29	14,29
Mp	7,51	14,64	14,29	14,29
S	39,91	14,29	14,29	14,29
C	17,84	13,57	14,29	14,29
Fp	7,04	14,29	14,29	14,29
Kds	4,23	14,64	14,29	14,29
M	19,72	14,64	14,29	14,29

Table 6.2. Parties´ power (Banhzaf's index) and alternative elections systems 1982.

raises the question how an equal distribution of power with no political centre affects political initiatives, preconditions for coalitions and a strong government.

V. Concluding remarks

It Would Have Been Different...

The main result of the study is that the election results differ with alternative electoral systems, also when voter preferences are held constant. The allocation of parliamentary seats would have been considerably more balanced if the proportional plurality method had been replaced by any of the other three methods. A lower percentage of the voter support and fewer numbers of the parliamentary seats would have been awarded to both the Social Democrats and the Conservatives. For the Social Democratic Party the reduction would have been considerable. The parties in the middle of the party political spectrum would have gained a larger percentage of the parliamentary seats if the Swedish electoral system had been modelled on the principles that underpin either of the other three electoral systems.

The degree of fragmentation in parliament would also have been different. If the plurality method had been replaced by any of the other methods, the fragmentation would have increased, which in turn could have led to a less strong and efficient government.

The combination of the parties into two competitive alliances, a socialist and a non-socialist (liberal/conservative), would also have looked differently. The degree to which the Social Democrats would have lost parliamentary seats would not have been compensated by an equal increase in seats for the Left Party, resulting in a weaker socialist block. The conservative/liberal block would have been the larger of the two.

The distribution of power would have been different, and again the plurality method displays the greatest variation. This method favours some parties when votes are transformed into parliamentary seats, most notably the Social Democratic Party, and these differences increase even further in the power-analyses using the Banzhaf index of power. Other electoral systems distribute power more evenly between the parties.

Why do these differences occur? Electoral systems use different amounts of information about how the voters rank their parties' preferences. The Social Democratic Party comes out as number one on the ranking of many voters, but there are also many voters who place the party as the second worst alternative; this figure was as high as 17 per cent in 1982 and 20 per cent in the election year of 1985.[26] The Conservative Party also gains many first rankings, but our analysis shows that an almost equal number rank them last. Since the plurality method only takes first rankings into account, the considerable amount of suspicion of these parties does not affect the allocation of parliamentary seats. The other group of parties does not feature as much on the top of the voter rankings, but they do not end up last either. Consequently, these parties stand to gain from electoral systems that take the full list of voter preferences into account. The Left Party is almost always placed last or second last. There is, however, a group of voters that rank the Left Party as second best. These voters most likely make up the left wing of the Social Democratic Party supporters.[27]

Multidimensional Proportionality

We can thus conclude that politics differ with the choice of electoral systems; the allocation of parliamentary seats in turn affect the distribution of power, the formation of strategic party alliances, etc. The question then arises: which method is most fair? How can we conceptualise fair representation? Such normative questions will not be addressed here. Ours is mainly a technical analysis of how alternative electoral systems produce different parliamentary majorities. In order to depart from our position of neutrality in relation to which system is better or more just we would have needed a different framework of analysis altogether. Such an analysis would also have demanded a greater number of alternative electoral systems as well as a set of more refined criteria of evaluation than the basic democratic criteria that are discussed.

However, proportionality is a multidimensional concept. Without making a normative argument, formal theory and our empirical analyses nevertheless allow us to comment critically on current political and scholarly debates. It would seem that both political commentary and more traditional research on electoral systems have taken the plurality method too much for granted. Empirical analyses of electoral systems and their ability to generate fair representation show that it should not be taken for granted that the plurality rule is superior in a democratic sense. There are other electoral systems than the plurality rule that equally well fulfil basic democratic criteria, for instance the approval method and the Borda method. This study shows that the concept of representation is far from unambiguous or simplistic; its full meaning is a function of the nature of the electoral system.

Proportionality or Strong Governments?

A related question is how much larger the parties should be over-represented in order to create conditions for strong governments. This question is also central in the discussion on the perceived advantages of the majority method: one man—one vote. Our analysis shows that some parties are favoured also within a proportional system. Our comparison of alternative methods shows that the plurality method boosts the representation of a few larger parties at the expense of smaller parties.

In our introduction we juxtaposed the dual purposes of the electoral system to give a just representation of the voter preferences and to produce strong governments. However, the anxious debates on the electoral systems are perhaps due to our exaggerated expectations on this particular institutional arrangement; it cannot both ensure a fair representation and strong governments. And yet, a country needs a government. So how are we to resolve this apparent paradox in multiparty democracies? It is perhaps not necessary to apply the consociational solution, or to favour other types of broad coalitions. One way to put the argument is to say that the challenge to the *elec-*

toral system is fairness: voter preferences shall be reflected as correctly and fair as possible through the electoral system. Our analysis has shown that this is far from a trivial problem. Since concepts such as proportionality and fair representation are multifaceted, we need additional criteria and guidance in choosing between different normative principles. The main concern in this study has been to describe how electoral systems allocate parliamentary seats. The next step of deciding on one over the others—of deciding on the criteria of fairness—is a political decision. A central challenge to democratic parliamentary regimes is, arguably, the formation of an executive government—a pursuit in which the choice of electoral system is fundamental.

Notes

1. Riker (Riker, 1982, p 51) argues that "undifferentiatedness" is a more precise concept: "The best name for the condition is undifferentiatedness because this is primarily what it provides, namely that one vote cannot be distinguished from another. This feature allows for anonymity and anonymity in turn allows for equality." See Härd, 1999, p 33 for a description of the anonymity criterion and its effect on the British election system.
2. See Härd, 1999, pp 34-37 for a discussion on the neutrality criterion.
3. This is identical with the *non-negative response*. A more demanding criterion is the *strong monotonicity* or *positive response*; see May, 1952; Plott, 1976, pp 557ff; and Nurmi, 1987, pp 66ff. See also Härd, 1999, pp 35ff for an elaborated description of the monotonicity criterion.
4. The standardised utility method does not satisfy the criterion of equality.
5. Steven Brams and Peter Fishburn introduced approval voting. Brams & Fishburn, 1982 gives the best description and discussion of the approval voting.
6. Riker & Ordeshook, 1973, pp 111f., von Neumann's and Morgenstern's (von Neumann & Morgenstern, 1944) utility indicator is one suggestion to overcome the problem of interpersonal comparisons.
7. Several authors illustrate the incapability of the decision methods to identify one unique winner. See for example Nurmi, 1982 and 1988 or Riker, 1982, chapter 2.

8, The preference structure is based on Nurmi, 1988, p 196 and Härd, 1999, pp 57ff. See also Brams, 1976.
9. Riker, 1982, pp 8-14 and 238-239.
10. Riker, 1982, p 238.
11. All possible election systems are not included in this study. The theoretical starting- point is the social-choice theory and the collective-decision methods proposed in this theoretical discourse.
12. See for example McLean, 1982; Riker, 1969 and 1982.
13. Härd, 1999 studies the effects of the choice of election systems in Sweden 1982 to 1991. In Lewin, 1995, pp 108-111 and Lewin, 1997. I calculate the distributions of seats according to the Borda count 1991. See also Steven Brams' and Peter Fishburn's analysis of the 1976 election of a majority leader in USA's House of Representatives. Based on voting data combined with assumptions regarding preference structures ("single-peakedness"), Brams and Fishburn test variants of approval voting and the plurality rule. They use the same methods on the American presidential election in 1982 (Brams & Fishburn, 1982, pp 59-77). See also Riker's examples from France in Riker, 1982, pp 21-28.
14. Swedish electoral surveys include a national representative sample of individuals and are performed every election year by the department of Political Science, Gothenburg University.
15. See Härd, 1999, pp 87-102 for a detailed technical description of data, scales and programmes for calculations.
16. This is of course a problematic strategy since it is impossible to say "how it would have been if..." with any certainty. Three objections should be kept in mind: Firstly, the existing election system probably affects data in electorate surveys. The existing election system has generated a parliament situation which in various ways affects the voters' preferences. The party structure and parliamentary configuration probably have an impact on individual preferences and attitudes. Secondly, voters act strategically. They adapt to the voting with respect to the functioning of the election system. Thirdly, it is likely that even parties behave strategically with regard to the election system. The most rational campaign strategy is probably dependent on the characteristics of the electoral system. See Härd, 1999, pp 83-86 for a discussion. See also Tetlock & Belkin, 1996 for an elaborated analysis of the contra-factual method.
17. One could argue that this is old data and that a single year cannot give us valid and reliable results. Other studies, however, show that other election years generate identical results. See Härd, 1999.
18. Herfindahl's and Hirschman's concentration index (HH) is calculated by HH = $\Sigma P^2 I$. For a comprehensive description of this index and other related indices, see Coulter, 1984.
19. The number of parties effects HH.

20. Lane & Stenlund, 1989, p 48.
21. Shapely & Shubik, 1954, Banzhaf, 1965. For overviews, descriptions and mathematical definitions, see Hermansson, 1990, pp 320ff, Lane & Stenlund, 1984 and 1989, pp 49ff or Nurmi, 1987, pp 184ff.
22. Lane & Stenlund, 1989, p 50.
23. Analyses of electorate data from other years generate the same overall pattern.
24. Hermansson, 1993, p 83 and Härd, 1999, p 73-75.
25. In order to calculate the index all possible coalitions have been defined. In this study the number of parties is 7 and the number of possible coalitions is 128.
26. Härd, 1999, p 172.
27. Härd, 1999, pp 163-185.

References

Arrow, K, 1963, *Social choice and individual values*. New York: Wiley, 1963 (2nd edition).

Banzhaf, J F, 1965, "Weighted voting doesn't work : a mathematical analysis", in *Rutgers Law Review*, 19, pp329-330.

Brams, S J & Fishburn, P C, 1981, "Reconstructing voting processes : the 1976 House majority leader election", in *Political Methodology,* vol 7, 3-4, pp 95-108.

—, 1983, *Approval voting*. Boston: Birkhäuser, 1983.

Coulter, P B, 1989, *Measuring inequality : a methodological handbook*. Boulder, San Francisco & London: Westview Press, 1989.

Hermansson, J, 1990, *Spelteorins nytta : om rationalitet i vetenskap och politik*. Stockholm: Almqvist & Wiksell (Acta Universitatis Upsaliensis), 1990.

—, 1993, *Politik som intressekamp : parlamentariskt beslutsfattande och organiserade intressen i Sverige*. Stockholm: Norstedts Juridik, 1993.

Härd, S, 1990, "På jakt efter folkviljan : en konfrontation mellan teorin om det kollektiva beslutsfattandet och svensk politik". Department of Government, Uppsala University, 1990.

—, 1999, *Den godtyckliga demokratin : en studie av olika metoder att tillgodose kravet på proportionalitet*. Uppsala: Uppsala University Library, 1999.

Lane, J-E & Stenlund H, 1989, *Politisk teori*. Lund: Studentlitteratur, 1989.

Lewin, L, 1995, *Votera eller förhandla : om den svenska parlamentarismen*. Stockholm: Norstedts Juridik, 1995.

—, 1997, "Majoritarian and consensus democracy : the Swedish experience", in *Scandinavian Political Studies,* vol 21, no 3, pp 195-206.

May, K O, 1952, "a set of independent, necessary and sufficient conditions for majority decision", in *Rational Man and Irrational Society?* (eds Barry & Hardin). Beverly Hills: Sage, 1982.

McLean, I, 1982, *Dealing in Votes.* Oxford: Martin Robertson, 1982.

von Neumann, J & Morgenstern O, 1953, *The theory of games and economic behavior.* Princeton: Princeton University Press, 1953.

Nurmi, H, 1982, "Problems of Voting Procedure", *Academia Scientarum Fennica—Year Book 1984-1982.*

—, 1987, *Comparing voting systems.* Dordrecht: Reidel, 1987.

—, 1988, "Discrepancies in the outcomes resulting from different voting schemes", in *Theory and Decision,* 25, 1988, pp 193-108.

Plott, C, 1976, "Axiomatic social choice theory : an overview and interpretation", in *American Journal of Political Science,* 20, pp 511-596.

Riker, W H, 1969, "Arrows theorem and some examples of the paradox of voting", in *Mathematical applications in political science 1 (ed* J M Claunch). Dallas: Southern Methodist University Press, 1969.

—, 1982, *Liberalism against populism : a confrontation between the theory of democracy and the theory of social choice.* San Francisco: W H Freeman, 1982.

Riker, W H & Ordeshook, P, 1973, *An introduction to positive political theory.* Englewood Cliffs: Prentice-Hall, 1973.

Shapely, L S & Shubik, M, 1954, "A method for evaluating the distribution of power in a committee system", in *American Political Science Review,* 48, pp 787-792.

Tetlock, P & Belkin, A (eds), 1996, *Counterfactual thought experiments in world politics: logical, methodological and psychological perspectives.* Princeton [N J]: Princeton University Press, 1996.

Economic Effects of Political Institutions, with Special Reference to Constitutions[1]

Niclas Berggren
Peter Kurrild-Klitgaard

I. Introduction

One of the major questions in economics is what causes the growth of wealth: what explains that some countries experience higher economic growth than others? The idea here is to explore the linkage between political institutions, on the one hand, where the constitution is at the centre of our interest, and economic performance, on the other.[2] Is it the case that certain sets of institutions are more conducive to economic growth and sound fiscal affairs than others—through their influencing the way political decision-makers act? If so, which are these institutions? The present paper presents both a theoretical analysis of these issues, and the results from a number of real-world studies.

Below, some theoretical considerations will be presented, stemming from two perspectives—the new institutional economics and constitutional economics—which argue that political institutions matter for, among other things, how an economy functions (section II). A survey of empirical studies that look into this is given next, the purpose of which is to clarify the degree to which the theoretical implications can be confirmed. Among the things covered are the following: the effects of economic freedom, the rule of law and secure property rights, the effects of different budget rules, the effects of electoral systems, the length of legislative terms, federalism, popular initiatives and referendums (section III). Lastly, some concluding and summarizing remarks are offered, reflecting, among other things, on the potential for improving the working properties of an economy through reforming political institutions.

It should be noted at the outset that it is quite difficult to isolate the effects of particular constitutions on economic performance, since many factors, institutional and non-institutional, play a role for the actual policies. But even though much more work needs to be done in this area, the studies discussed here, in conjunction, seem to indicate the clear relationship between certain institutions and economic outcomes, a result that must be included into any earnest and comprehensive constitutional discussion. The selection of institutions is an important matter.

II. The Importance of Political Institutions: A Theoretical Perspective

Underlying many, or most, theories in the social sciences is some conception of man, at least with regard to what determines his actions. Not least is this the case in economics, with a view of man as a rational, largely self-interested actor who does his best, given his endowments and *given the rules, or institutions, under which he acts*. But whereas classical economists paid much attention to the role of rules for human behaviour, this aspect has largely been ignored in the post-war literature, at least as an explicit factor to be studied. Rather, man has been seen as a utility-maximiser without a possibility to change the rules under which he goes about his business. Of course, the idea behind institutions is to direct human action in certain ways—and hopefully in ways productive of human well-being—which seems in effect to presume that institutions are completely exogenous and hence not objects with which social scientists need to concern themselves.[3]

However, institutions can both be seen as exogenous and binding, on the one hand, and as possible (and, sometimes, desirable) to alter, on the other. The latter insight is important and, as mentioned, neglected in much economic analysis. As clarified by Buchanan and Tullock (Buchanan & Tullock, 1962, pp 77-80) and Brennan and Buchanan (Brennan & Buchanan, 1985), in many contexts there are two distinct levels of choice, *e g* in choosing a constitution and in making everyday political decisions. If so, this implies that rules instituted by lower-level decisions in some practical sense are exogenous *to those to whom these rules apply* albeit possible to change for those given the authority, in line with some higher-level rules, to do so. But it bears noting that the higher-level rules are not totally exogenous: although they are more difficult to change, they can be changed. Hence, alterability is a continuous variable, not a dichotomous one.[4] This is in fact what underlies the research programme of constitutional economics; as stated by Buchanan (Buchanan, 1990, pp 1, 7),

> Constitutional political economy is a research program that directs inquiry to the working properties of rules, and institutions within which individuals interact, and the processes through which these rules and institutions are chosen or come into being. The emphasis on the choice of constraints distinguishes this research program from conventional economics. ... [E]mphasis is centered directly on the selection of rules, or institutions, that will, in turn, limit the behavior of the persons who operate within them. Institutions, defined broadly, are variables subject to deliberate evaluation and to explicit choice.

The logic behind institutions is hence at base one of ensuring that the incentives facing those making choices, to the highest degree possible, are such as to make it more probable that certain actions, considered desirable, are taken rather than others (Elster, 1985 and Brennan & Kliemt, 1990). Just as a person may wish to exercise self-constraint by choosing to impose on himself a certain set of behavioural restrictions, ultimate democratic decision- makers may likewise think it prudent not only to put constraints on themselves (admittedly, only binding in an imperfect manner) but on their fellow present and subsequent rulers as well.[5]

The realization that institutions matter has been stressed by several economists, not the least Adam Smith, as remarked by Coase (Coase, 1977, p 320):

> [T]hroughout the *Wealth of Nations* one finds Adam Smith discussing the appropriate institutional framework for the working of a price system. Whether one agrees or disagrees with his views on apprenticeship laws, land tenure, joint-stock companies, the administration of justice, or the educational system, what distinguishes Adam Smith's approach from much of what has come since is that he obviously thinks this is a proper and important part of the work of an economist. It is, I believe, only recently that economists in any number have come to realize that the choice of an institutional framework is a subject which deserves to be studied systematically.[6]

And in that tradition we follow.

However, there is a theoretical critique of this view, as formulated by, *e g*, Boudreaux (Boudreaux, 1998) and Voigt (Voigt, 1998). In a somewhat nihilistic tone, these critics seem to assert that the specific contents of a written constitution are more or less unimportant for the way politics is actually carried out. The reason is that those deciding on the written constitution are the ones who must obey it, and if they wish to act in ways which the constitution do not allow, they either change it to suit their desires or simply agree not to follow it.[7] Above, some theoretical counter-arguments have been presented to this dichotomous way of analysing the issue, and Buchanan (Buchanan, 1999) sums it up well,

> Constitutional rules have the effect of increasing the costs of taking certain actions. It is more costly to take action in violation of a rule than it is to take the same action in the absence of the rule. If this much be acknowledged, then rules must matter if the basic law of economics is accepted. An increase in the cost of any choice alternative will reduce the resort to that alternative.[8]

We largely agree with this statement.[9] But ultimately, this is an empirical matter, hopefully to be settled in section III below. Before delving into the real-world effects of political institutions, this section will present some theoretical insights from new institutional economics and constitutional economics.

Institutions, Politics, and the Economy

One of the major questions in economics and economic history has been the basis for the growth of wealth. What explains that some countries have experienced higher economic growth than others? In older, more traditional neo-classical economic models, economic growth was largely, if not completely, a question of natural endowments: economic output simply flowed from combinations of such inputs as land, labour and capital, and faster—or slower—growth would then just be a question of the amount or efficient use of the input. In contrast, newer economic theories have emphasized the role played by institutions, and hence by institutional design. Specifically, one approach is represented by the so-called *new institutional economics*[10] which stresses that man acts under uncertainty for lack of perfect information about the world and because of a limited capacity for processing information. This implies that there are transaction costs in connection with human action, which among other things have an inhibiting effect on economic activities. Among these costs can be mentioned search costs, contractual costs, and controlling costs.[11] In such a reality, institutions in the sense of formal and informal rules, the violation of which entails some sort of penalty, tend to arise to reduce uncertainty and transaction costs.[12] Typical institutions of this kind are judicial systems, accounting systems, insurance, and the existence and protection of private property rights, which entail a set of rules within which the ownership of property is delineated and which stipulate how conflicts on such issues are to be resolved. If property rights are clearly defined and enforced, we should expect this to facilitate welfare-enhancing interactions between individuals, as well as the internalisation of externalities, and hence to stimulate economic growth.[13]

An *efficient* institution can thus be defined as one that guides human action in such a way that productive activities are favoured instead of unproductive, or even destructive, activities and which therefore leads to economic growth. To achieve economic progress, efficient institutions are required. It is hence of central importance to realize that economic development is highly affected by the institutional structure, as it affects how humans choose to behave both in economic and political contexts. As Coase (Coase, 1998, p 73) puts it,

> Adam Smith explained that the productivity of the economic system depends on specialization (he says the division of labor), but specialization is only possible if there is exchange—and the lower the costs of exchange (transac-

> tion costs if you will), the more specialization there will be and the greater the productivity of the system. But the costs of exchange depend on the institutions of a country: its legal system, its political system, its social system, its educational system, its culture, and so on. In effect, it is the institutions that govern the performance of an economy.

This insight—especially the connection between political institutions, decisions in the political process, decisions in the market, and economic performance—is partly captured in *figure 7.1* on the next page..[14]

The political institutions define the rules of the political game and thus heavily influence the working properties of the political process. Among these institutions, the foremost is the *formal constitution*, which lays down such basic things as voting rules, the electoral system, a catalogue of rights, the central political units (not the least the relationship between the legislature, the executive, and the judiciary).[15] But there are also other political institutions, and they may also be quite important. Examples are the internal organization of the legislature, the budgetary process, and the structure of the bureaucracy, which together with the formal constitution may be seen as constituting what could be called the *'extended' or 'effective' constitution*. This concept allows for unwritten rules as well: it may be that political decisions do not follow the formal rules, perhaps in a setting where "all" actors regard this as prudent. In such cases, the formal and the efficient constitutions are not identical but probably overlap considerably.[16]

Furthermore, the central actors when it comes to deciding on political institutions in a democracy are, ultimately, the politicians themselves: it is their goals and the constraints put upon them (by themselves or other politicians on previous occasions) as they strive towards reaching those goals that determine the

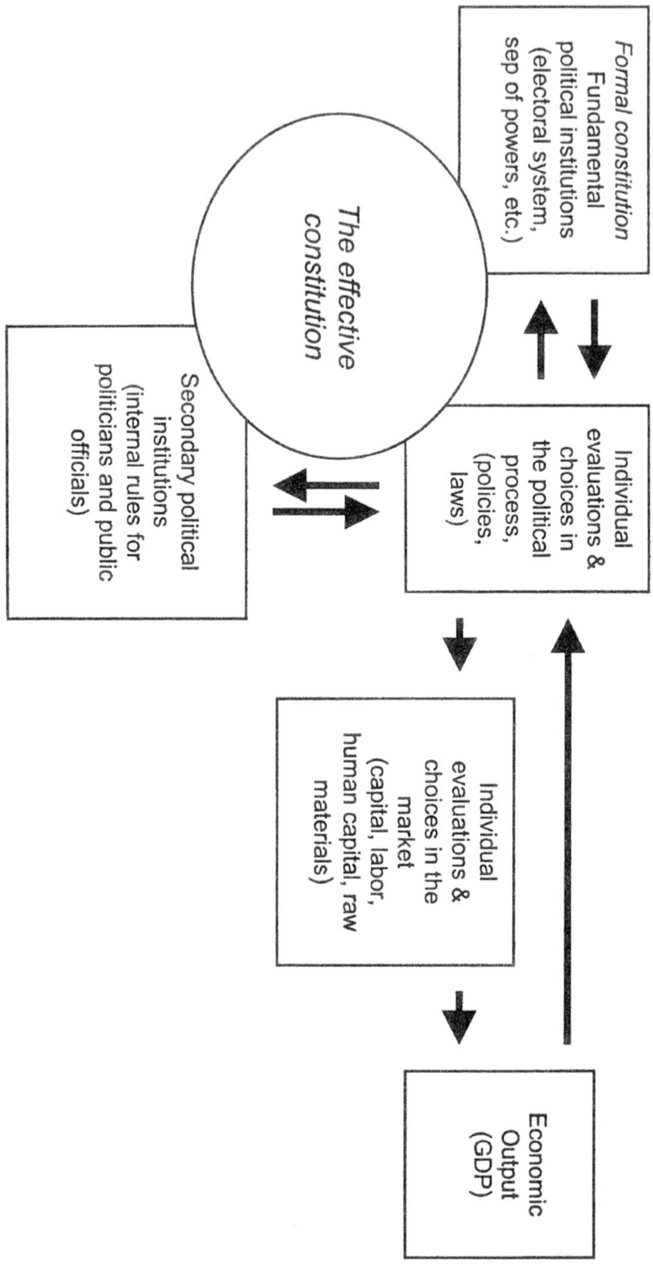

Figure 7.1. How political institutions interacts with the economy. Note: An arrow should be interpreted as □ *influence(s)*□ .

institutional set-up. Politicians, in turn, of course often decide on the basis of taking voter and interest-group concerns into consideration, also on institutional and constitutional issues. As clarified in the figure, in this some, probably considerable, constraint is exercised by the existing political institutions.

The laws and policies imposed in the political process in turn have an effect on, among other things, the evaluations and choices made in the economic markets. This affects such central factors as the capital-formation process and the functioning of the labour market—not least through the incentive effects on the economic actors and through affecting the transaction costs—and hence the development of economic output, *e g* in the form of Gross Domestic Product (GDP).[17] Economic growth, lastly, enters as a factor in the political process: a poor growth record may induce the decision-makers to introduce some institutional changes—both constitutional and non-constitutional—or, more frequently, some policy changes to make the economy work better.[18]

Constitutional Economics

Whereas the new institutional economics discusses a large number of different institutions, and whereas it primarily views the emergence of institutions as a response to uncertainty and transaction costs, *constitutional economics* has concentrated more on the basic political institutions, not least those at the constitutional level, and on viewing these as having a potential for guiding the political decisions so that they are not plagued by shortsightedness or special interests.[19] According to this latter view, political institutions may very well be implemented to *increase* political transaction costs. At the forefront is the motivation of the central actors and how this affects the need for and choice of constitutional rules.[20]

The underlying analysis stems from a theoretical view of the political game which essentially identifies three main groups of actors: politicians, voters, and interest groups, and which assumes that each strives towards realizing its own goals in a rational manner, *i e* gaining as many private benefits as possible for themselves, while letting others bear the costs.[21] The goal of the politicians could be to maximize the number of votes or to implement some programme on the basis of an ideological conviction, the goal of the voters to maximize their disposable incomes, and the goal of the interest groups to secure various sorts of favours. Policies are formed in a process where the politicians pay heed to how (oftentimes less well-informed and less well-organized) voters and (oftentimes well-informed and well-organized) interest groups can be expected to react to decisions. Due to the way in which politics works, in particular in modern media settings, with a focus on the short-sighted distributional effects of different decisions, with the influence of interest groups over the political process, and with a possibility for politicians to gain electoral support by offering parts of the electorate various pecuniary advantages, quite a few decisions will be characterized by short-sighted and special interests rather than a long-term public interest, and *e g*, with the result that political decisions are made with growth-retarding effects.[22] This may be considered undesirable from the point of view of *the long-term interests* of the polity, as illustrated in the following figure, based on Buchanan and Congleton (Buchanan & Congleton, 1998, p 23).

	B_1	B_2
A_1	1,1 I	-1,2 II
A_2	2,-1 III	0,0 IV

Figure 7.2. Payoffs with a simple-majority rule

The logic of the game that underlies *figure 7.2* is somewhat similar to that of the prisoners' dilemma game. The numbers signify payoffs for different individuals in different outcomes, which are the result of political decisions. The left-hand number in each pair denotes the payoff for decision-maker *A* and the right-hand number that of decision-maker *B*. These can be seen as perfect representatives for a deciding simple majority. The one in power can choose between four decisions, represented by the Roman numbers in the boxes. When *A* is in power, he will choose box III, and when *B* is in power, he will choose box II, as these choices reward them the most. This illustrates how the simple-majority rule gives rise to sub-optimal social outcomes, as it is possible, in each period, to obtain a total payoff of 2 (box I) instead of the total payoff of 1 given by boxes II and III. The problem is that the majority in power at any point in time always chooses that which gives their own group the highest payoff. The challenge is to devise the rules of the political game in such a way that the off-diagonals are eliminated from the choice set by the decision-makers—clearly in part a constitutional issue, of how to make it easier for the politicians to withstand short-sighted pressure from the public opinion and interest groups.[23]

Choosing Constitutions

This perspective entails a largely instrumental view of how a democracy should be designed. The basic idea is that democracy is desirable but that it will only be sustainable in the long run if it gives rise to good results—as evaluated by the citizens themselves. This in turn implies that the choice of democratic building blocs, within a framework of 'minimal' basic principles of democracy, is a rather open question being dependent on to what extent the alternative arrangements contribute to this satisfaction of the citizens' preferences.[24] This starting-point for the analysis can be used to generate more precise insights, some general examples of which will now be mentioned. Specifically, we will distinguish between (1) rights, (2) decision rules, (3) electoral systems, and (4) the separation of powers.[25]

Rights

If we conceive the rights of the individuals as being what has traditionally been called 'negative' rights, *i e*, as restrictions upon what others may do to an individual, then constitutionally protecting the individual rights from the interference of temporary political majorities, as well as from other individuals, may have a number of positive effects on human cooperation and hence human welfare. Most fundamentally, they limit—if successfully protected—the costs which other actors, private and political, can impose on individuals, and hence make it worthwhile for economic actors to invest their time and resources in productive efforts. This is, most obviously, the case with such classical 'negative' rights as the right to own property, to contract and trade, etc., without the interference of the government. But protecting such individual rights furthermore lowers the costs of the collective decision-making through a decrease in the decision-making costs of individual action by according to each individual a sphere within which he can ultimately act according to his own judgement. Also, the expected external costs of the choices made by others become lower, *cf* Buchanan and Tullock (Buchanan & Tullock, 1962).

It may, in contrast, be argued that the constitutional 'guaranteeing' of so-called 'positive' rights may have exactly the opposite effect. If the citizens of a state through the constitution have a 'right' to, *e g*, a certain living standard or other politically provided special benefits, this will per definition entail that others must bear the cost, and hence be restricted in their enjoyment of their (negative) rights. To the extent that such constitutionally mandated 'positive' rights are successfully implemented, the result may easily be a redistribution far beyond what an economy can bear and with significantly negative effects on wealth and productivity. Furthermore, by opening up for constitutional mandates for redistribution, the lid may be taken off a Pandora's Box of rent-seeking, whereby special interest groups may gain a considerable interest in ensuring that exactly their narrow benefits are institutionalized on a permanent basis.[26] In this way the 'positive' rights will increase both the external costs and the collective decision-making costs of the constitution.

The concept of economic freedom can be used to assess the degree to which negative rights are upheld and the degree to which positive economic rights are absent in an economy and also to analyse how this affects the economy. It is important to note that this is only partly a question of a relationship between institutions and economic performance; economic freedom may indeed prevail in many different institutional settings and is also a function of other things than institutions, *e g*, regular policies which, in turn, are also influenced by such things as external shocks and political preferences. But one could perhaps argue that these latter things are, in turn, influenced by institutions, and thus it seems appropriate to posit that institutions largely determine the degree of economic freedom, which in turn affects the working properties of an economy.

Decision rules

The specific types of decision rules may have a significant effect on the types of choices made as well as on the outcomes; on this, see Mueller (Mueller, 1989, part II). For example, the simple-majority rule may very well contribute to facilitating decisions where majorities exploit minorities or where influential groups manage to steer politics in ways favourable to them but not to others, which, among other things, can have negative efficiency effects. One implication is that qualified-majority rules or institutions which complement the simple-majority rule in the decision-making procedure could be preferable.[27] Legislative institutions, such as a particular budget process or a committee system, may steer the outcomes in ways more conducive to a sound economic policy.[28]

Electoral system

The electoral system itself may also have effects on the policies adopted. In an analysis of how parliamentary democracies with proportional electoral systems work, Moberg (Moberg, 1998) argues that they have a relatively strong innate tendency for a constant expansion of public expenditures and taxes, which leads to a dysfunctional economy. A central mechanism for this is that the party system typical of such constitutional settings, with a number of homogeneous, disciplined parties, facilitates the forming of majority coalitions which ally themselves with interest groups and voter groups requiring higher expenditures.[29] A change of the electoral system to a "first-past-the-post", or plurality system, in combination with an independently elected executive, would plausibly dampen this tendency.[30]

Separation of powers

Finally, the organization of the state may have effects on the choices made. Persson, Roland and Tabellini (Persson, Roland & Tabellini, 1997) show that the separation of powers with "checks and balances" between the executive and the legislature, in conjunction with a constitutional court which supervises that the constitution is upheld, can increase social utility, primarily because such an arrangement creates conflicts of interest between the two power centres while they, at the same time, must agree. Thereby, they monitor each other and contribute to the denouncement of power abuse, such as in the budgetary process (where the constitution can divide the process into two steps while requiring that both instances of power agree at each step: the first one entails one of them proposing a budget size and the second one entails the other proposing how to allocate budget resources between alternative uses). This implies that to the degree that monistic constitutional arrangements are thought to have too weak a mechanism for assuring that long-term and general interests are properly taken into account in political decision-making, a constitutional reform is a possible avenue forward.[31]

Referendums may also serve as a check-and-balance, in particular if such a measure can be initiated by the citizens as so-called 'voter initiatives'. It has, *e g*, been argued by Romer and Rosenthal (Romer & Rosenthal, 1979) that referendums generally will tend to restrain public agencies from overspending. This point has been extended theoretically by Gerber (Gerber, 1996), who has developed a uni-dimensional model showing that the existence of a possible threat of a referendum will tend to move public policy closer to the position of the median voter. The implication would then be that if the citizens have the right to demand that issues be put to a popular vote, the policies would be closer to those of the median voter.[32] Naturally, as noted below, this might yield policies that do not enhance long-term economic performance; but, depending on how the system of referendums and initiatives is designed, the opposite can also be obtained.

Federalism, lastly, can also be expected to influence the character of the political decisions taken. Hamlin (Hamlin, 1985, p 189) defines it as an institutional structure with "a multiplicity of competing government units within a single nation." The main purposes of such a system is to provide decentralization in order to "attain a better correspondence between the package of goods and services provided by government and the preferences of individuals by allowing the content of the package to vary across regions" (Hamlin, 1991, p 194) and competition, which leads to increased efficiency as "a multiplicity of governments will compete with each other both with respect to resources (seen as tax bases) and with respect to voter-citizens." (Hamlin, 1991, p 194).[33]

III. An Empirical Survey

Let us now see what empirical support there is for the contention of the previous section: do constitutions *de facto* matter for how economies function and, if so, how?[34]

Rights

Given the theoretical perspective adopted a fundamental question must be how important formal rights, as partly captured by the concepts of economic freedom and political freedom, are for economic growth and prosperity.[35] Research in economic history has shown that in societies which have obtained a high and enduring level of material wealth, well-defined and protected private ownership rights have been of central importance, not the least when the Western world was industrialized and when growth accelerated in the beginning of the 19th century.[36]

Political freedom

Studies of the possible relationship between political freedom and economic growth have been relatively frequent for some decades, no doubt due to the wide availability of obvious data (*e g* the annual Freedom House reports). For the present purpose we may view political freedom as consisting of two essential components: political rights and civil liberties.[37] Political freedom in the form of political rights are typically in the form of such 'positive' rights as, *e g*, the rights of the citizens to participate in the elections (*i e* universal franchise), free and open elections (*i e* between alternative parties), etc. Furthermore such 'positive' political rights may also be seen as including the various types of politically provided entitlements, *e g* to social security, medical care, housing, work, etc. In contrast, political freedom in the form of civil liberties is typically conceived of as 'negative' rights (other than economic rights), *e g* freedom of religion, freedom of speech, freedom of the press, freedom of association, freedom against unreasonable searches, due process, etc, *i e* what we would often associate with the 'rule of law' broadly conceived.[38]

There is hardly any consensus on the possible relationship between political rights and economic growth, with conclusions ranging from a positive relationship over no relationship at all to a negative one, no doubt partly due to the fact that such a very wide and complex set of concepts is subsumed under the broader concept (see Wu & Davis, 1999, p 40). There would, however, in recent studies seem to be an emerging conclusion that while civil liberties may play an important role (*cf infra*), political freedom as such does not lead to economic growth.

Vanssay and Spindler have in two studies examined data from a sample of approximately 100 countries for the period 1960-90.[39] They have done so by transforming the presence or absence of a number of political and economic rights into a set of dummy-variables as well as the general, over-all level of freedom, and the political structure. They found that political rights, *i e* the political structure and various forms of constitutional 'guarantees' of positive rights (entitlements), have no significant effect on economic growth and economic wealth.

Similar conclusions have been reached by others who have investigated the possible correlation and/or causality between political freedom and economic growth and prosperity, *e g* Farr, Lord and Wolfenbarger (Farr, Lord & Wolfenbarger, 1998) and Wu and Davis (Wu & Davis, 1999). Most recently Barro (Barro, 1997 and 2000) has similarly concluded that the extent of democracy as such has little effect on subsequent economic performance.[40]

In partial contrast, Lane (Lane, 1996) has found that positive rights may have some significant effect on prosperity and economic growth, albeit a negative one. He found, studying a comprehensive set of institutional data from the OECD countries, that states with more 'universal' welfare state entitlements tend to have less economic growth than states with more 'selective' transfers (*e g* on the basis of some estimate of 'need'). In the period 1965-80, economic growth (measured as change in GNP per capita) was 2.3 per cent vs. 1.8 per cent in the two types of systems respectively, and in the period 1980-91 the corresponding figures were 2.3 per cent and 1.8 per cent. This suggests that the inclusion of 'positive' rights to specific entitlements into the constitutional framework will have a growth-retarding effect over time.[41]

Economic freedom

The importance of good institutions has also been observed in studies looking at the connection between the degree of economic freedom, on the one hand, and economic wealth and economic growth, on the other hand. But while many studies have attempted to find a possible relationship between political freedom and economic growth, it is only within very recent years that something similar has been done in regard to economic freedom.[42] This has no doubt been due to the lack of systematic data, but at least three such attempts have been developed in recent years, *e g* the Scully-Slottje index of economic liberty (1994), the *Economic Freedom of the World Index* (1996 ff.), and the Wall Street Journal/Heritage Foundation *Index of Economic Freedom* (1996 ff.).[43] With economic freedom one would typically associate a free market economy, *i e* the property rights of individuals, freedom of choice and voluntary exchange, freedom of contract and the enforcement of contracts, the absence of taxation, regulation, etc.[44]

By now the studies seem to be almost unanimous in their verdict: Countries which have higher economic freedom (lower taxes, smaller public sector, more deregulated markets and trade, lower inflation, etc.) tend systematically to have greater wealth and higher economic growth than other countries.[45] In fact, no matter which of the three major attempts at indexing economic freedom is used, there is a statistically significant positive relationship between economic freedom and per capita national income.[46]

Vanssay and Spindler (Vanssay & Spindler, 1994 and 1996) have, in their studies of political and economic rights and their effect on growth and prosperity, found a significant positive relationship between economic freedom and economic growth. Furthermore, economic freedom together with the savings ratio, population growth and education, explain more than 75 per cent of the cross-country variation in per capita income.

The studies by Vanssay and Spindler were, however, among the first to attempt an investigation of the possible relationship between economic freedom and economic growth, and they accordingly did not compare the results of their use of the Scully-Slottje index with those resulting from other measures. An important study by de Haan and Siermann (de Haan & Siermann, 1998) has considered not only whether economic freedom has any effect on economic growth, but also which kinds of economic freedom may have a larger or smaller effect.[47] Their conclusion is that the robustness of the results depends on the specific indices used; for some measures of economic freedom, there is a positive relationship—and a strong one—while for others there is no relationship. They also found that some forms of economic freedom seem to have larger effect than others.[48]

Similarly Grubel (Grubel, 1998) has used some relatively simple comparisons to find some quite clear positive relationships between the levels of economic freedom and wealth (measured as GDP per capita) and between the levels of economic freedom and economic growth (measured as growth of real GDP per capita 1985-96). He has also, by relying on data from 20 OECD countries 1993-96, established similar, but negative, relationships between levels of economic freedom and unemployment rates.

The two freedoms

An important question relating to the importance of the various types of rights to growth and prosperity is how much importance they have together and relatively to each other. Wu and Davis (Wu & Davies, 1999) have examined data from approximately 100 countries in the period 1975-90 by using log-linear models to test the association and hence possible relationship between four variables: economic freedom, political freedom, levels of income (GDP per capita) and rates of economic growth. The results indicate, on the one hand, that given economic freedom, economic growth has no association with political freedom and the level of income, while on the other hand, given the level of income, political freedom is independent of economic freedom and the rate of economic growth. The analysis thus provides suggestive evidence for the theoretical argument that economic growth leads to an increase in political freedom, and further suggests as a general hypothesis that economic freedom promotes economic growth, and that an increased level of income leads to political freedom.

It would thus seem that what really matters for economic growth is *de facto* economic freedom, while the connection between political freedom and economic growth is, at best, fragile and highly dependent on the exact content of political freedom. And to the extent that there is a relationship between economic growth and political freedom it would seem more likely that the former leads to the latter than the reverse.

The results found by Wu and Davis are reflected in a study by Farr, Lord and Wolfenbarger (Farr, Lord & Wolfenbarger, 1998), which has attempted not simply to measure any possible correlation between economic freedom, political freedom and economic growth/economic wealth, but has investigated the possible direction of causality between the variables. The results may be summarized as done in *figure 7.3*, on next page, where the arrows symbolize an empirically detected causality:

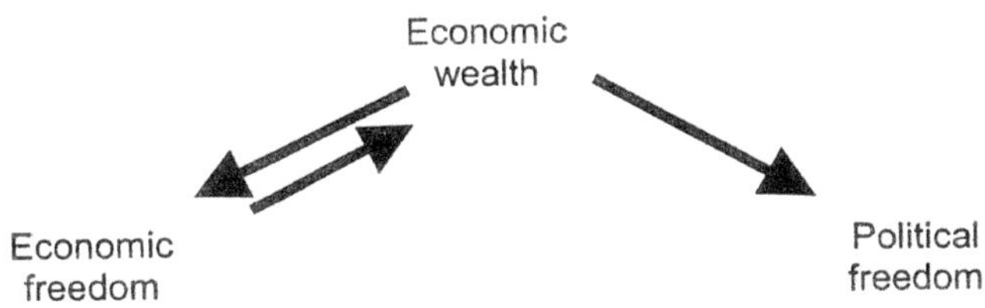

Figure 7.3. Causal relations between economic freedom, political freedom and economic wealth

The same pattern characterized both industrialized and non-industrialized countries: economic freedom at one time significantly causes economic wealth at a later time, and economic wealth at one time similarly causes both economic freedom and political freedom at a later time. There is, in other words, a feedback effect between economic freedom and economic wealth and through this an indirect effect of economic freedom upon political freedom. Political freedom, in contrast, seems to have no significant effect upon economic freedom or economic wealth, directly or indirectly.

The results may all together seem to indicate that some freedoms are of great importance, but what is important is not the formal enumeration of *de jure* rights or the summarization of what rights the citizens have, but the *de facto* protection of the rights.

The rule of law

Thus, more important than the formal constitutional guarantees of various rights seems to be the real protection of such rights, and here some would seem to be more important than others, in particular the rule of law and the protection of the property rights.

Vanssay and Spindler did not, in their studies, find any significant effect of, *e g*, traditional civil liberties, independent supreme courts, etc., on growth and prosperity. But the authors themselves suggest that the reason for this may be that what is important is not the formal constitution itself but rather the extended, 'effective' constitution.

Furthermore, the important role of the rule of law, broadly conceived, in stimulating prosperity has indeed been emphasized in a number of studies, historical as well as contemporary. De Long and Shleifer (De Long & Shleifer, 1993) have, for example, shown how the absence of arbitrary absolutism was very important in stimulating economic growth in medieval Europe; in general, the more absolutist, the less growth. North and Weingast (North & Weingast, 1989) specifically demonstrate how the Glorious Revolution of 1688 led to the creation of institutions credibly securing property rights, protecting wealth and eliminating confiscation, which resulted in a stimulation of economic growth.

More contemporary data would seem to point in the same direction. While Barro (Barro, 1997 and 2000) found that the extent of democracy as such has little effect on prosperity, he also—and in somewhat contrast—found that the most important factor for the developing countries is the rule of law. And even for non-developing countries the rule of law is important. This is a finding, which is also supported by, *e g*, Scully (Scully, 1992), who in a study of 115 market economies between 1960 and 1980 shows that politically open societies respecting the rule of law display higher economic growth during the period; *cf* Scully (Scully, 1988 and 1991).

In a recent study Olson, Sarna, and Swamy (Olson, Sarna & Swamy, 2000) have investigated the importance of good governance in the developing countries on the basis of a hypothesis that differences in governance explain why most developing countries grow more slowly than high income countries, while a few developing countries grow faster. They did so by considering GDP per capita data for 68 developing countries in the period 1960-87, and by comparing these with variables such as indices measuring the risk of expropriation and nationalization by foreign enterprises, the risk that governments will renege on contracts with foreign investors, the quality of the bureaucracy, the level of corruption and the level of national respect for public authority (*e g* the strength of the court system and the political stability). The analysis showed that all the variables had a significant effect, but that the most important were the risk of expropriation and of repudiation of contracts, *i e* of violations of property rights. If countries such as Haiti and Syria had had a rule of law such as that of Hong Kong, their annual growth in productivity would have been 2-3 per cent higher than it actually was.

Similar results are obtained in Knack and Keefer (Knack & Keefer, 1995), where property rights are found to have a great impact on investment and growth, sometimes even higher than the impact of education. The effect of the institutions of growth persists even after controlling for investments, which implies that secure property rights not only affect the size of the investment but also the efficiency with which the inputs are allocated. The rates of convergence to U S level incomes also increase notably when the property rights variables are included in the growth regressions; *cf* Keefer (Keefer, 1999).

Another study, by Norton (Norton, 1998), highlights that well-defined and enforced property rights seem to be particularly important to the well-being of the poorest people in the world.[49] The stronger the delineation and constitutional protection of property rights, the smaller the poverty and the higher the extent of 'human development', which may be interpreted as a clear sign that the safer the property rights, the greater the opportunity to engage in wealth-maximizing behaviour. For example, in societies with strong property rights the proportion of people not expected to live to the age of 40 is 6-9 per cent, while it is more than 25 per cent in societies with weak property rights (see Norton, 1998, p 243).

Decision Rules

One group of studies has investigated the effects of procedural design: whether there are any relationships between the types of decision rules and the types of decisions made, *e g* the level or types of spending. Not all of these rules are constitutionally mandated, but some are and most could be seen as being at least a part of the 'effective' constitution.

Budget rules

Attempts have been made at testing how the budget process rules may affect the size of budget deficits and public debt. Hagen (Haagen, 1991) has compared the budget processes in the individual U S states, and concluded that the more restrictive the rules governing the budgetary process, the smaller the budget deficit and the public debt. But the restrictions also have some effect in simply shifting the debt from restricted to non-restricted areas.

Similar results have been found by Krol (Krol, 1997), who has also studied the effects of various budget rules in the US states. Specifically, Krol has surveyed the effects of limitations on how much taxes and expenditures can increase per year, the line-item veto where governors can veto and reduce the spending on a line-by-line basis, and balanced-budget laws in the states. He found that all these measures have the intended effect: they reduce state spending, state taxes and state debt. Not all of these restrictions are in the form of formal constitutional rules in a narrow sense; some are simply in the form of statutory laws, and the empirical evidence suggests that the former are more effective than the latter, just as it seems as if restrictions on spending are more effective than restrictions on taxation.[50]

Other studies, *e g* Alt and Lowry (Alt & Lowry, 1994) and Poterba (Poterba, 1994), have focused on budget rules limiting the possibility of transferring budget deficits from one year to another, as well as substantive restrictions in the form of fixed limits on taxes and spending. These studies have demonstrated that such rules do have an effect, for instance by leading to a more rapid reconstruction following sudden fiscal crises. Another study by, for example, (Lopez-de-Silane and others (Lopez-de-Silane *et al*, 1995), have shown that states with strict budgetary restrictions also tend to privatise more than states with less strict rules.[51]

These findings would together with the many studies finding a negative relationship between the level of government spending and the level of economic growth seem to suggest that there is an empirical basis for expecting that tax and spending restrictions over time will tend to favour economic growth.

The size of the constitution

It may finally be noted that there seems to be an empirical relationship between the length of a constitution and economic wealth, and a negative one. Specifically, Montenegro (Montenegro, 1995), in a study of 38 countries in the late 1980's, shows that. There is a clear negative relationship between the length of the constitution (measured by the number of articles as a proxy) and the level of GDP per capita. In fact, the conclusion is that no country with a high GDP per capita has a long constitution.

This is a finding which is in partial agreement with other studies concluding that the formal enumeration of rights in a constitution has no positive effect on economic wealth.[52] The obvious interpretation is that the formal *de jure* enumeration of rights is irrelevant to the factors resulting in economic growth; in fact, a complicated and detailed constitution may rather be seen as the result of the amount of influence exerted by various rent-seeking, special interest groups. What is relevant is a simple and understandable constitution and the actual *de facto* protection of those rights supporting wealth-creating activities.

Electoral Systems

The many studies, which have investigated the possible relationship between the presence of a democratic system and economic wealth and growth, have not found any significant evidence of a relationship between the two. To the extent that democracy is seen as entailing such other aspects as a rule of law, etc., there may be a connection in this broader sense, but not between a democratic political system as such and economic wealth (*cf* Barro, 2000). Similarly, democracy may be seen as being caused by previous wealth, which again may be seen as being caused by economic freedom, but the causality does not run in the reverse direction.[53]

But while there is no necessary connection between democracy and prosperity, the specific forms of electoral systems in democracies may have some effects. Grilli, Masciandaro and Tabellini (Grilli, Masciandaro & Tabellini, 1991) investigate the possible relationship between political and monetary institutions and public finance policies. These policies, they argue, reasonably differ because governments of different countries are subjected to different political and economic incentives. They found that in political systems with a proportional representation system and a fractionalized party system, the budget deficits and public debt tend to be higher than in democracies with majoritarian electoral systems.

In another study de Haan, Sturm and Beekhuis (de Haan, Sturm & Beekhuis, 1999) demonstrate that coalition governments tend to find it more difficult to remain within their budgets after an adverse economic shock than is the case with one-party majoritarian governments. Furthermore, there is evidence that the number of political parties tend to go along with a growth in the size of the government debt. Since coalition governments tend to be more prevalent in systems with proportional representation, there would seem to be good reasons to believe that an electoral system that creates clear choices between alternative majority governments would tend to have a positive effect on sound fiscal behaviour. This is also supported by de Haan and Volkerink (de Haan & Volkerink, 2000), who find that more fragmented governments have higher deficits, and by Ashworth and Heyndels (Ashworth & Heyndels, 2000), who find that the larger the fragmentation of the government, the greater is the persistence of deviations, after shocks, from the desired tax structure. Fragmentation, in turn, is reasonably a direct result of the type of electoral system in use, as argued by Moberg (Moberg ,1998 and 2000 a); *cf* Härd (Härd, 2000).

Separation of Powers

Quite often, a constitutional separation of powers will not in itself guarantee that the separation will remain in place. It is, for example, the US and Swiss experience that constitutional safeguards are not completely immune to changes in the preferences and the behaviour of rent-seeking special interest groups, especially not in times of crises and war.[54]

Nonetheless, the fundamental constitutional structure may have important effects. Lane (Lane, 1996) has conducted a comprehensive study comparing a wide range of data from the OECD countries spanning several decades. Lane found some significant relationships—and some less significant ones. The study shows that by 1991, OECD countries characterized by federalism, presidentialism and bicameralism had significantly less public spending and greater wealth (measured as GDP per capita) than countries which did not. The results, however, were not completely unequivocal since economic growth was less in countries with presidentialism and federalism during the period 1965-91.

Crain (Crain, 1999) has undertaken a study comparing data from 47 countries from the 1970's and 1980's with regard to the possible relationship between institutional characteristics and the character of public investment, specifically whether or not certain types of institutions promote 'political business cycles', *i e* the oversupply of policies with pre-election benefits and post-election costs. The analysis compared, on the one hand, the length of the legislative terms, the number of chambers in parliament (one or two), the formal separation of powers, and whether legislators are elected simultaneously or with overlapping terms, and on the other hand the relative weight of the different types of public expenditure (consumption or investment). The finding was that the institutional set-up had some effects, among other things that longer legislative terms led to an increase in public investment relative to public consumption. In other words, the time horizon of the legislators is extended. In contrast, a formal separation of powers between the legislative and the executive branch seems to have a negative effect on the share of the public investments.[55]

Federalism

In a federal state there is, per definition, a specified division of authority—a vertical separation of powers—between the various levels of government, which is not necessarily present in a unified single-level state, and there seems to be evidence that the federal element has systematic effects on the nature of public spending.

Vaubel (Vaubel, 1996) has examined data from 65 countries, primarily from 1989-91, and he finds that federalism has an impact on the total size and relative centralization of government spending, and hence possibly also on the economy. Specifically, federal states on average tend to be more decentralized in their composition of public spending than non-federal states, and the share of the central government is significantly smaller, if the income per capita and the area of the state are large.[56]

Federal states do, however, often exhibit a tendency of gradual centralization, with the power shifting away from the individual states to the federal state. Vaubel's study indeed shows that the most important factor when it comes to constraining the federal government is the presence and independence of a constitutional court.

Moser (Moser, 1994) has similarly evaluated the experience from both the U S and Switzerland, and concluded that it is very difficult to constrain the federal government by its own federal institutions alone. What seems to be effective are precise and narrow rules limiting what can be done.

Popular initiatives and referenda

While democracy as such seems to have no systematic effect on economic growth and prosperity, one particular aspect of democracy, direct democracy in the form of referendums, seems empirically to work as a form of separation of powers.

Matsusaka (Matsusaka, 1995) has empirically demonstrated—drawing upon extensive data from the 50 states of the USA in the period 1960-90—that total public spending, state and local, has a systematic tendency to be lower in states that have voter initiative referendums than in states where the political decision-making lies exclusively with the legislature. Furthermore states with voter initiative had more decentralized spending and utilized less redistributional spending. Matsusaka's reasoning is that direct democracy will result in the adoption of policies favoured by the median voter in the electorate as a whole, while this may not necessarily be the case with representative democracy. In that respect the findings seem similar to a number of others, concluding that the use of direct democracy may tend to lower the level of public debt and—at least—coincide with a higher GDP per capita.[57]

Research by Feld and Matsusaka (Feld & Matsusaka, 2000) further indicates, in the form of a panel-data study of Swiss cantons, that where new government spending programmes must be approved by mandatory citizen referendums, this reduces the size of the budget by 15 per cent for the median canton.

The logic of Matsusaka does, however, cut both ways in practice: if the median voter wants higher spending, more regulation, etc., the institution of public initiative could counteract growth-supporting policies. Matsusaka (Matsusaka, 1999) has indeed demonstrated, by looking at data from the US states for the period 1900-49, that the voter initiative in the first half of the century seemed to have had the opposite effect: public spending was higher in states which had the possibility of voter initiatives than in states which did not. The empirical results then seem less than unequivocal in terms of whether referendums generally will have one result or another, and Matsusaka (Matsusaka, 1999) has hence suggested that the explanation may be that the preferred policy of the median voter has changed during the 20th century and thus does not have a consistent effect on the overall size of state and local public spending. But one important finding is that the voter initiative does systematically lead to more decentralized public spending, *i e* at the local rather than the state level.

IV. Conclusion

Institutions matter; this presumption is at the centre of attention in institutional and constitutional economics. Here, we look at political institutions, in particular constitutional ones, and predict that they influence the character of political decision-making, which, in turn, strongly influences economic outcomes.

At the basis of this prediction is an incentive-based understanding of human action, which stresses that institutions constitute constraints and rights that direct choices in a systematic fashion. If there is a rule prohibiting action *x*, and if there is some type of sanction attached to breaking this rule, then, all else equal, action *x* is less probable than in the absence of the rule. The issue at hand: is this in accordance with the facts?

There are indications that if a government is constitutionally unlimited and expands greatly, it will have a negative effect on the economy, and that, in contrast, there may be significant rewards to reap for society by moving towards a more constitutionally limited government (see, *e g* Gwartney, Lawson & Holcombe, 1998, and Gwartney, Holcombe & Lawson, 1998). Certain sets of political institutions hence seem more conducive than others to a good economic development and good macroeconomic policies.

Clearly, constitutions are complex documents with a number of different components, and one can imagine a great number of combinations that function equally well. Also, other things than constitutions shape policies and economic outcomes. However, based on the survey above, we posit that if a government contemplates reforming its constitution, and to the extent that economic progress is made a high priority, it is wise to consider the following institutional arrangements:

- Upholding negative economic rights, especially secure private property rights.
- An electoral system favouring strong, non-fragmented majorities.
- Some form of a decentralized—hierarchical or federal—structure in the public sector, with a vertical separation of powers.
- Some form of horizontal separation of powers at each level of the government.
- Levels on spending, taxes, and public debt.

- The possibility of popular initiatives for certain types of decisions, *e g* taxes, or the possibility of requiring referendums on expropriation, new taxes, regulation, etc.
- Strict budget processes in legislatures.

What is important to note is, however, that the specific effects of a particular, new, constitutional arrangement may be highly dependent on where and when reforms are introduced. Some institutions, which may work favourably in terms of making it more difficult to enact policies with growth-retarding effects, may under different circumstances have the opposite effects. A bicameral system and a strong separation of powers may, for example, be important in deterring narrowly redistributive policies and hence be effective in maintaining a limited government. But if the point of departure is an expansive welfare state instead, such as found in the Nordic countries, the effect could conceivably be the opposite, *i e* the institutions may make it difficult to adopt policies that will favour general growth and prosperity at the cost of narrow special interests. This factor has to be kept in mind when considering constitutional engineering.

It should also be stressed that there are other goals for the political system than economic ones. But we submit that economic goals are important—both in themselves and in that the realization of other goals often hinges upon there being sufficient economic resources available—and that, as a consequence, constitutional reforms should note what economic effects some of their reform choices entail. Only then can proper trade-offs between various goals be made.

Notes

1. The authors wish to thank Fredrik Bergström, Jørgen Grønnegard Christensen, Dan Johansson, Nils Karlson and Andreas Peterson for valuable comments and suggestions.
2. As clarified in Kasper and Streit (Kasper & Streit, 1998, pp 30-31), there are external (or formal) institutions, created and maintained by the government, and internal (or informal) institutions, such as conventions, ethical norms, customs, and professional practices. Focus here is on the former. It should also be noted from the outset that the institutional and constitutional focus does not preclude other determinants of economic variables, but it does hypothesize that all else equal, institutions and constitutions play an important role.
3. This is a rationalist-constructivist approach to institutional change that we largely adhere to, but there is also much merit in the evolutionary theories of institutions, analyzing their unplanned, spontaneous emergence and persistence—*cf* Hayek (Hayek, 1973). These two perspectives need not be viewed as substitutes; rather, they can, in our view, largely be seen as complementary.
4. There is no infinite series of levels: in all cases, there is some highest level of rule- making, which is never, in itself, exogenous. From the point of view of those who are able to change these rules, *all* rules stemming from the political sector are, indeed, at base changeable. However, political transaction costs are generally higher when it comes to changing higher-level rules, due to more stringent decision mechanisms. Clearly, these costs are never infinitely high, which is why overarching rules, as well as other rules, *are* suitable study objects. They can be changed, and they affect human behaviour. *Cf* Kasper and Streit (Kasper & Streit, 1998, ch 12), who analyze how constitutions evolve through choices induced by economic and political competition between jurisdictions.
5. The precise form of such constraints may vary and be either procedural or substantial, see Wagner and Gwartney (Wagner & Gwartney, 1988), and Aranson (Aranson, 1988). The former concern the rules for the political process—*e g* those regulating how decisions are made in the legislature—while the latter refer to specific requirements on political outcomes—*e g* that the national debt may not exceed a certain share of the GDP.
6. For more on the institutional insights of Adam Smith, see Rosenberg (Rosenberg, 1960), Buchanan (Buchanan, 1990, p 11), and Berggren (Berggren, 1993).
7. This is akin to the old question: who guards the guardians?
8. *Cf* Brennan & Buchanan, 1985.
9. *Cf* Mueller, 1989, ch 17.

10. See, *e g* North, 1981 and 1990; Eggertsson, 1990; Myhrman, 1994, chs 2 & 8, and Kasper & Streit, 1998.
11. See, *e g* North, 1990, ch 5.
12. See Heiner, 1983 and Vanberg, 1994.
13. See, *e g* Coase, 1960; North & Thomas, 1973; North, 1981; and Eggertsson, 1990. *Cf* also North & Weingast, 1989.
14. Cf *figure 2.4* in Myhrman, 1994.
15. It bears noting that the effects of a constitution on politics can be direct (in defining the formal properties of the political system) or indirect (in that the formal properties may have secondary effects on the political system). The latter may not be easily understood. Both types of effects in turn affect how the judicial system and the economy function. On the importance of analyzing the indirect effects, see Moberg (Moberg, 2000 a), which explores how the constitution influences the party system without dealing with it explicitly and how this, in turn, influences the type of decisions that are made in politics.
16. We may thus distinguish between the *formal constitution*, understood as, *e g* the formal document so named, and the *effective constitution*, where this is the constitution broadly conceived and the set of rules, which are enforced *de facto*, *i e* including, for example the level of regulation, taxation, etc. *Cf* Vanssay & Spindler, 1994, pp 360, 266-367 notes 3 and 4; 1996, pp 12.
17. *Cf* Eliasson (1998, pp 56) for a specification of formal institutions that create incentives to industrial dynamics and economic growth.
18. Such considerations can be expected to play an important role no matter what motivates political decision-makers. If they are self-interested, a growing economy is important to retain popular and interest-group support; and if they are more altruistically inclined, they probably value a growing economy because it makes the lives of the citizens more enjoyable. On how considerations such as these vary with political systems, see Olson, 2000.
19. By "constitution" is meant a set of overriding, durable rules which define the political game. For general presentations of constitutional economics, see, *e g* Buchanan (Buchanan, 1987 and 1990), Brennan and Buchanan (Brennan & Buchanan, 1985), Mueller (Mueller, 1996), and Berggren (Berggren, 1997). On a central issue of the research programme, see Buchanan (Buchanan, 1993). On the relationship between the new institutional economics and constitutional economics, see Voigt (Voigt, 1999, pp 2-3).
20. Generally, in this line of literature, following Buchanan (Buchanan, 1959 and 1987, pp 585), it is not seen as worthwhile to try to persuade politicians to revise their policy as long as the institutional setting does not give them incentives to act in accordance with such attempts of persuasion. Rather, focus should first be on trying to devise better rules.

21. *Cf* Downs, 1957; Olson, 1971; and Peltzman, 1976.
22. A conclusion from the empirical research on the interaction between politicians, voters, and interest groups is that the latter are quite influential in the political process and that they are prepared to invest substantial amounts in lobbying. See, *e g* Mueller (Mueller, 1989: parts 3, 4), Crain and Tollison (Crain & Tollison, 1990), Potters and Sloof (Potters & Sloof, 1996), Tollison (Tollison, 1997), Bergström (Bergström, 1998), Shleifer and Vishny (Shleifer & Vishny, 1998, pp 53-90), and Dahlberg and Johansson (Dahlberg & Johansson, 1999). On 'institutional sclerosis' and its negative effect on economic growth and prosperity, see Olson (Olson,1982).
23. In order to achieve this, Buchanan and Congleton (Buchanan & Congleton, 1998) propose that the simple-majority rule be complemented with the generality principle, requiring all political decisions to treat all citizens equally *qua* citizens. *Cf* Buchanan, 1993. For an application of this approach to Swedish industrial policy, see Berggren & Bergström (1999 a). On the desirability of a constitutional reform in Sweden, in order to induce long-term efficiency, see Åberg, 1997.
24. For an elaborated argument, see Berggren & Bergström, 1999 b. This view presumes that citizens primarily do not value a particular institution for its own sake but only proportionally to its ability to generate well-being. Overall, political legitimacy is then a positive function of how the *set* of relevant institutions contribute to this goal. It bears noting that there are different normative bases for this line of reasoning, *e g* a contractarian one and a utilitarian one. On the former, see Coleman, 1990; on the latter, see Berggren, 1999.
25. Other categorizations of the constitutional aspects could be made; this is only for heuristic purposes.
26. On rent-seeking, see, *e g* Tullock, 1993.
27. See, in general, Riker (Riker, 1982), and on the simple-majority rule in particular, Buchanan and Tullock (Buchanan & Tullock, 1962, pp 63-91).
28. This line of inquiry is akin to the one addressed in the literature on structure-induced equilibria (*e g* Shepsle & Weingast, 1981; Shepsle, 1986; and Weingast & Marshall, 1988. There, the issue is how institutional arrangements that complement the pure majority rule, primarily in the form of the way the legislature is organized, can instill legislative stability. The idea is to restrict the domain and the content of legislative exchange.
29. A somewhat similar conclusion has been reached in a sophisticated game-theoretical analysis (Austen-Smith, 1998). The somewhat stylized equilibrium model demonstrates that there is a tendency for political systems with proportional representation and more than two parties to result in higher taxes (but also flatter distributions of income) than is the case in political systems with "first-past-the-post"

systems and only two parties. The reason is that since no political party has an absolute majority of the votes, the parties need to engage in legislative bargaining, which drives up redistribution.

30. *Cf* Grilli *et al*, 1991. For a general discussions of pros and cons of the two alternative electoral systems, see, *e g* Cox, 1997 and Dummett, 1997.
31. On the division of power more generally, see, *e g* Dorn, 1988, Vile, 1998, and Nergelius, 1999.
32. For a systematic treatment of the basis for referendums and initiatives in constitutional democracies, see Moberg, 1999.
33. *Cf* Wildavsky, 1990 and Casella & Frey 1992. For a more critical perspective of federalism and institutional competition, but in agreement insofar as the principle that federalism affects the working properties of politics is concerned, see Moberg, 2000 b.
34. For a broader survey of the consequences of various institutional setups, see Moser, 1999.
35. For a discussion of some of the conceptual problems involved in distinguishing between economic freedom and political freedom, as well as of some of the problems involved in measuring and comparing freedoms, see Hanke & Walters, 1997 and de Haan & Sturm, 1999.
36. See North & Thomas, 1973 and 1977; Rosenberg & Birdzell, 1986; Hodgson, 1988; Jones, 1988; and North, 1992. *Cf* Olson, 1996.
37. *Cf* Farr, Lord, & Wolfenbarger, 1998, p 253; de Haan & Siermann, 1998, pp 364-365), and Wu & Davis, 1999, pp 41.
38. *Cf* Hayek, 1960.
39. See Vanssay & Spindler, 1994 and 1996, who used the Scully-Slottje index as well as other sources. The data relating to income and growth used in the two studies were different, but the results of the two studies are more or less consistent.
40. Barro (Barro, 1997; 2000) used the Gastil index to measure the extent of democracy. Barro also finds that democracy does not have a strong effect in fostering the rule of law and hence not even in this way an indirect effect on economic growth.
41. See Lane, 1996, pp 209-211.
42. For a survey and comparison of the various major attempts, see Hanke & Walters, 1997.
43. See Scully & Slottje, 1991; Gwartney, Lawson & Block, 1996; Gwartney & Lawson 1997 and 2000; Johnson & Sheehy, 1996; Holmes, Johnson & Kirkpatrick, 1997; and O'Driscoll, Holmes & Kirkpatrick, 2000.
44. *Cf* de Haan & Siermann, 1998, pp 364-365; and Wu & Davis, 1999, pp 40-41.
45. See, *e g* Scully, 1992; Vanssay & Spindler, 1994 and 1996; Grubel, 1998; de Haan & Siermann, 1998; de Haan & Sturm, 1999; Wu & Davis, 1999; and Gwartney & Lawson, 2000.

46. See Hanke & Walters, 1997.
47. The authors employed the *Economic freedom of the world index* by Gwartney, Lawson & Block, 1996.
48. For analyses of how government expenditure levels affect the economic growth, see Gwartney, Lawson, & Holcombe, 1998, Gwartney, Holcombe & Lawson, 1998, and Fölster and Henrekson, 1988 and 1999. Barro (Barro, 1997) has similarly examined the effects of what he calls "nonproductive government spending" (*i e* total government spending minus defence and education) and found a significantly negative relationship between the level of government spending and the growth in GDP per capita.
49. Norton tests the level of extent and character of poverty by using the UN Human Development Index and Human Poverty Index also utilized by Grubel and by testing these against several measures of the extent of protection of property rights derived both from the *Economic freedom of world index* by Gwartney & Lawson, 1997, and from the *Index of economic freedom* by Holmes, Johnson & Kirkpatrick, 1997.
50. See also, *e g*, Stansel, 1994.
51. It should be noted that not all studies have found a relationship between constitutions and the economy. Abrams and Dougan (Abrams & Dougan, 1986) found that the types of constitutional rules in operation do not affect the total level of public expenditure. But against this it might conceivably be countered that not all constitutional rules are equally effective in practice; some may be circumscribed more easily than others.
52. See Vanssay & Spindler, 1994 and 1996.
53. *Cf* Farr, Lord, & Wolfenbarger, 1998.
54. See Moser, 1994. *Cf* also Higgs, 1987.
55. See Crain, 1999, pp 10-11.
56. Grossman (Grossman,1989 and 1992) and Vaubel (Vaubel, 1994) find that the higher the degree of fiscal centralization, *i e* the share of public expenditures controlled by the central government, the larger the public sector.
57. For a review of some of these studies, see Moser (Moser, 1999).

References

Åberg, C J, 1997, *Ett svårskött pastorat : hur förnya svensk politik?* Stockholm: SNS Förlag, 1997.

Abrams, B A & Dougan, W R, 1986, "The effects of constitutional restraints on governmental spending", in *Public Choice*, 49, pp 101-116.

Alt, J E & Lowry, R C, 1994, "Divided government, fiscal institutions, and budget deficits : evidence from the States", in *American Political Science Review*, 88, pp 811-827.

Aranson, P H, 1988, "Procedural and substantive constitutional protection of economic liberties", in *Public choice and constitutional economics* (*eds* Gwartney, J D & Wagner, R E). Greenwich: JAI Press, 1988.

Ashworth, J & Heyndels, B, 2000, "Political fragmentation and the evolution of national tax structures in the OECD" (paper presented at the Annual Meeting of the European Public Choice Society". April 26-29, 2000, Siena, Italy.

Austen-Smith, D, 1998, "Redistributing income under proportional representation." Dept of Political Science (unpublished manuscript), Northwestern University, 1998.

Barro, R J, 1997, *Determinants of economic growth : a cross-country empirical study*. Cambridge: MIT Press, 1997.

—, 2000, "Rule of law, democracy, and economic performance", in *2000 Index of Economic Freedom* (*eds* O'Driscoll, G P, Holmes, K R & Kirkpatrick, M). Washington [DC] & New York: Heritage Foundation and *Wall Street Journal*, 2000.

Berggren, N, 1993, "The role of institutions in economic analysis : from Smith to North." Department of Economics (unpublished manuscript), George Mason University, 1993.

—, 1997, "Proem", in *Essays in constitutional economics*. Stockholm: The Economic Research Institute, 1997.

—, 1999, "A preference-utilitarian foundation for the generality principle", in *Constitutional Political Economy*, 10, pp 339-353.

Berggren, N & Bergström, F, 1999 a, "A constitutional analysis of selectivity in economic policy making", in *Makt utan motvikt: om demokrati och konstitutionalism* (*eds* Berggren, N, Karlson, N & Nergelius, J). Stockholm: City University Press, 1999.

—, 1999 b, "Den otämjda demokratins problem" in *Skatter & Välfärd*, 4, pp 34-41.

Bergström, F, 1998, *Essays on the political economy of industrial policy*. Stockholm: Ekonomiska forskningsinstitutet, 1998.

Boudreaux, D J, 1998, "What is the american constitution?", in *The Freeman* 48 (7).

Brennan, G & Buchanan, J M, 1985, *The reason of rules : constitutional political economy*. Cambridge: Cambridge University Press, 1985.

Brennan, G & Kliemt, H, 1990, "Logo logic", in *Constitutional Political Economy,* vol 1 (1), pp 125-127.

Buchanan, J M, 1959, "Positive economics, welfare economics, and political economy", in *Journal of Law and Economics*, vol 2, pp 124-138.

—, 1987, "Constitutional economics," in *The new Palgrave : a dictionary of economics* (eds Eatwell, J, Milgate, M & Newman, P). New York: Stockton, 1987.

—, 1990, "The domain of constitutional economics", in *Constitutional Political Economy*, vol 1 (1), p 1-18.

—, 1993, "How can constitutions be designed so that politicians who seek to serve 'Public interest' can survive?", in *Constitutional Political Economy, vol* 4 (1), pp 1-6.

—, 1999, "Why do constitutions matter?", chapter in this book (lecture presented at the City University of Stockholm conference "The Constitutional Challenge," September 1).

Buchanan, J M & Congleton, R D, 1998, *Politics by principle, not interest : towards nondiscriminatory democracy*. Cambridge: Cambridge University Press, 1998.

Buchanan, J M & Tullock, G, 1962, *The calculus of consent : logical foundations of constitutional democracy*. Ann Arbor: University of Michigan Press, 1962.

Casella, A & Frey, B, 1992, "Federalism and clubs : towards an economic theory of overlapping political jurisdictions", in *European Economic Review*, vol 36 (2-3), pp 639-646.

Coase, R H, 1960, "The problem of social cost", in *Journal of Law and Economics, vol* 3, pp 1-44.

—, 1977, "The wealth of nations", in *Economic Inquiry,* vol 15, pp 309-325.

—, 1998, "The new institutional economics", in *American Economic Review*, vol 88 (2), pp 72-74.

Coleman, J, 1990, "Constitutional contractarianism" in *Constitutional Political Economy*, vol 1, pp 135-148.

Cox, G, 1997, *Making votes count : strategic coordination in the world's electoral systems*. Cambridge: Cambridge University Press, 1997.

Crain, W M, 1999, "Sources of inefficiency in representative democracy : evidence on public investments across nations" (paper presented at the Annual Meeting of the Public Choice Society, March 12-14,1999, New Orleans).

Crain, W M & Tollison, R D (eds), 1990, Predicting politics : essays in empirical public choice. Ann Arbor: The University of Michigan Press, 1990.

De Long, J B & Shleifer, A, 1993, "Princes and merchants : European city growth before the industrial revolution", in *Journal of Law and Economics*, vol 36 (2), pp 671-702.

Dahlberg, M & Johansson, E, 1999, "On the vote purchasing behavior of incumbent governments". Uppsala University, Dept of Economics (Working paper no 24, see http://www.nek.uu.se/research/pdf/1999wp24.pdf).

Dorn, J A, 1988, "Public choice and the constitution : a madisonian perspective", in *Public choice and constitutional economics* (*eds* Gwartney, J D & Wagner, R E). Greenwich: JAI Press, 1988.

Downs, A, 1957, *An economic theory of democracy*. New York: Harper and Row, 1957.

Dummett, M, 1997, Principles of electoral reforms. Oxford: Oxford University Press, 1997.

Eggertsson, T, 1990, *Economic behaviour and institutions*. Cambridge: Cambridge University Press, 1990.

Eliasson, G, 1998, "From plan to markets", in *Journal of Economic Behavior and Organization*, vol 34, pp 49-68.

Elster, J, 1985, *Ulysses and the sirens : studies in rationality and irrationality*. Cambridge: Cambridge University Press, 1985.

Farr, W K, Lord, R A, & Wolfenbarger, J L, 1998, "Economic freedom, political freedom and economic well-being : a causality analysis", *Cato Journal*, vol 18 (2), pp 247-262.

Feld, L P & Matsusaka, J G, 2000, "Budget referendums and government spending : evidence from Swiss cantons" (paper presented at the Annual Meeting of the European Public Choice Society, April 26-29, 2000, Siena, Italy. See http://www-rcf.usc.edu/~matsusak).

Fölster, S & Henrekson, M, 1998, "Growth effects of government expenditure and taxation in rich countries". Stockholm: The research institute of industrial economics (Working paper no 503), Sweden.

—, 1999, "Growth and the public sector : a critique of the critics", in *European Journal of Political Economy*, vol 15 (2), pp 337-358.

Gerber, E, 1996, "Legislative response to the threat of popular initiatives", in *American Journal of Political Science*, vol 40 (1), pp 99-128.

Grilli, V, Masciandaro, D & Tabellini, G, 1991, "Political and monetary institutions and public financial policies in the industrial countries", in *Economic Policy*, vol 13, pp 341-392.

Grossman, P J, 1989, "Fiscal decentralization and government size : an extension" in *Public Choice*, vol 62, pp 63-69.

—, 1992, "Fiscal decentralization and public sector size in australia", in *The Economic Record*, vol 68 (202), pp 240-246.

Grubel, H G, 1998, "Economic freedom and human welfare : some empirical findings", in *Cato Journal*, vol 18 (2), pp 287-304.

Gwartney, J D, Holcombe, R & Lawson, R, 1998, "The scope of government and the wealth of nations", in *Cato Journal*, 18 (2), pp 163-190.

Gwartney, J D & Lawson, R, 1997, *Economic freedom of the world : 1997*. Vancouver: Fraser Institute, 1997.

—, 2000, *Economic freedom of the world: 2000 annual report*. Vancouver: Fraser Institute, 2000.

Gwartney, J D, Lawson, R & Block, W, 1996, *Economic freedom of the world: 1975-95*. Vancouver: Fraser Institute, 1996.

Gwartney, J D, Lawson, R & Holcombe, R, 1998, *The size and functions of government and economic growth*. Washington: Joint Economic Committee of the US Congress, 1998.
de Haan, J & Siermann, C L J, 1998, "Further evidence on the relationship between economic freedom and economic growth", in *Public Choice*, vol 95, pp 363-380.
de Haan, J & Sturm, J-E, 1999, "On the relationship between economic freedom and economic growth" (paper presented at the European Public Choice Meetings in Lisboa, 1999).
de Haan, J, Sturm, J-E & Beekhuis, G, 1999, "The weak government thesis : some new evidence", in *Public Choice*, 101, pp163-176.
de Haan, J & Volkerink, B, 2000, "Fragmented government effects on fiscal policy : new evidence" (paper presented at the Annual Meeting of the European Public Choice Society, April 26-29, 2000, Siena, Italy).
von Hagen, J, 1991, "A Note on the empirical effectiveness of formal fiscal restraints", in *Journal of Public Economics*, vol 44, pp199-210.
Hamlin, A P, 1985, "The political economy of constitutional federalism", in *Public Choice*, vol 46 (2), pp 187-195.
—, 1991, "Decentralization, competition, and the efficiency of federalism", in *The Economic Record*, vol 67 (198), pp 193-204.
Hanke, S H & Walters, S J K, 1997, "Economic freedom, prosperity, and equality : a survey", *Cato Journal*, vol 17 (2), pp 117-146.
Härd, S, 2000, "Arbitrary democracy", chapter in this book.
Hayek, F A, 1960, *The constitution of liberty*. Chicago: University of Chicago Press, 1960.
—, 1973, *Law, legislation and liberty* (vol I). London: Routledge, 1973.
Heiner, R A, 1983, "The origins of predictable behavior", in *American Economic Review,* 73, pp 560-95.
Higgs, R, 1987, *Crisis and Leviathan : critical episodes in the growth of American government*. Oxford: Oxford University Press, 1987.
Hodgson, G M, 1988, Economics and Institutions: A Manifesto for a Modern Institutional Economics. Philadelphia: University of Pennsylvania Press.
Holmes, K R, Johnson, B T & Kirkpatrick, M, 1997, *1997 Index of Economic Freedom*. Washington & New York: Heritage Foundation and Wall Street Journal, 1997.
Johnson, B T & Sheehy, T P, 1996, *1996 Index of Economic Freedom*. Washington: Heritage Foundation, 1996.
Jones, E L, 1988, *Growth recurring : economic change in world history*. Oxford: Clarendon Press, 1988.
Kasper, W & Streit, M E, 1998, *Institutional economics : social order and public policy*. Cheltenham: Edward Elgar, 1998.
Keefer, P, 1999, "Does one size fit all? : fitting economic reforms to political institutions", in *Journal for Institutional Innovation, Development, and Transition*, vol 3, pp 5-14.

Knack, S & Keefer, P, 1995, "Institutions and economic performance : cross-country tests using alternative institutional measures", in *Economic and Politics*, vol 7 (3), pp 207-227.
Krol, R, 1997, "A survey of the impact of budget rules on state taxation, spending, and debt", in *Cato Journal*, vol 16 (3), pp 295-307 (see http://www.cato.org/pubs/journal/cj16n3-2.html).
Lane, J.E, 1996, Constitutions and Political Theory. Manchester: Manchester University Press.
Lopes-de-Silane, F, Shleifer, A & Vishny, R W, 1995, "Privatization in the United States" (Working paper no 5113, NBER).
Matsusaka, J G, 1995, "Fiscal effects of the voter initiative : evidence from the last 30 years", *Journal of Political Economy*, vol 103 (31), pp 587-623.
—, 1999, "Fiscal effects of the voter initiative in the first half of the twentieth century" (paper presented at the Annual Meeting of the Public Choice Society, March 12-14, 1999, New Orleans).
Moberg, E, 1998, "The expanding public sector : a threat to democracy?", in *The limits of government : competence and economic growth* (*eds* Eliasson, G & Karlson, N). Stockholm: City University Press, 1998.
—, 1999, "Positive and normative aspects of direct democracy : the case of Sweden in a general context", in *Makt utan motvikt : om demokrati och konstitutionalism* (*eds* Berggren, N, Karlson, N & Nergelius, J). Stockholm: City University Press, 1999.
—, 2000 a, "Democracy : constitutions, politics, and welfare effects". Unpublished manuscript (see http://www.mobergpublications.se).
—, 2000 b, "Federalism", chapter in this book.
Montenegro, A, 1995, "Constitutional design and economic performance", in *Constitutional Political Economy*, vol 6, pp 161-169.
Moser, P, 1994, "Constitutional protection of economic rights : the Swiss and US experience in comparison", in *Constitutional Political Economy*, vol 5 (1), pp 61-79.
—, 1999, "The impact of legislative institutions on public policy : a survey", in *European Journal of Political Economy*, vol 15, pp 1-33.
Mueller, D C, 1989, *Public choice II*. Cambridge: Cambridge University Press, 1989.
—, 1996, *Constitutional democracy*. Oxford: Oxford University Press, 1996.
Myrhman, J, 1994, *Hur Sverige blev rikt* [How Sweden grew rich]. Stockholm: SNS Förlag, 1994.
Nergelius, J, 1999, "Maktdelningsbegreppet", in Makt utan motvikt : om demokrati och konstitutionalism (*eds* Berggren, N, Karlson, J & Nergelius, J). Stockholm: City University Press, 1999.
North, D C, 1981, Structure and change in economic history. New York: Norton, 1981.

—, 1990, Institutions, institutional change and economic performance. Cambridge: Cambridge University Press, 1990.
—, 1992, *Transaction costs, institutions, and economic performance*. San Francisco: International Center for Economic Growth, 1992.
North, D C & Thomas, R P, 1973, *The rise of the Western world : a new economic history*. Cambridge: Cambridge University Press, 1973.
—, 1977, "The first economic revolution", in *Economic History Review*, vol 30 (2), pp 229-241.
North, D C & Weingast, B R, 1989, "Constitutions and commitment : the evolution of institutions governing public choice in seventeenth-century England", in *Journal of Economic History*, vol 49 (4), pp 803-832.
Norton, S W, 1998, "Poverty, property rights, and human well-being : a cross-national study", in *Cato Journal*, vol 18 (2), pp 233-246.
O'Driscoll, G P, Holmes, K R & Kirkpatrick, M, 2000, *2000 Index of economic freedom*. Washington: Heritage Foundation & New York: Wall Street Journal, 2000.
Olson, M, 1965, *The logic of collective action : public goods and the theory of groups*. Cambridge: Harvard University Press, 1965.
—, 1982, The rise and decline of nations : economic growth, stagflation, and social rigidities. New Haven: Yale University Press, 1982.
—, 1996, "Big bills left on the sidewalk : why some nations are rich, and others are poor", in *Journal of Economic Perspectives*, vol 10, pp 3-21.
—, 2000, *Power and prosperity : outgrowing communist and capitalist dictatorships*. New York: Basic Books, 2000.
Olson, M, Sarna, N & Swamy, A V, 2000, "Governance and growth : a simple hypothesis explaining cross-country differences in productivity growth", in *Public Choice*, 102, pp 342-164.
Peltzman, S, 1976, "Towards a more general theory of regulation", in *Journal of Law and Economics*, vol 19, pp 221-240.
Persson, T, Roland, G & Tabellini, G, 1997, "Separation of powers and political accountability", in *Quarterly Journal of Economics*, vol 112, pp 1163-1202.
Poterba, J M, 1994, "State responses to fiscal crises : the effects of budgetary institutions and politics", in *Journal of Political Economy*, vol 102, pp 799-821.
Potters, J & Sloof, R, 1996, "Interest groups : a survey of empirical models that try to assess their influence", in *European Journal of Political Economy*, vol 12 (3), pp 403-432.
Riker, W H, 1982, Liberalism against populism : a confrontation between the theory of democracy and the theory of social choice. Prospect Heights: Waveland Press, 1982.
Romer, T & Rosenthal, H, 1979, "Bureaucrats versus voters: on the political economy of resource allocation by direct democracy", in *Quarterly Journal of Economics*, vol 93 (4), pp 563-587.

Rosenberg, N, 1960, "Some institutional aspects of the wealth of nations", in *Journal of Political Economy,* vol 68, pp 557-570.
Rosenberg, N & Birdzell, L E (Jr), 1986, *How the West grew rich : the economic transformation of the industrial world.* New York: Basic Books, 1986.
Scully, G W, 1988, "The institutional framework and economic development", in *Journal of Political Economy,* vol 96, pp 652-662.
—, 1991, "Rights, equity, and economic efficiency", in *Public Choice,* vol 68, pp 195-215.
—, 1992, *Constitutional environments and economic growth.* Princeton: Princeton University Press, 1992.
Scully, G W & Slottje, D J, 1991, "Ranking economic liberty across countries", in *Public Choice,* vol 69, pp 121-152.
Shepsle, K A, 1986, "The positive theory of legislative institutions: an enrichment of social choice and spatial models", in *Public Choice,* vol 50, pp 135-178.
Shepsle, K A & Weingast, B R, 1981, "Structure-induced equilibrium and legislative choice", in *Public Choice,* 37, pp 503-519.
Shleifer, A & Vishny, R W, 1998, *The grabbing hand : government pathologies and their cures.* Cambridge: Harvard University Press, 1998.
Stansel, D, 1994, "Taming Leviathan : are tax and expenditure limits the answer?". Washington: Cato Institute (Cato Policy Analysis no 213), 1994.
Tollison, R D, 1997, "Rent Seeking", in, *Perspectives on public choice : a handbook* (ed Mueller, D C). Cambridge: Cambridge University Press, 1997.
Tullock, G, 1993, *Rent seeking.* Cheltenham: Edward Elgar, 1993.
Vanberg, V J, 1994, *Rules and choice in economics : essays in constitutional political economy.* London: Routledge, 1994.
de Vanssay, X & Spindler, Z A, 1994, "Freedom and growth : do constitutions matter?" in *Public Choice,* vol 78, pp 359-372.
—, 1996, "Constitutions, institutions, and economic convergence : an international comparison", in *Journal of Studies in Economics and Econometrics,* vol 20 (3), pp 1-20.
Vaubel, R, 1994, "The political economy of centralization and the European community", in *Public Choice,* vol 81 (1-2), pp 151-90.
—, 1996, "Constitutional safeguards against centralization in federal states : an international cross-section analysis", in *Constitutional Political Economy,* vol 7, pp 79-102.
Vile, M J C, 1998, *Constitutionalism and the separation of powers.* Indianapolis: Liberty Press, 1998.
Voigt, S, 1998, "Implicit constitutional change : changing the meaning of the constitution without changing the text of the document", in *European Journal of Law and Economics,* vol 7 (3), pp 117-144.

Wagner, R E & Gwartney, J D, 1988, "Public choice and constitutional order", in Public Choice and Constitutional Economics (*eds* Gwartney, J D & Wagner, R E). Greenwich: JAI Press, 1988.
Weingast, B R & Marshall, W J, 1988, "The industrial organization of congress : or, why legislatures, like firms, are not organized as markets", in *Journal of Political Economy*, vol 96 (19), pp132-163.
Wildavsky, A, 1990, "A double security : federalism as competition", in *Cato Journal*, vol 10 (1), pp 39-58.
Wu, W & Davis, O A, 1999, "The two freedoms, economic growth, and development : an empirical study", in *Public Choice*, vol 100, pp 39-64.

*The Evolution of Constitutional Qualities under the Influence of Global Competition**

Wolfgang Kasper

I. A Necessary Preamble: Some Definitions

Any veteran of preaching the virtues of institutional economics knows of the dangers of not defining the key terms up-front. Let me therefore begin in a somewhat tedious way by spelling out the following definitions as I will use them:

Institutions are rules of human conduct whose violations attract sanctions of some sort. Appropriate institutions can help people with limited cognition to make sense of the complex and evolving reality, in other words help to ease the knowledge problem (*figure 8.1* on page 215). They also help to constrain selfish, opportunistic behaviour, promote order, avert conflict and help to settle unavoidable conflicts expediently. All this serves to reduce the transaction costs in markets (as well as the costs of running organisations). This is an important consideration since these costs now make up about half of all costs of producing and distributing the national product.

We distinguish between two basic types of institutions, according to their genesis (Kasper-Streit, 1998, pp 92-118): *Inter-*

* This text was also the contents of a lecture by Wolfgang Kasper at a City University seminar in Stockholm, 23 November, 1999.

nal institutions evolve within a community in the light of experience. Conventions, ethical norms, customs and professional practices tend to become norms of behaviour when people interact regularly and discover that certain arrangements expedite business. These are imitated, gain critical mass and then become community-wide norms, in short: new internal institutions.

External rules are, by contrast, designed and imposed by a political authority (collective action), and their violations incur formal, *i e* organised, sanctions. Legislation, regulations and administrative practices are examples of external institutions (*figure 8.1* on next page).

The term "institution", as used here, must not be confused with *organisations*, which are more or less durable associations of production factors. Organisations may, of course, embody certain institutions that affect their effective operation (for example company-specific work practices).

Constitutions are sets of overriding, durable rules, frequently of an abstract, general character. Political and economic constitutions should create order among individual rules and provide *meta* rules that guide us in how to interpret and reconcile specific rules (Kasper-Streit, 1998, pp 332-334).[1]

Written constitutions tend to contain external institutions, but in many countries important components of the constitution are not written down. Thus, the *Magna Carta* is part of Australia's constitution, although it is not contained in our Constitution of 1901. Black-letter lawyers often stress the external-rule components of constitutions; yet, their interpretations often draw on internal rules, such as natural law or *Volksrecht*. Any living constitution has to stand on two legs—external and internal rules.

The close logical relation of constitutions and institutions has in recent years led to the practice of speaking of *constitutional economics* when one discusses collectively chosen rules and their effect on economic performance (Voigt, 1997). The presumption is

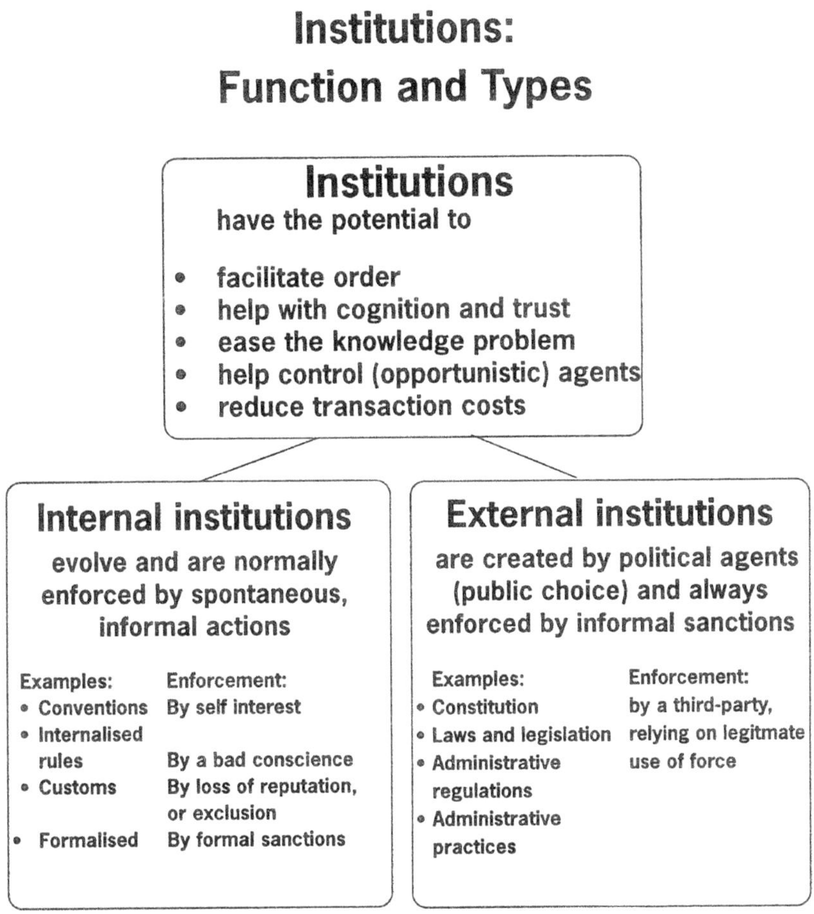
Institutions:
Function and Types
Institutions
have the potential to
• facilitate order
• help with cognition and trust
• ease the knowledge problem
• help control (opportunistic) agents
• reduce transaction costs
Internal institutions
evolve and are normally enforced by spontaneous, informal actions
Examples:
• Conventions
• Internalised rules
• Customs
• Formalised
Enforcement:
By self interest
By a bad conscience
By loss of reputation, or exclusion
By formal sanctions
External institutions
are created by political agents (public choice) and always enforced by informal sanctions
Examples:
• Constitution
• Laws and legislation
• Administrative regulations
• Administrative practices
Enforcement:
by a third-party, relying on legitmate use of force

Figure 8.1

that communities with good constitutions, in the sense of overriding rule systems, enjoy healthy economic constitutions, in the sense of resilience to change and good performance. The journal *Constitutional Politcal Economy* deals with comparisons between existing systems, which shape the underlying institutional constraints in the interest of better outcomes, and with measuring the economic consequences of certain rules.

Constitutional and other rules are not a purpose in its own right. They are tools to achieve individual human aspirations, specifically a plurality of *fundamental human values*, which define a well-run society: freedom, security, justice, equity, peace, prosperity and the conservation of a liveable environment (Kasper-Streit, 1998, ch 4). Institutions that hinder the attainment of these values need to be changed, but often are not.

The key quality of institutions to look out for if one wants effective rule systems is *universality*, as defined by the great Italian jurist Bruno Leoni (Leoni, 1962) and the Austrian economist-philosopher Friedrich Hayek (Hayek, 1960 and 1971-79). An institution is universal if it is

- certain and simple, making the institutions knowable and predictable—ad hoc regulations and 'legislative diarrhoea' violate this maxim;
- abstract and general, *i e* avoiding case-specific rules and discrimination amongst people—industry-specific decrees and preferential policies for well-connected interest groups violate this maxim; and
- open in the sense that existing rules give guidance in as-yet-unknown future situations—Russian-style *ukases* or arbitrary rulings that do not apply open-ended to the same conditions fail to create entrepreneurial confidence.

In addition, there should be consistency among rules and the orders they create: highly regulated labour markets are incompatible with open, competitive product markets, for example.

II. Evolution and Evolving Norms

Adaptability versus Rigidity

Any institution (or set of institutions) can only have a normative effect on human behaviour if it remains reasonably stable over time. There is much truth in the conservative adage that "old rules are good rules". People are familiar with old institutions and have adapted to them. Therefore old institutions better assist individuals in the attainment of fundamental values—Mao's perpetual revolution of the rules inflicted untold harm on the Chinese.

Yet, the world changes ceaselessly, and today's circumstances may require that we modify yesterday's known rules. Institutional evolution is part and parcel of the never-ending drama of human existence. It inflicts costs, but in certain circumstances the costs of rigidly upholding old institutions may exceed the adjustment costs. This fundamental conflict between adaptation and continuity deeply affects the degree to which fundamental values are attained. History shows time and again that both inertia in constitutional change and dramatic reversals in the rule system can endanger social peace, prosperity and freedom. Contemporary Russia is a telling example of the costs of poor institutional evolution.

To sum up the argument thus far: we have to weigh the costs and the benefits of the stability of rules against those of adaptation, and the relevant standard of valuing the costs and the benefits should be the individual human values we listed above. This can be stated glibly, but the matter involves complex empirical issues of individual cognition, collective choice and relative political power. It is desirable to have constitutional provisions in place which facilitate the process of re-evaluation and which act as a framework for re-tuning the rules in orderly, non-violent ways.

Openness

Experience shows that a community's social and economic life is a most complex process of open-ended evolution. The feedbacks and side effects of decisions are such that no human mind can grasp or plan society or the economy. Life is full of surprises. Models of society which are closed to evolutionary changes in technology, transport and communications, demography etc. are useless to analysing open-ended evolution (in other words, my criticism applies most economic models—Kasper, 1998 a)[2].

Of particular interest for the topic at hand is the openness of the system to international influences. This covers not only the openness to international trade in goods and services (the Internet now for the first time makes many services internationally tradable), but also to international factor flows. Thanks to technical and organisational progress, capital, knowledge, highly skilled people and enterprise are now becoming increasingly mobile amongst countries (globalisation). This means that the owners of these resources increasingly have an "exit option" if their home location promises relatively poor rates of return. We see, for example, the exit of numerous manufacturing ventures from OECD countries to those new industrial countries which have been made attractive by lower cost prices, great eagerness to work productively and improving economic institutions in these new locations (Kasper, 1998 b).

Openness has frequently been the driving force of changes in economic and political constitutions, if it is not even the main driving force of constitutional evolution. In early modern times, jurisdictions in western Europe were faced with the exodus of gifted, skilled people, capital and enterprises when they insisted on religious intolerance, arbitrary taxes and worse (*e g* the exodus of the Jews from Inquisition Spain to NW Europe and Turkey, the movement of the Huguenots to England, Prussia and Russia). Jurisdictions that offered a constitution which credibly safeguarded equality before the law, secure property rights and the freedom of contract made economic gains by attracting these valuable resources for growth.

Economic openness often presents an affront to the positions of established political power. Even in fairly democratic regimes, entrenched interest groups will defend the old rule system if it serves their interests, whatever the "voice" of the people (see the degeneration of many electoral democracies under the influence of ruthless group egotism and biddable parliamentarians and high-court judges). But if "voice" is supplemented by "exit", the pressures for constitutional evolution mount (Hirschman, 1970/80). The degree of openness now reached by many countries under the influence of globalisation imposes a discipline on rule-makers to keep the institutions in a form that allows mobile individuals and firms to operate with confidence and at low transaction costs. The fact that elected parliaments are subject to the discipline of capital markets may enrage some. But it is conveniently forgotten that parliamentarians, once elected, easily become self-serving or opportunists in pursuing party and interest-group privileges, rather than the common good of the citizens. With openness, citizens are normally empowered by the international competition among jurisdictions and are frequently protected from parliamentary opportunism by it.

The ways in which the disciplines of openness impact on the evolution of the underlying rules of the civic and economic game differ between internal and external institutions. We shall discuss these in turn.

Inertia and the Evolution of Internal Rules

Changing circumstances that impact on individuals typically elicit experimentation with alternative institutional arrangements. Some may spontaneously try out new arrangements that breach old rules, even possibly accepting reprimands. If successful, imitation and the gaining of critical mass will lead to the emergence of new internal institutions.

Frequently, such changes will affect specific rules. But if sufficient numbers of rules are altered, then the overriding rules—the constitutional provisions—will also be adapted for the sake of rule consistency. Thus, Princes in the European Renaissance initially tried to lure mobile merchants their way (to enhance their revenue base) by granting them specific laws and guarantees. As these privileges multiplied, they introduced incompatibilities into the system, so that the rulers began to adopt high-level general guarantees of private property, free contracts and the rule of law, as well as other fundamental liberties. Out of the rivalry of jurisdictions grew the constitutional state and the rule of law.

The history of humankind can be described from the angle of constitutional evolution, as the German Historical School (the Old Institutionalists) did one hundred years ago. As social and trading contacts intensify and spread further afield thanks to lower transport costs, new institutional arrangements evolved, many of which were of the internal variety. Globalisation, the ongoing constitutional reforms and the conflicts of the present day are but the latest stage in this historic process (*figure 8.2* on next page).

Nowadays, many developing countries are faced with the need to put the constitutional layers of regional, national and global exchange on top of their traditional, village-level rule systems, and all this within one generation. It is, for example, fascinating to observe how the internal rules of Confucian ethics

Development and Institutional Evolution

A Reader's Digest of the Historical School

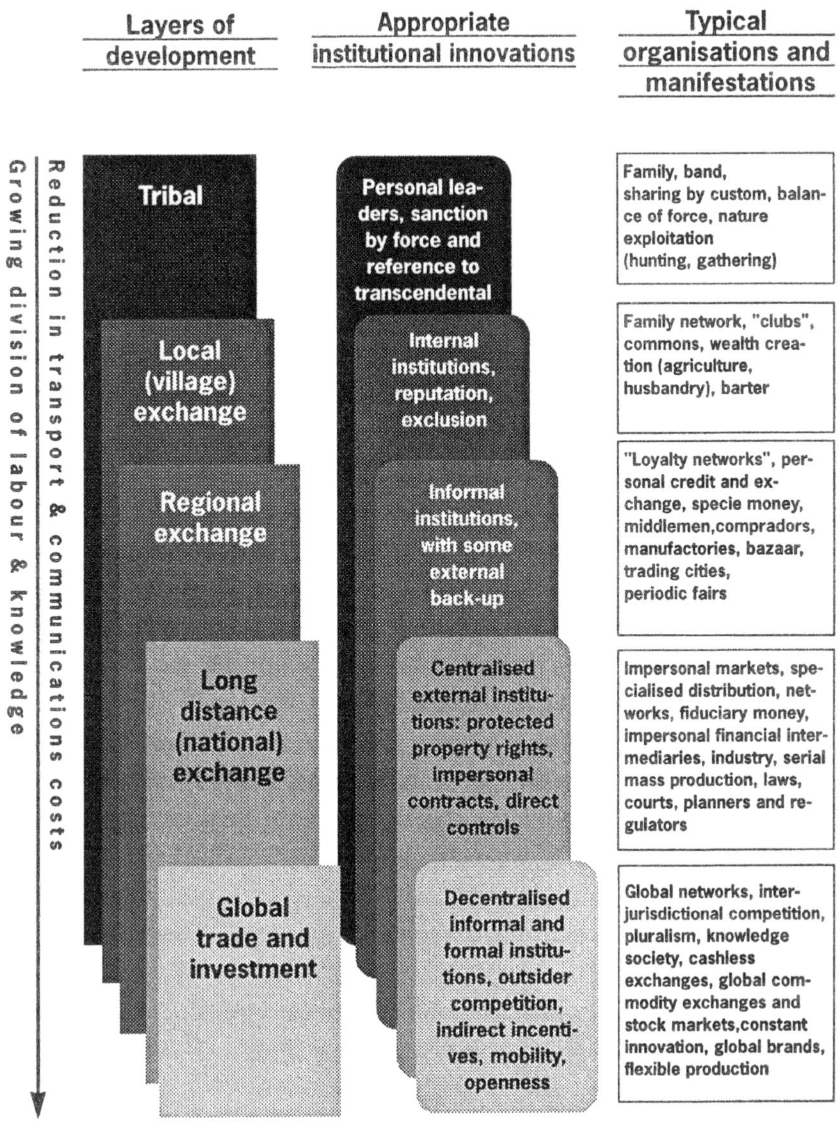

Source: Kasper (1997),12

Figure 8.2

have been adapted in East Asia by trial and error. In the process, a static, hierarchical order was transformed into one with future-oriented, evolutionary and performance-based ground rules (Hofstede-Bond, 1988; Rozman, 1991). Confucianism, which Max Weber once considered to be an immutable handicap to modern development, has been pragmatically changed into a major asset of economic growth, by "a million little rebellions"—as the novelist Naipaul once put it.

However, internal constitutional rules do not always evolve so smoothly and in ways that benefit individual welfare. There is considerable inertia in many rule systems that have, after all, been practiced since Palaeolithic times. The constitution of the inward-looking tribal society is alive and well in most affluent societies, underpinning the welfare state. The tribal mentality is driving well-organised attacks on globalisation, as was for example manifested recently in the NGO campaign against OECD's failed Multilateral Investment Agreement (MIA) and against the free-trade rules of the WTO at the failed Seattle summit of December 1999. In the coming decade, we will observe numerous clashes of deeply engrained institutions with the demands of global competition, and we cannot be sure which of these incompatible forces will gain the upper hand.

Inertia in institutions leads to tensions in society and to inter-generational conflicts. It may even lead to cultural and economic decline and civil war. If you live in a society where people believe that the old rules have been ordained for all times by God or the gods, economic stagnation, or even a decline will follow—as *e g* witnessed in present-day Iran. Over time, the costs may become more visible, even intolerable. Then, constitutional changes become possible. Internal constitutional rules may then first be altered within sub-societies. The outcome of those limited experiments will then influence the conventions, ethics and practices of other sections of society.

But institutional adjustment to new circumstances is far from inevitable. Examples of pent-up constitutional evolution are the long, relative decline of China (1600 to 1950, as compared to the far-western peninsula of Eurasia) and the extended agony of the 'sick man on the Bosporus' before Kemal Atatürk imposed reforms from above, by decreeing modernised external institutions. In some instances, entire communities have vanished rather than abandon their traditional rules, which gradually became harmful. This has been the fate of many ethnic communities and explains the present difficulties of groups such as Australian aborigines.

Evolution of External Constitutions: Exit versus Power

Constitutional evolution becomes even more problematic when we deal with external rules. This is so because of the information feedback to the rule-makers from the impact of changed circumstances which individuals experience is more roundabout, because it involves cumbersome collective choices and hard-to-reach compromises, and because "lumps" of organised interests are involved. We deal here with a many-faceted process of economic and political competition (Streit, 1996; also see Kasper-Streit, 1998, ch 12).

When external institutions are involved, we typically observe the following interactions (*figure 8.3* on next page):

i. Lower transport and communications costs impact on the degree of openness, facilitating new trade competition and inducing owners of internationally mobile production factors to compare constitutional ground rules here and abroad. As long as the underlying rules guarantee free trade, free factor mobility and free currency convertibility (and as long as individualist values support the maintenance of openness), competitors make eco-

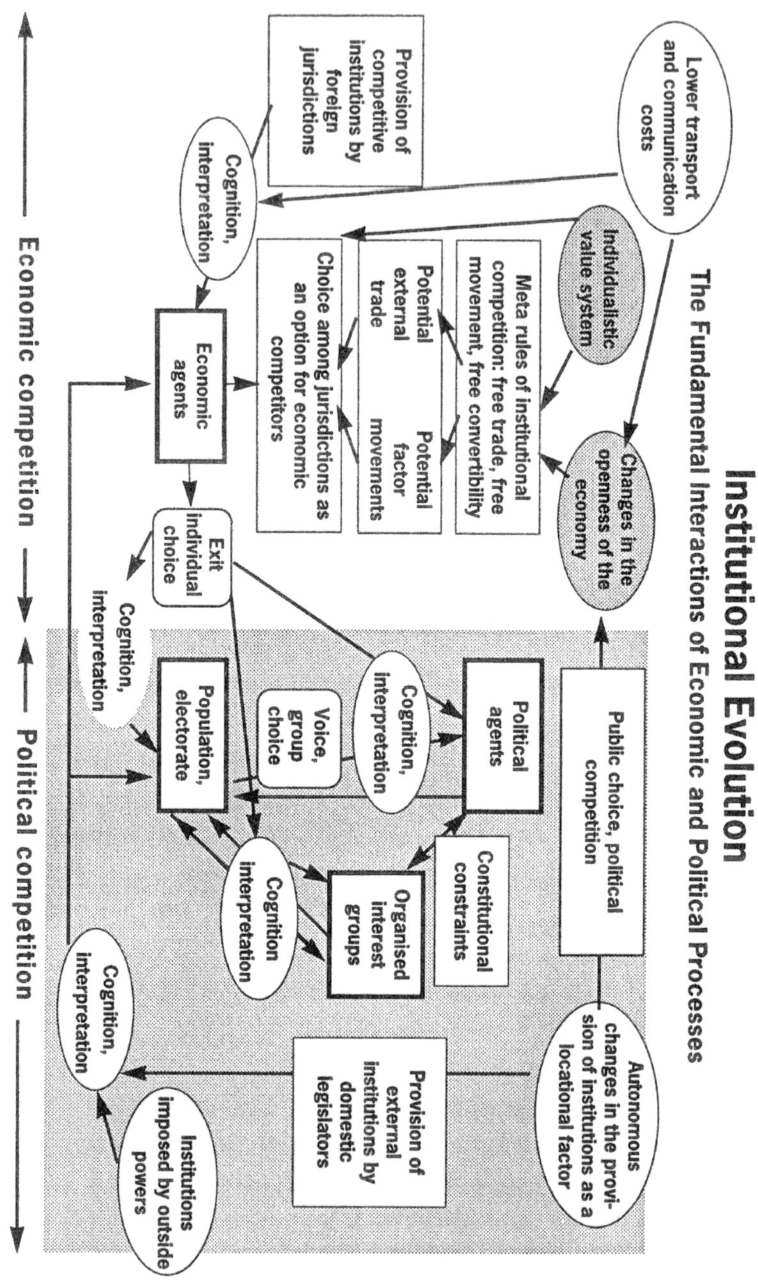
Institutional Evolution
The Fundamental Interactions of Economic and Political Processes
Lower transport and communication costs
Individualistic value system
Changes in the openness of the economy
Meta rules of institutional competition: free trade, free movement, free convertibility
Potential external trade
Potential factor movements
Choice among jurisdictions as an option for economic competitors
Provision of competitive institutions by foreign jurisdictions
Cognition, interpretation
Economic agents
Exit individual choice
Cognition, interpretation
Public choice, political competition
Political agents
Cognition, interpretation
Voice, group choice
Population, electorate
Constitutional constraints
Organised interest groups
Cognition interpretation
Autonomous changes in the provision of institutions as a locational factor
Provision of external institutions by domestic legislators
Cognition, interpretation
Institutions imposed by outside powers
Economic competition
Political competition
Adapted from Kasper-Streit, 1998. p 402.

Figure 8.3

nomic decisions among alternative countries. They may exit when they become aware that foreign jurisdictions offer better rules. Such a new awareness does not come about automatically, since economic agents do not always recognise and correctly interpret the signals and their causes. Even in the present circumstances, trade and relocation across the institutional discontinuities of national borders, demand risk-laden, complex entrepreneurial choices.

All this is a matter of *economic competition* and individual, private choice, a kind of locational arbitrage amongst given alternative constitutions.

ii. But constitutions are not inalterably given, they can be reshaped by *political competition*. The agents of collective action in various jurisdictions may compete by producing alternative rule sets—or they may refuse to do so (*figure 8.3*).

Much depends on the cognition and interpretation of emerging economic facts. The population may not be aware that companies and plants are migrating out, or they may believe that this does not affect them much. Then, they will not voice their concerns and collective agents, such as parliamentarians and union leaders, may persist in denial mode and do nothing. Political leaders may also have cognitive limits and fail to interpret the causes of "exits" correctly. Organised interest groups who are almost always a fossil of past power structures and a source of defending past constitutional arrangements, will influence politicians and the public to ignore the connections between "exit" and bad (*i e* non-universal) rules. Who can, for example, prove the link between the discriminatory *Systembolaget* in Sweden and locational choices by financial professionals who wish to drink cheap Australian red wine of a quality that *Systembolaget* does not import? Which German parliamentarian who voted for a new law to ensure that workers in precision mechanics plants must not work more than 5 m from a window realised that this would lead to the migration of tens of thousands of jobs to Asia? Given the complexity of modern economies, the unintended side effects of selective political choices are notoriously hard to trace.

iii. As a consequence, outdated constitutional provisions—even when they have become harmful to attaining fundamental values—are often retained. Prosperity, freedom, social peace and security then deteriorate, as we now observe in the more sclerotic societies of Europe. The rigidity may possibly persist to a point where aggressive neighbours impose new rules and the country loses its sovereignty (example: Tibet in the 1950's coming under the constitution of the PRC).

iv. In other cases, political inertia is overcome by political entrepreneurs, often belonging to a new generation. They fashion political programmes and seek electoral support for a reform agenda, pointing to the harmful consequences of existing underlying arrangements. They may of course be defeated. An example where constitutional innovation was partially successful is New Zealand, long the "sick man of the South Pacific". Between 1984 and 1994, it became suddenly the creator of the arguably best economic constitution of any OECD country (Kasper, 1996). The new leaders of both major political parties adopted more universal fundamental rules and threw out a plethora of regulations; a laggard productivity performance turned into economic growth and a cheerful, more enterprising society[3].

When the reason for capital flight is correctly perceived by parliaments and the public and is remedied by autonomous reforms, the economic decision-makers will turn capital flight into inward investment, though not necessarily so.

Figure 9.3 signals "cognition, interpretation" as a frequent filter and obstacle in the processes of institutional evolution. This is so because (i) politics works in a world of fuzzy, indirect and imperfect knowledge of the real world, (ii) political self-interest often militates against universal rules and their consistent enforcement, and (iii) public choices are always multi-lateral, non-reciprocal, laden with externalities and cumbersome.

Academics, think tanks, journalists, and jurists can play an important role in enhancing the reform process by assisting with better cognition and correct interpretation of the facts. To do that they have to go beyond their narrow fields of specialisation and base their analyses on an integrated view of moral philosophy, psychology, history, geography, sociology, politics, law and economics. A difficult task indeed! In reality, they all too often fall prey to inertia and the uncritical acceptance of interest-group rhetoric.

When "exit" and "voice" fail to shift the institutional system in a jurisdiction (or an organisation), there is a danger that the citizens lose loyalty (Hirschman, 1980). The resulting demoralisation then reinforces the drift to a poorer attainment of fundamental human values—a vicious circle from which there are no easy escapes.

Institutional and administrative creativity and open channels of communication about evolving circumstances are therefore valuable assets. They deserve cultivation as a preference of public choice. One can think of constitutional *meta* rules that promote these qualities, for example a commitment to minimal, constitutional government, the protection of a free press, or a commitment of the courts to fundamental human rights. The task is made easier if the constitution fulfils its most fundamental function: to create an abstract framework, in which institutions are changed expediently, and peacefully, maintaining order in the process. Constitutional rules can do much to maintain confidence and trust during times of transition, in that they make the rule changes transparent and predictable.

We can therefore stipulate that a constitution appropriate to today's fast-changing world must enhance the collective capacity for recognising changing circumstances and for altering the shared external rules. Given the innate inflexibilities of public choice, it also seems useful to reduce the areas, which are subject to collective rules by deregulation and privatisation and to foster the creation and enforcement of internal rules (deregulation, liberalisation and small government). In the coming global competition among jurisdictions, successful states are likely to concentrate on protective government, shedding many productive functions and most redistributive functions.

III. Conclusion

What has been said *in abstracto* has great bearing for the Old Continent. For long, European constitutions were shaped by the fairly self-contained nation state in which governments could wield considerable powers. At the same time, modern industry seemed the sole, safe possession of the "white race". This is no longer the case. The number of workers in modern industries that compete in world markets has more than doubled over the past generation—and most of the new faces are brown, yellow or black. This has imposed enormous adjustment pressures, many of which have been delayed by defensive protective action at the national and increasingly the Brussels levels (example: Europe's agricultural policies, efforts at subsidising selective old and new industries, attempts to use environmental, health and cultural arguments to hinder the progressive openness of European countries, the Luddite scare campaign against gene-modified foods, and so on). It is true that there is a movement from the hierarchical, national to a more competition-friendly, individualistic order. But, on the whole, it seems to this observer from far-away that the tribalist-corporatist 'modèle rhénanien' of capitalism seems to gain the upper hand in Europe over the alternative 'modèle anglo-saxon' and the (by world standards half-hearted) Dutch 'Polder model'.

If the slow-growing European economies are to achieve any reform, constitutional changes must occur in external and internal institutions. Any sustained reform must walk on these two legs. At least as seen from afar, the response of European rule-makers seems haphazard, a bit like occasionally hopping on one leg. The partial deregulation, selective strengthening of property rights and half-hearted reduction in redistributive political interventionism run parallel to a drift towards a more formally organised, more centralised, more *dirigiste* Europe trying to weaken its openness (Weede, 1992). All around the world we can now observe a trend to local responses to globalisation and to decentralisation (competitive federalism). Only Europe is drifting into a bigger, hence more closed, more politically run unit.

One can therefore not be sure whether the Old Continent will go the way of ancient Greece or Ottoman Turkey, or whether there will be an outburst of constitutional rejuvenation of the sort observed in Germany in the late 1940's and 1950's, many East Asian countries in the 1960's and 1970's, and in places like New Zealand in the 1980's and early 1990's.

Notes

1. An aside: Many economists and jurists these days are following the Swedish economist Knut Wicksell (1851—1926) and the bulk of the public choice school (James Buchanan etc.) in that they assert that constitutions are the result of a social contract. I find the contractarian approach entirely implausible and fraught with logical problems (Kasper-Streit, 1998, pp 334-335). No one ever asked me to vote on a constitution.
   A more plausible theory of constitutions than the contractarian explanation is the evolutionist theory of origin made popular by F A Hayek (Hayek, 1960) and more recently by P Ordeshook (Ordeshook, 1992). It says that constitutions are sets of overriding, fairly durable rules. Such constitutional rule sets can evolve from experience, maybe codified or imposed by "fathers of constitutions" in order to promote a consistent order among the various rules.
2. In contrast to the prevailing neoclassical economic paradigm, which is closed to future evolution, the new constitutional economics looks at

the rules and values, which facilitate constructive adaptation to such changes.

3. Even such economic success is not a guarantee that the institutional reforms are durable: New Zealand's left government elected in 1999 is busying itself with a massive stop-go turn in institutional evolution.

References

Hayek, F A, 1960, *The constitution of liberty.* London: Routledge, Kegan, Paul, 1960.

—, 1973-79, *Law, legislation and liberty.* Chicago: Chicago University Press, 1973-1979.

Hirschman, A O, 1980, *Exit, voice, and loyalty : responses to decline in firms, organisations, and states.* Cambridge [MA]: Harvard UP (first published in 1970).

Hofstede, H & Bond, M H, 1988, "The confucius connection : from cultural roots to economic growth", in *Organizational Dynamics (*vol 16, Spring), 1980, pp 5-21.

Kasper, W, 1996, *Free to work: the liberalisation of New Zealand's labour markets.* Sydney & Wellington: Centre for Independent Studies, 1996.

—, 1997, "Transitions and institutional innovation : reflections on the current economic setback", in *Malaysian Journal of Economic Studies* (vol. xxxiv, ns 1 & 2, special issue on the financial crisis), 1997, pp 5-14.

—, 1998 a, "Ignorance, discovery and choice : a requiem for economic rationalism?", in *Australian Journal of Legal Philosophy* (vol 22), 1997, pp 1-14.

—, 1998 b, "Rapid development in East Asia : institutional evolution and backlogs", in *Malaysian Journal of Economic Studies* (vol 45, no 1 & 2), pp 45-66.

Kasper, W & Streit, M E, 1998, *Institutional economics : social order and public policy.* Cheltenham, E Elgar, 1998.

Ordeshook, P, 1992, "Constitutional stability", *in Constitutional Political Economy* (vol 3, no 2), 1992, pp 137-175.

Rozman, G (*ed.*), 1991, *The East Asian region : Confucian heritage and its modern adaptation.* Princeton [NJ]: Princeton University Press, 1991.

Streit, M E, 1996, "Competition among systems as a defence of liberty", in *Libertarians and liberalism : essays in honour of Gerard Radnitzky* (*ed* H Bouillon) Aldershot: Avebury, 1996, pp 236-252.

Voigt, S, 1997, "Positive constitutional economics : a survey", in *Public Choice* (special issue on constitutional political economy, vol 90) pp 11-53.

Weede, E, 1999, "Kapitalismus und Solidarität : Arbeit und Wachstum in westlichen Industriegesellschaften : Einfache Berechnungen und widersprüchliche Resultate", in *Zeitschrift für Politik* (vol 46, no 1), pp 30-49.

Competition in Government by Federalism: a Discussion of the Idea[1]

*Erik Moberg**

In this paper I will treat the two subjects of *federalism* and *competition in government*, and in particular I will focus on their bearing on each other. Certainly the two subjects may be treated separately, and that has also been done to a considerable extent. A lot may be said about federalism without mentioning competition, and a lot may be said about competition in policy without having federalism especially in mind. Still there are strong reasons for treating the two subjects together. Thus, governmental competition may be particularly beneficial when taking place within a federal framework, or at least that is sometimes argued. It should therefore be interesting to discuss that idea in some detail, and that is the main purpose of this paper. I will also try to make the discussion relevant to Swedish politics. That, as we will see, means addressing two main questions. The first one is about the idea of arranging policy competition within Sweden, by making the country federal in some way. The other one is about the idea of creating, for instance within the EU, some kind of policy competition in which many countries, among them Sweden, may participate.

*For other texts by Erik Moberg, see http://www.mobergpublications.se

I. Hierarchies and Federations

Multilevel Decision-making

It is a well-known phenomenon that public decisions, depending on their nature, are taken at different levels. Almost all nations do, for example, have a central, or national, level, as well as a level of local communes. Some nations also have a federal level, and a state level. Above the nations there is furthermore the possibility of a supranational level and there are, in the real world, at least some rudimentary signs of actual supranational decision-making. The existence of different levels is thus obvious, but in spite of this the basic principles behind these multilevel structures are hardly obvious and, in fact, not even well understood in the relevant social sciences. What is the *raison d'être* of these structures? Which purposes do they serve?

A first important point is that there are different kinds of multilevel structures. A main distinction is the one between hierarchies and federations. Below, I will mainly deal with federations, but even so it is expedient to describe hierarchies carefully in order to make the distinction clear. Looked upon superficially the two types of structures are quite similar, and they are actually sometimes treated interchangeably, even in scientific texts. I will give some examples of that later on.

But even if the emphasis is on federations, I will start by describing hierarchies since they are easier to understand.

Hierarchies in General[2]

Let us consider the task of building a big highway, within a scheduled time and according to specified criteria of quality, through a nation with varying climatic and terrain conditions. Clearly, this task requires the participation of a large amount of people, and obviously the activities of all these people must be coordinated in some way. For this type of operation a hierarchy, like the one in *figure 9.1*, is a fitting organization. At the summit there is a chief executive, who is responsible for the overall planning as well as for the division of the complete task into subtasks, such as the building of parts of the highway. Heading these sub-tasks are the functionaries at the level immediately below the chief executive. Similarly, these functionaries may have officers below them and finally, at the bottom line, are all the individual workers actually building the highway. Thus, the lower a level is, the more people it contains. Furthermore, at each level people are obeying orders from those at the level immediately above, but they are also given a considerable latitude for acting according to their own judgements. Such action, however, is expected to be in line with, and to serve, the common, overall goals, of the entire operation.

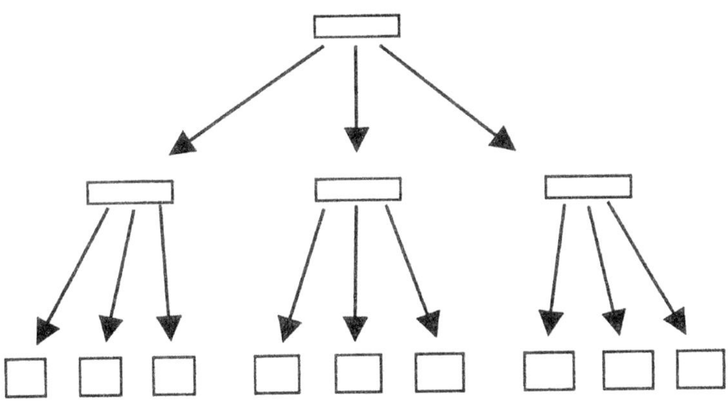

Figure 9.1.

The example illustrates the basic purpose of a hierarchy. Assume, for instance, that all the individual workers were left on their own, without any superior command; then their behaviour would be chaotic and uncoordinated, and thus ineffective. Assume, on the other hand, that the orders of the chief executive were utterly detailed and gave no latitude at all for individual action at lower levels; then the individual worker would be constrained, and without any possibilities to adapt his behaviour to the needs of his individual situation, which only he himself is familiar with. So clearly, there is a lot to be achieved by allocating the decision-making to a number of levels, and by giving the people at each level a considerable freedom to act upon the particular information they happen to have at their own particular level. It is precisely this possibility that is provided for by a hierarchy. At the same time, however, it is important to note that the decisions taken at any level are always intended to serve the goals of the entire structure as formulated by the leadership at the summit. Basically, the hierarchy is a command structure. The reason for the delegation of decisions to lower levels is just expediency. The organization works better, with reference to its own goals, if the power to take decisions is distributed in a proper way to the functionaries at the different levels.[3]

The purpose of the hierarchy in the example above was to build a highway and there are, of course, countless similar hierarchies created for the execution of big and complex tasks. Such hierarchies are, for instance, omnipresent in industry. Even military hierarchies, which make big defensive or offensive operations possible, are of interest here. At the top of such an hierarchy there is a commander in chief with responsibility for the activities along the whole front line; immediately under him there is a small number of sub-chiefs, each one responsible for his rather large section of the front; and so forth down to the individual soldiers, each one responsible for just a few meters of the entire front. As in other hierarchies, considerable latitude is given to the decision-makers at each level. The individual soldier, for instance, decides himself about the exact pointing of his gun, and perhaps about the exact moment of shooting. What is interesting about the military hierarchy, in contrast to many other hierarchies, is that it has an enemy; and the enemy is likely to concentrate his efforts at those parts of the front where, whatever the reasons, the hierarchy is weakest. In a similar sense some governing hierarchies have enemies, for example citizens trying to escape a tax-collecting hierarchy.

So far I have taken for granted that the orders given in a hierarchy are transmitted effectively downwards to the functionaries they are intended for, and that those functionaries obey the orders completely. In reality, however, neither assumption is likely to be valid. First, orders will always, to some extent, be distorted or misunderstood and, second, the functionaries will always have some goals of their own and will therefore try to serve these goals rather then to implement the given orders completely. Together these two mechanisms put a practical limit on the size of a hierarchy. If it becomes big enough, for instance in terms of the number of levels, the lowest level will act independently of the orders given at the hierarchy's summit. This phenomenon is sometimes described as *bureaucratic free enterprise* (Tullock, 1965).

Hierarchies for Governing

Governing a country involves, among other things, the enforcement of laws. This task, in turn, contains the obligations of making the laws known to people, of supervising people's conduct, including obedience to tax laws, and of reacting when laws are broken. These tasks are reasonably more demanding the bigger the nation is (in terms of area, or population, or both). They are also more demanding the more reluctant people are to stick to the rules.

Let us assume, for a beginning, that we have a very small nation. If so, it seems quite likely that a single uni-level government for the whole country would serve perfectly well. Since the area and the population are assumed to be very small, such a government will be able to govern on its own. If, however, the nation is considerably bigger in terms of area and population, the governing tasks may be too demanding for a single government. In such a situation a hierarchy is a likely solution. The nation may be divided into a number of regions or districts, each one with a chief, who, as an agent of the central government-principal, is responsible for the law enforcement within the district. At some still bigger size it may be rational to divide the districts into sub-districts, each one with its own chief, and so on. Sheer size may thus justify a hierarchy for governing.

In reality these kinds of hierarchical patterns are omnipresent. It is common to divide nations into administrative districts, which are run on instructions from the central government in order to make the central power more effective. In France there are, for example "les départements", and in Sweden we have our "län". These are important components of typical hierarchies.

In many governing hierarchies levels are defined in terms of areas or geographical districts. There are, however, also other kinds of hierarchies in government, which are not necessarily so defined and which may be used for slightly different purposes. In public administration, in particular, there are two purposes that are of interest in this context, namely the quest for general overview, and the quest for uniformity.

As an example of the first purpose we may consider the energy policy of a country. Here the legislature may decide about the broad lines and allocate specified amounts of money to solar energy, nuclear energy, energy saving, and so forth, and these sums may be handed out to authorities that are specialized in these various fields. The authorities, in turn, may distribute the money to their own departments, which are further specialized, and these departments, perhaps, will finally send the money to the intended receivers—for example people engaged in various kinds of relevant energy research. A system like this is obviously hierarchical since all decisions are intended to serve the national energy policy. The system also gives the decision-makers, and in particular those at the top of the hierarchy, a good overview of what is happening. The other side of the coin, however, is an obvious element of central planning. In many areas, such as for example energy policy, the merits of the whole arrangement can thus be disputed. Still, hierarchies of this particular kind, serving the purpose of overview, are common in public administrations.

As an example of the second purpose we can consider a national judicial system. In such a system there are often courts at several levels and, if so, it may be possible to appeal against the ruling of a particular court at a court at the next level upwards. Even if this system is not hierarchical in the sense that higher courts give orders to lower courts, it is so in the very similar sense that higher courts may, first, change individual verdicts of lower courts and, second, thereby sometimes also create precedents that constrain future action of lower level courts. One rationale for this system is its likelihood to enhance the quality of the verdicts, but the uniformity that it fosters is usually also, since it means equality before the law, considered a value by itself.

The size of the hierarchies used in governing do not usually have natural size limits as, for instance, the hierarchy created for building a highway. The latter's size was determined by the task to be performed. A public hierarchy does not have a natural size limit like that. Consider, for instance, the quest for overview. It could always be argued that a better overview could be obtained by putting more policy areas under the same hat—environmental policy could for example be linked to energy policy—with fewer and bigger hierarchies as a result. Thus, bureaucratic free enterprise may be a permanent threat, and a quite likely phenomenon, in public hierarchies used for governing.

Federations[4]

A federation, like a hierarchy, has several levels, although, as in *figure 9. 2*, the number is usually limited to two—a national or federal level, and a state level. The relationship between the levels differs, however, completely from that in a hierarchy. In a federation there is no such thing as a common, all-pervading goal. On the contrary, the very idea is that the entities at the various levels should be free, within specified limits, to decide about their own goals and activities. An example may be illustrative. Imagine that there are a number of adjacent but separate nations, each one characterized by its own history, its own culture, and its own language. Imagine furthermore that these nations are threatened by a common enemy, which is much bigger and stronger than anyone of them individually. If so, it seems a good idea for the nations to engage in some kind of common defence. One possibility is to create an ordinary defence alliance. That kind of solution may be enough, although it has some shortcomings. Since, in such an alliance, there is no common

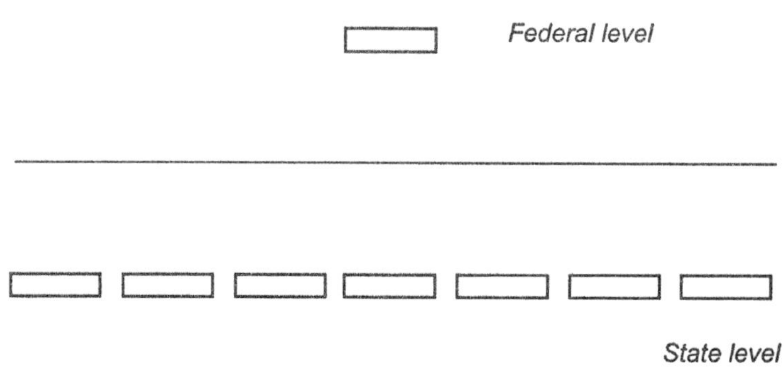

Figure 9.2.

central authority with power to tax the member-nations for building an efficient military organization, there will be incentives to free-riding and risks of failure. This may be avoided by going one step further and creating a common authority with power to tax and to act in the military area. At the same time, however, the member nations, because of their different characters, have all reasons to keep their remaining powers intact. Thus, the result is a federation in which military decisions are taken at the central, federal level, and all other decisions at the level of the former nations, or states.

Riker gives the following definition of a federation (Riker, 1964, p 11): "A constitution is federal if *i.* two levels of government rule the same land and people, *ii.* each level has at least one area of action in which it is autonomous, and *iii.* there is some guarantee (even though merely a statement in the constitution) of the autonomy of each government in its own sphere." The opposite of a federal government is a unitary government.[5]

A few comments on the meaning and implications of the autonomy concept may be added. First, since Riker talks about two levels of government ruling the people, I interpret him as saying that the autonomy, at both levels, includes the power to legislate (within the specified limit). Second, since the autonomy of the two levels is crucial in a federation, and since the borderline between the two levels has to be clear, a constitutional court seems to be a natural part of a federation. This position is in fact quite common. Bealey (Bealey, 1999, the entry "federal government"), for instance, maintains that "a constitutional court must act as an arbitrator between the different authorities."

Federalism is thus associated with a legal structure. In particular, there are laws that divide the power between the levels, and there is also, in all likelihood, a court for settling conflicts between the levels. Each level has also a capacity to legislate within specified limits. When these legal conditions are fulfilled we may talk about *a real federation*. Even without these legal prerequisites a levelled structure may, however, have great similarities with a federation in the real sense. There may be a division of power between the levels that holds in practice, even if not specified in law. And the lower level may have considerable independence without having, in particular, the capacity to legislate. In such cases we may speak about *quasi-federalism*.

Obviously federations may differ with respect to the amounts of power, generally speaking, which are allocated to the federal level, and to the state level, respectively. If most power is allocated to the federal level we speak about a *centralized federation*. If, on the contrary, the power basically rests with the states we are dealing with a *peripheralised federation*. The terminology is taken from Riker (Riker, 1964, p 5f).

There are many federal nations in the real world. In 1964 Riker (Riker, 1964, p 1) made the following lists for different parts of the world:

North America—Canada, Mexico, the United States.
South America—Argentina, Brazil, Venezuela.
Europe—Austria, the Soviet Union, Switzerland, West Germany, Yugoslavia.
South Asia—Australia, India, Malaysia, Pakistan.
Africa—Congo, Ethiopia, Nigeria.

Since he was concerned only with federalism as such, Riker had both democracies and dictatorships in his list.[6] In 1999 Arendt Lijphart, who was concerned only with democracies, made another list. He classified 36 nations in the world as democracies. Among these he labelled some as federal and some as semi-federal in this way (Lijphart, 1999, p 189):

Federal—Australia, Austria, Belgium after 1993, Canada, Germany, India, Switzerland, the United States, Venezuela.
Semi-federal—Belgium before 1993, Israel, the Netherlands, Papua New Guinea, Spain.

Lijphart's definitions of federalism and semi-federalism, it should be noted, do not exactly correspond to the notions of real federalism and quasi-federalism above. They are, to put it briefly, somewhat less legalistic and somewhat more sociological.

Here I have used the term "state" for the entities at the lower level, but in reality the vocabulary is shifting on this point. In the United States, India, Australia and Venezuela they are, in fact, called states, but in Canada they are called provinces, in Germany and Austria Länder, in Switzerland cantons, and in Belgium regions (according to Lijphart, 1999, p 187).

Mixtures of Hierarchical and Federal Elements

Hierarchical and federal structures sometimes appear side by side, and sometimes almost imperceptibly so. Consider for example the local communes in Sweden. They have two sectors, or two areas of decision-making, which are usually called the bounded sector, and the free sector, respectively. Within the bounded sector the communes essentially do things that they are required by the state to do—they are, for example, running schools as prescribed by the national laws. In this area the communes are local extensions of the central national administration, and thus operating within a hierarchical structure. In the free sector the situation is completely different. There the communes undertake any activities they want, subject only to the obvious restriction that they have to remain within the boundaries of relevant laws. They may, for instance, build various kinds of sporting grounds, or they may keep away from such activities completely. Within the free sector the communes are thus operating within a federal structure, or, more precisely, within a quasi-federal structure.

Having mentioned the coexistence of hierarchical and federal elements in the Swedish municipalities it should also be mentioned that not even federal nations are always as federal as they may appear. In Argentina, Brazil and India, for example, there are constitutional rules about "federal intervention to govern states that fail to perform satisfactorily (when of course, the federal government is judge of what is satisfactory performance)" (Riker, 1964, p 120). The implication, of course, is that the states are not really free, and that, to that extent, we are in effect dealing with a hierarchy rather than a federation.

II. The Unitary System

The Border

In order to be able to discuss the properties of two-level federal systems, it seems expedient to consider one-level systems, *i e* unitary systems, first. An understanding of unitary systems is, I think, a prerequisite for a good understanding of multilevel systems. In the discussion about unitary systems I will consider both the mechanisms behind the outer limits, or the borderlines, of such systems, and the problems of governing within those limits. These two kinds of problems may to a large extent be treated separately, but nevertheless they are also closely related to each other.

As regards the discussion of the outer limits I will start by quoting Riker. "National decision making", he argues (Riker, 1964, p 146), "is in the abstract more efficient than local decision making on every issue. That is, ... , it is cheaper on any subject of legislation to have a uniform rule, ... , than not to have uniformity." This is an argument about advantages of scale. Some things benefit from being done on a large scale rather than on a small scale. Among these things, according to Riker, are legal rules and legislation.

This argument by Riker may be systematized and generalized. For that purpose I will use the "map" in *figure 9 3*, which represents two different cultural-linguistic areas with a common border. The area *A*, which is divided into a number of sub-areas, is a bit larger than *B*, and we may also assume the same about its population. Let us at first confine the discussion to *A* and start by considering traffic law, for instance about traffic lights, which is discussed by Riker. Two possible arrangements may be compared. In the first one each of the nine sub-areas decide about their own rules, whereas in the other one the rules are common to the whole *A* area. Which are the advantages and disadvantages of these two arrangements that we may call the local arrangement and the encompassing arrangement respectively?

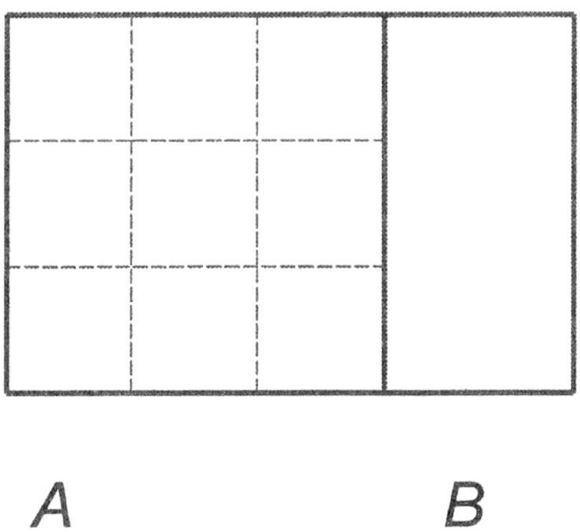

Figure 9.3.

This question is important but even so it is not clear how it should be answered. One method, which has been used in slightly different variations by Riker as well as by Buchanan and Tullock, for treating this kind of problem, is to identify and take into account different kinds of relevant costs. I will follow the pioneers on this track even if my method, in turn, is a slightly new variation: the list of costs is not exactly the same.

I will start with *the decision-making costs*, which is a concept introduced by Buchanan and Tullock. These costs, basically a kind of transaction costs, are the costs associated with arguing, building coalitions, and so forth, in order to achieve a decisive constellation.[7] If we assume that both the local and the encompassing arrangement utilize some kind of democratic decision-making, with a specified type of representation and a specified decision rule, then the total decision-making costs, per capita, will be lowest in the first case. Thus, from this point of view, the local arrangement comes out better than the encompassing one. But there are more aspects to the problem than this.

Another kind of costs, discussed by Riker, is *the costs of law enforcement*. These costs, according to Riker, are higher in the first case. "If a red light meant different things in different localities", he says, "it is highly likely that the costs of enforcement of road rules would increase enormously." Riker is certainly right here and this aspect thus favours the encompassing arrangement rather than the local one. But even so it is important to make clear exactly why Riker is right. Law enforcement is necessary because people sometimes tend to break the law. The reasons for not following the rules may, however, vary considerably. People may break the law since they derive some kind of advantages from it, or they may break the law by mistake, due to ignorance. Furthermore, in a heterogeneous cultural-linguistic environment many people may break laws simply because they do not acknowledge them. In the example here, since we are dealing with a homogenous cultural-linguistic environment, the first two reasons are the most likely. It is also likely that the distinction between the local and the encompassing arrangements is irrelevant to breaks on purpose, whereas it is highly relevant to breaks by mistake. The costs of law enforcement in a homogenous environment are therefore related to another factor that Riker also mentions, namely people's efforts to learn the law.

The *costs for those affected of learning the laws* are obviously smaller the fewer the laws are. If we consider, for instance, traffic rules and take for granted that people, to a large extent, drive around in the whole linguistic-cultural area, and not just in their own local sub-area, the local arrangement means that they will have to learn nine laws, whereas the learning of one law is enough in the encompassing arrangement. As there are many people involved, these costs are likely to be considerable, and this factor thus strongly favours the encompassing arrangement. It should be added that those who have to learn a law, since they are affected by it, are not only ordinary people but lawyers as well. This may be more obvious if we turn from traffic to trade, for example. In this case not only the traders but also, and especially, their legal advisors have to be familiar with the legal preconditions.

The factors so far brought into the discussion thus indicate that the encompassing arrangement is better than the local one. There is, however, in the traffic law example, one important prerequisite for this conclusion, namely that technology permits large numbers of people to leave their local area and travel freely in a wider region. The conclusion favouring the encompassing arrangement is thus technology-dependent, and this result may perhaps be generalized. If technology develops, and makes activities of various kinds possible over wider and wider areas, the case for more and more encompassing laws becomes concomitantly stronger.

This being so, it is straightforward to continue by asking about the prospects for laws that are still more encompassing, and whose application thus transcends the borders of the linguistic-cultural areas. Consider, for instance, a suggested law for an area consisting of all of *A* plus all of *B*. In such a case the costs of learning will obviously decrease, since it is enough for those affected to learn one law rather than two. The costs of the decision-making may however increase enormously, especially if the two cultures are different enough, and the same is true for the so-called *external costs*, in Buchanan-Tullock's sense, which are the inconveniences from a decision hitting those who do not support it. Imagine, for instance, that the tolerance for alcohol differs considerably in the two cultures, and that this is relevant in relation to traffic and driving as well as in other ways. If so, and if a majority rule is used, the external costs may become very high. If, for instance, a majority from *A* overrules a minority from *B,* the inconveniences for the latter may be considerable. In this case, since the law is not generally accepted, the costs of enforcement are also likely to be considerable. If, on the contrary, some more demanding decision rule, for example some qualified majority rule, is used, the decision-making costs may raise to very high levels since it may be very difficult to find a compromise, perhaps including a scheme for side-payments, which gets the necessary support. Consequently it may not pay to extend the law across cultural-linguistic borders.

For many laws the homogenous cultural-linguistic area is thus a natural area of application. The explanation, as we have seen, is that the expansion of the application to the cultural-linguistic borders is easy and profitable, whereas further expansion may meet considerable obstacles. Having said this we have also provided an answer to a question that is almost never asked, but nevertheless deserves a serious treatment, namely the question of the nature of the nation. At least on the surface, this question has similarities with Coase's seemingly innocuous question about the nature of the firm. As for nations we may ask why they are there at all, and why they look the way they do. Why do their borders usually, and at least to a large extent, coincide with the borders of cultural-linguistic areas? Why does not nation-building follow other principles, which disregard the cultural-linguistic borders? What exactly makes these particular borders so important? A likely answer, as we have seen, is that the cultural-linguistic area is often optimal to legislation. Furthermore, we may now assert that the state is the entity within the nation that provides the legislation. This, thus, is the basic rationale for the state. Other common notions of the state, for instance that its raison d'être is the provision of public goods, are at best misleading. True, laws are public goods, but they are a very particular kind of such goods, and there are many other kinds of public goods. So the rationale for the state, within the nation, is the provision of laws and law enforcement, not the provision of public goods in general.

The importance of this result, in this context, is that it indicates an absolute scale for the allocation of levels in a multilevel system. After this we can do more than just order the different levels relatively, as being below or above each other. The national level serves as a base level, or a level of departure, when considering other levels, upwards or downwards.

Legislation and Implementation by Hierarchy

After having considered hypothetical mechanisms behind the delimitation of nations, I will now consider the problem of governing a nation. This, of course, is a giant complex, and I will just concentrate on a few aspects of relevance in relation to federalism.

A first point is that not only the top-level position of legislation, but the bottom-level position of the practical implementation of various tasks as well, are supported by some general principles. To illustrate this, I will use an example inspired by Buchanan and Tullock (Buchanan & Tullock, 1962, pp 111 f). Suppose that a school is to be built and run for the people living in a certain area. Suppose, furthermore, that the school is to be public rather than private, and that it shall be financed collectively rather than by vouchers (a case considered below). If so, the decisions about the school—for example about its location, about the building, about which teachers to employ, and so forth—are to be taken collectively. So the problem is: which collective is the appropriate one?

Let us assume that there is a limited group of people who start thinking about the school since they want it for their children, and that these people are indicated by the hatched innermost part of *figure 9.4*. These people obviously should be members of the decision-making group, or at least they should be represented in it. Now, since the school is assumed to be run as a collective good there are, in all likelihood, also other people who may benefit from it, and who are thus likely to use it for their children when it is built and ready. It therefore seems to be a good idea that these people, who are marked by the dotted area

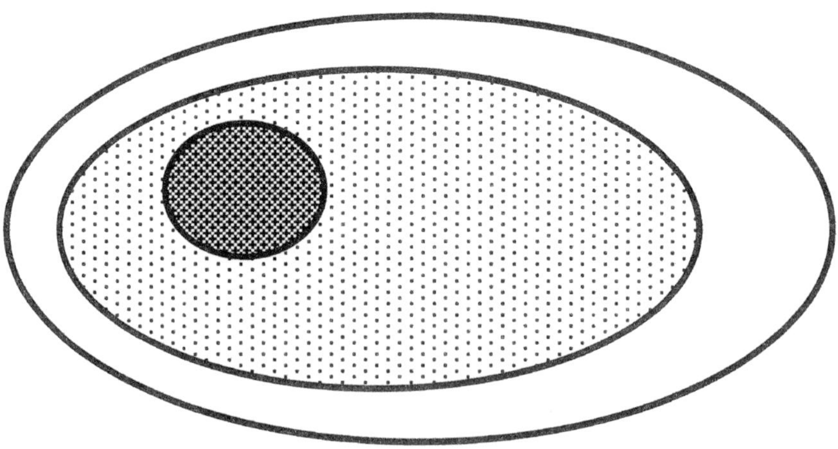

Figure 9.4.

in the figure, are brought into the decision-making group as well. More specifically, and according to the argument by Buchanan and Tullock, two things happen when the decision-making group is expanded. One is that the decision-making costs per individual increase, since it requires more efforts, per individual, to reach a decision in a big group than in a small one. On the other hand however the risks of harmful, or bad decisions, or in other words the external costs become smaller the more of those affected by the decisions take part in them. This effect may very well compensate for the former one and thus, to a point, justify the expansion of the decision-making group. After that point however, since the people who still are affected by the school either are too few, or too little affected, the increased decision-making costs which follows from a further expansion of the decision-making group, for instance to the outer borderline in the figure, will not be fully compensated for by better decisions. The collective activity should thus, according to Buchanan and Tullock, be organized "in the smallest units consistent with the externality that the collectivisation is designed to eliminate."

This reasoning, which uses the same general kind of arguments as the discussion about laws in the preceding section, thus leads to the conclusion that a lot of practical, administrative and public activities can, and should, be organized on a small scale locally. In addition to schools this may be valid for roads, harbours, bridges, parks, museums, and so forth.

Now I have come to a position where it is possible to put Riker's argument about the benefits of legislating on a large scale, and Buchanan-Tullock's argument about the benefits of handling practical administrative tasks on a small scale, into a common framework. There is, in fact, a passage by Milton Friedman where his main concern is to argue in favour of school vouchers, but where, incidentally, he also happens to supply exactly the kind of framework I am interested in here. "I distinguished", he recalls in his memoirs (Friedman, 1998, p 347), "among three levels of government involvement in schooling: requiring schooling, financing schooling, and administering schools. I argued that a case could be made for both the imposition of a minimum required level of schooling and the financing of this schooling by the state. However, I went on, a third step, namely the actual administration of educational institutions by the government ... is difficult to justify on any grounds. Governments could require a minimum level of schooling financed by giving parents vouchers redeemable for a specified maximum sum per child per year if spent on 'approved' educational services. Parents would then be free to spend this sum and any additional sum they themselves provided on purchasing educational services." This argument for a voucher system in education is interesting here for three reasons.

First, Friedman explicitly describes education as a complex undertaking involving legislation, financing and the running of individual schools, and argues that these different tasks belong to different levels. This is in sharp contrast to simplistic notions such that, for instance, education *is* a local government service. Public tasks, as well as private ones for that matter, are often complex in this sense. Friedman obviously has a hierarchy in mind, although he does not mention that particular word, and some basic characteristics of that hierarchy are noteworthy. Thus, legislation takes place at the top level, which is in accordance with the principles formulated in the preceding section. This is very much as the general staff at the top of a military hierarchy formulating the general strategic and tactical principles for an impending operation. Furthermore, the practical implementation of the principles in the law, for example the running of individual schools, takes place at lower levels, which is also in accordance with the principles presented above. In the military analogy this corresponds to the individual platoons, and even soldiers, performing their practical assignments, down to earth tasks, at the low levels of their hierarchy.

Second, Friedman's argument makes an explicit case for private alternatives, even as hierarchical elements, since the schools that receive the vouchers may very well be private enterprises. This is something that should be kept in mind whenever tasks to various actors are assigned.

Third, when Friedman says that parents should be free to spend the voucher sum, and any *additional sum*, on educational services, he introduces a further and different kind of private activity. The voucher sum belongs to the hierarchical system, whereas the additional sum, which is not compulsive, is a result of an initiative from the parents. Initiatives of the state, as represented by the hierarchy, are thus mixed with private initiatives from the customers-consumers.

This example from Friedman illustrates a kind of hierarchy that is omnipresent in public affairs. At the upper level legislation takes place, at the lower levels implementation. The activities at the lower levels, although always publicly financed, may otherwise be either public or private. Furthermore, the introduction of private consumer initiatives may be tolerated by the hierarchy, and may even be important. This kind of hierarchies is, I think, not only a common but also a very useful, and often even necessary, governing device.

The existence of hierarchies of this type does however not imply that all local, public, and administrative undertakings are components of such hierarchies. There are, obviously, also a lot of activities which are run as independent enterprises on their own merits. Buchanan-Tullock's principle regarding the benefits of small units may thus sometimes concern activities that belong to hierarchies, sometimes independent activities.

The Principle of Subsidiarity

Buchanan-Tullock's principle is, in fact, closely related to, or rather a variety of, a principle saying that "the responsibility for functions should be allocated, as far as practicable, to the lowest levels of society". This frequently invoked principle, usually called the *principle of subsidiarity*, is in fact very old and attributed to Thomas Aquinas (1225-1274). He had the problem of protecting the Catholic Church from the infringements of the state, and to that end he proposed that all activities of the church should be performed at the longest possible distance from the threatening state, and thus at the lowest possible level. (Bealey, 1999, the entrance "subsidiarity"). But even if the principle dates back to the thirteenth century it is, as I have indicated, still going strong. It is, for instance, prominent in present thinking about European integration and, in fact, formally inscribed into the Maastricht Treaty (Oates, 1999, p 1122).

Here it is important to note that this principle is compatible with federal as well as hierarchical ideas. Thomas obviously thought along federal lines. He wished the church to enjoy real federal freedom in complete independence of the state. Even in an hierarchy it is however possible to argue that decisions should be placed at the lowest possible levels, since this is a way of placing the decisions where the information is, and thus of avoiding top-heaviness.

Risks for Bad Government

Governing, of course, is difficult and risky, and may go astray. In particular there are the risks that those in power satisfy their own wants at the expense of those of the citizens. One kind of threat is that hierarchies, although to a large extent necessary, become too large, and too top-heavy. There are also other ways in which the governing power may become too concentrated, too strong, too unrestrained, and too uncontrolled. Several imaginable means have been suggested for correcting such failures, among them the introduction of a certain amount of real federalism. Thus, the idea is that some of the problems of the unitary state may be alleviated by federalism. This idea will be discussed in chapter IV. Before that, however, I will discuss some general topics related to federations.

III. Federalism—Some General Aspects

Mistaking Hierarchies for Federations

We have seen that hierarchies and federations, although they are similar in being multilevel systems, are also strikingly different. In hierarchies lower actors get orders from higher actors, whereas, in federations, lower actors enjoy freedom, upheld by law, from intervention by higher actors. Considering this fundamental difference, it is interesting to note that the two kinds of systems nevertheless are often mixed up, even by experts.

Consider, for instance, the following passage from Riker in his work about federalism, under the headline "Transportation and communication" (Riker, 1964, p 68): "The usual rule (not always followed, of course) for the division of labour on this function among the several levels of government seems to have been: The smallest government that rules both terminals of the proposed line of transport or communication is the one to promote and supervise it. The operative effect of this rule is that initially the states were the main promoters, whereas in the last century or so the United States has become the main one. Even in the beginning, however, the central government had quite a bit to do and today the states have quite a bit to do. At no point is there an exclusion of one kind of government from the function. Rather, the function is fully shared. It is just that the recognized rule of division gave the states the preponderance of the task in the beginning and now gives the preponderance to the nation." What Riker describes here, in spite of his intentions, is not a federal system at all. Rather, and obviously, he talks about a hierarchy in exactly the sense defined and discussed above.

In another context Riker writes about Germany (Riker, 1964, p 123), that "... the federal government does not directly administer programs in many of the areas of action about which it legislates, ...". Here he is explicitly dealing with federal institutions and with degrees of centralization and peripheralisation. Still, he obviously describes a hierarchy: the federal government legislates about programmes that are administered by the "Länder". The hierarchy, in fact, fits very well into the pattern described in the section "Legislation and implementation by hierarchy" in the preceding chapter.

Or consider Buchanan when he writes (Buchanan, 1999 b, p 311) that: "Federalism,' 'devolution,' 'decentralization,' 'subsidiarity,' 'denationalism,' 'privatisation'—these are political terms of the 1990s. The current relevance of these terms stems from the widespread acknowledgment that, either directly or indirectly, regulatory authority has been too much concentrated in central governmental units, with the result that they have become omnipresent. The argument from organizational efficiency alone dictates institutional reform in the direction of decentralization." To me, at least, it seems that Buchanan here, in spite of what he says himself, is concerned with hierarchies rather than with federations. He purports to talk about "federalism", etc., but goes on with arguments about a too concentrated regulatory authority, and about organizational efficiency. What he criticizes here, I think, is top-heavy hierarchies that would benefit from more delegation downwards. The concepts of regulatory authority and organizational efficiency belong to hierarchical rather than to federal thinking. Hierarchies really exist in order to enhance efficiency. The basic purpose of federations, on the contrary, is the delimitation of areas of independence or freedom.

In the following I will give some further examples of hierarchies mistaken for federations.

Reasons for Two-Level Systems

But even if hierarchies are sometimes mistaken for federations there are real federations as well. Whenever we are dealing with such a system there is a problem about the reason for the two levels of decision-making. Why are the constituent states not, in all respects, acting as separate entities? Or, alternatively, why do they not merge all their activities, and thus form a common unitary state? Why do they find it important to keep their individuality in some respects? In the example in the first chapter the defence problem provided the answer to the first question. The individual states were not able to defend themselves. Had it not been for that problem the states would not have formed a federation. They would have remained as separate unitary nations in all respects. As for the second question the answer is in terms of the different cultures and histories of the constituent states. Had it not been for those differences the states could as well, together, form a single, big, unitary nation.

These points certainly go a long way towards explaining the two levels, but still there are some unanswered questions. The most important one is why the military problem requires a fusion of the constituent states into a federation. Why is an ordinary defence alliance not enough? The answer given in chapter one is that the threat of free-riding is countered much more effectively in a federation than in an alliance, and this is certainly true. Still, even this answer is not complete.

The problem is that the group of nations forming the federation is quite small, whereas free-riding, according to Mancur Olson's logic of collective action (Olson, 1965), is usually much more of a problem in large groups than in small ones. Therefore, if free-riding is to become a real threat, there must be something which makes it especially tempting even in a small group of nations. The fact that military expenses are usually extremely high may account for that.

Two factors thus basically explain the defence federation. First, the constituent states are too small for defending themselves, and therefore they have to cooperate. Second, since defence expenditures usually are very high, a federation is a better solution than a defence alliance. Now, it is of course interesting to ask about the possibilities to generalize this result. Are there, besides military affairs, any other policy areas which call for federations for the same reasons? Are the conditions of scale, and of costs, fulfilled in any other policy areas?

Consider for instance environmental policy, and suppose that global warming due to carbon dioxide emissions is a real threat. If so, cooperation between nations is a necessity. Furthermore, since it may be very costly to avoid emitting carbon dioxide, there may be a very strong incentive for free-riding, and thus a justification of large federations, and ultimately a global one. The problem, which we shall not deal with here, is that the threat of global warming is sometimes disputed.[8] But even if this threat is a real one I fail to see a lot of similar cases. Usually, and introducing a normative argument, I think, international cooperation could, and should, take place in ordinary organizations, such as for example Interpol, rather than in federations.

Problems with Two-Level Systems

Having thus discussed some rationales for two-level systems it is appropriate to consider some problems as well. In the literature some such problems are discussed and they are usually related to the interaction between the different parts of a federation, for instance the interaction between the states, or between the two levels.

Riker warns that legislation in the states, in a federation, often is tantamount to minority rule. One example is about minimum wages (Riker, 1964, p 146). He assumes that one state (in the US) has a lower minimum-wage level than all the other states have, and want to have. If so, capital that yields more in a low minimum-level environment will migrate to the low level state, and all other states would suffer. The only way to counter this, apart from national decision-making, is to follow the single state and decrease, in all other states, the minimum- wage level. This means that the single state with the initially low minimum wage sets the national norm, and thus the minority rules.

Another example is about divorces (Riker, 1964, p 147). There are according to Riker a few states in the US, in particular Nevada, which grant divorce "on the most trivial grounds and after only the briefest periods of residence". He argues that these rules have been motivated mainly by a wish to attract tourists, and that they have "the effect of imposing easy divorce on all jurisdictions." ... Therefore "(t)he external costs of the existence of what most citizens of most states regard as low moral standards are thus very high for the probably overwhelming majority that opposes easy divorce." Again, says Riker, a policy is imposed on the majority by a minority.

Riker's sharpest criticism of US federalism, and its tendency towards minority rule, is however related to the race issue. "The plea for states' rights or for maintaining the guarantees of federalism", he contends (Riker, 1964, p 142), "is simply a hypocritical plea for the special privilege to disregard the national majority and, of course, to permit one minority, segregationist Southern whites, to tyrannize over another minority, the Southern Negroes." Then (Riker, 1964, p 144) he concludes that: "For the last century approximately 10 per cent of the people have been denied civil rights. Those so denied have been a kind of lumpenproletariat and hence a drain on the whole society."

Surely some aspects of Riker's examples may be discussed. Thus it is obvious that his worries are not limited to the minority rule as such, but also include the particular results illustrated by the examples. In this latter respect there is, however, clearly room for other opinions. But even so the minority-favouring mechanism may clearly be a reality, and something to be concerned about.

Other kinds of ominous interaction between the parts of a federation are related to financial flows. Assume, for instance, that one of the constituent states tries to attract an enterprise by offering particularly favourable tax rules, and as a consequence gets a public finance deficit. If so the federal government, for one reason or another, may step in and cover the deficit. In the long run that kind of deficit-creation, and covering, may obviously ruin the whole federation. The mechanism described, which is related to the dynamics between the components of a federation, is an example of what is sometimes called "race to the bottom".

Some further problems with two-level systems are discussed in the section "The framework for the competition" in the next chapter.

Fusion, Fission and Equilibrium

The two levels of a federation are never, as it seems, created simultaneously. Either the upper level, or the lower level, comes into existence after the prior, original level. In the former case the federation is a result of fusion, in the latter a result of fission. These two cases are illustrated by the examples *1 a* and *1 b*, respectively, in *figure 9.5* on next page.

Riker has studied empirically the mechanisms by which the present federations in the world were created (the ones mentioned in the list taken from Riker in the first chapter above), and his results are therefore of great interest here. When formulating his hypothesis Riker conceives of a federation as a result

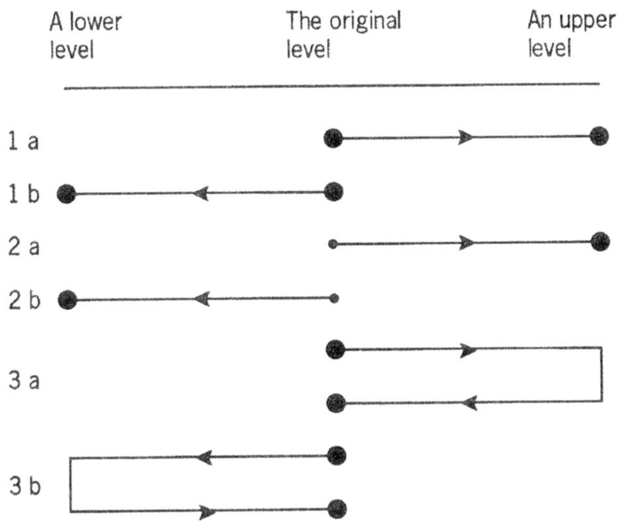

Figure 9.5

of a bargain according to which some actors create power at an emerging federal level, and others give up power at the state level. The motives of these two groups are described by Riker as follows (Riker, 1965, p 12):

> 1. The politicians who offer the bargain desire to expand their territorial control, usually either to meet an external military or diplomatic threat or to prepare for military or diplomatic aggression and aggrandizement. But, though they desire to expand, they are not able to do so

> by conquest, because of either military incapacity or ideological distaste. Hence, if they are to satisfy the desire to expand, they must offer concessions to the rulers of the constituent units, which is the essence of the federal bargain. The predisposition for those who offer the bargain is, then, that federalism is the only feasible means to accomplish a desired expansion without the use of force.
> 2. The politicians who accept the bargain, giving up some independence for the sake of the union, are willing to do so because of some external military-diplomatic threat of opportunity. Either they desire protection from an external threat or they desire to participate in the potential aggression of the federation. And furthermore the desire for either protection or participation outweighs any desire they may have for independence. The predisposition is the cognizance of the pressing need for the military strength or diplomatic manoeuvrability that comes with a larger and presumably stronger government.

Riker then hypothesizes that these motives are always present when a federation is created, and that the two points therefore can be regarded as necessary conditions for a federation. After the empirical investigation he finds that his hypothesis is confirmed. "On the basis of the evidence here set forth, he states (Riker, 1965, p 48), "we may conclude that the hypothesis is confirmed that the military and expansion conditions are necessary to the occurrence of federalism."

Being more detailed, Riker (Riker, 1965, pp xii, 1, 8, 10, 34) furthermore maintains that all existing federations apart from medieval Switzerland are creations of the 19th and 20th century and thus modern. They are inspired by the US constitution. The US federalism was centralized rather than peripheralised and this was, according to Riker, the main reason for its appeal and influence. Central federalism was invented in Philadelphia in 1787 and was a crucial event in the history of federalism.

Switzerland, which today is a unique federation (in being peripheralised), was originally not at all so. There were many of its kind, but the others were conquered and disappeared. Their military performance was inadequate since their federalism was peripheralised rather than centralized—in the same way as for the Greek city-state-federations long before. Or, in Riker's words (Riker, 1895, p 8): "In northern Italy and southern Germany medieval cities formed military federations to resist the encroachments of nascent nation states, all of which were essentially imperial in nature. These Italian and Suabian federalisms went through exactly the same cycle as the Greek federalism had done 1,500 years earlier and for exactly the same reasons. Only one of them survived into the modern world: the Swiss confederation—and it survived not because of its constitutional form but because of its unique geographic advantages for defensive military operations."[9]

Anyway, Riker's main result means that all existing federations were created for some kind of military or diplomatic reasons, and that all came about by fusion. The *1 a* pattern is thus common. On the contrary there are no historical examples, at least among the present federations, of the *1 b* type.

The frequent *1 a* process, as well as the infrequent *1 b* one, means that stable federations are created. Earlier in this chapter I mentioned the problem of the raison d'être of the two levels, and I indicated that stable federal multilevel systems are quite remarkable, and nothing to be taken for granted. One may say that there is a balance, or equilibrium, between the levels, which calls for an explanation. There are, in the literature, some examples of this kind of thinking. Thus Buchanan explicitly talks about equilibrium (Buchanan, 1999 a, p 182). "I like", he says, "to think of a federal structure in the following way, and I think it is applicable in the European context: Think of a satellite in orbit. A satellite in orbit is, of course, being maintained by the centripetal and centrifugal forces in equilibrium. So you can sort of think of federalism as a satellite being pulled always by two separate forces in opposite directions—namely, a force toward monolithic centralized authority and forces in the other direction toward a set of autonomous separate units. So federalism is a kind of equilibrium. It is shaky to maintain that equilibrium, but I think in the European context it may be the future likelihood or prospect."

A federal equilibrium, since it is a delicate thing, is by no means an assured result. If a process in the direction of federalism starts, whether upwards or downwards, it is not certain, and it may in fact not even be intended, that it should halt in a state with two coexisting levels. The central power may progressively impose its will on the lower level and thus reduce the original freedom there. In that way a federal system may gradually, and perhaps unnoticeably, turn into a hierarchical system. This is the *2 a* pattern in the figure, which represents a complete fusion or amalgamation of the original constituent parts. It is, however, also possible that the upper level is challenged, and loses. If so we have a case of the *2 b* pattern, which represents a complete fracturing or fission of a single original entity.

Probably there are many historical examples of the *2 a* pattern. What I am thinking of is the unification of the Netherlands, Italy and so forth. The *2 b* process may perhaps be illustrated by the disintegration presently taking place in the different parts of the prior communist world.

In the patterns *3 a* and *b* of the figure a process towards federalism, for one reason or another, finally proves untenable, and turns back. Here, the European unification may be used as an illustration. Mostly, I think, we tend to consider it as a process of type *1 a*. We thus tend to think about the EU as an emerging, viable and stable federation with two levels. That may however be premature. The alternative *3 a*, for instance, may still be open. This means that the unification fails, and that the nation-states fully reappear. In addition to that, and going back to the earlier patterns, *2 a* may also be open. If this alternative materializes, the European federalism turns into a European hierarchy. Buchanan does not predict this alternative, but he has described it vividly while criticizing the Maastricht treaty and the *dirigistes* from Brussels (Buchanan, 1999 a, pp 181 f.). "The danger", he argues, "is that the Brussels bureaucracy will dominate and that you will have excessive harmonization and regularization, which would mean a less prosperous Europe."

IV. Competition in Law

Competition in Policy

Market competition is usually considered beneficial. According to this view, the competition between firms for customers is a powerful mechanism for the enhancement of general welfare. In this process the firms are striving to maximize their profits, and the customers to maximize the satisfaction derived from their resources. This idea of competition is sometimes transferred to the realm of polities and citizens. It is imagined that polities, in analogy with companies, and by varying their policies, can compete for citizens, who are thus the analogues to the customers. It is furthermore imagined that the good polities, *i e* the polities in which the citizens lead relatively decent and happy lives, will somehow survive and prosper in the process, whereas the bad polities, if they don't change their policies, will somehow get marginalized. A basic process involved is migration. People leave the bad polities and move into the good ones.

Ideas like these have been expressed by several writers. Buchanan and Tullock argued for instance in *The Calculus of Consent* (Buchanan & Tullock, 1962, p 114), after having made the case for the smallest possible units of collective activity (as accounted for in chapter II above), that "If the organization of collective activity can be effectively decentralized, this decentralization provides one means of introducing market like alternatives into the political process. ... In concrete terms, this suggests that the individual will not be forced to suffer unduly large and continuing capital losses from adverse collective decisions when he can move freely to other units, nor will he find it advantageous to invest too much time and effort in persuading his stubborn fellow citizens to agree with him." After this Buchanan has remained faithful to the idea throughout the years. Thus he wrote very recently (Buchanan, 1999 a, p 179) that "If there is an exit option, if there is a chance to leave, this necessarily imposes discipline on those who would exploit you through a political structure or a bureaucratic structure."

Furthermore, Buchanan has explicitly associated this idea of competition with federalism. "For me", he thus writes (Buchanan, 1999 b, p 312), "the ideal political structure, especially in large polities, is one described by competitive federalism: the central government remains strong but severely limited in its range of powers, and the separate but integrated lower-level units compete with one another in providing for most of the collectively supplied services as demanded by the citizenry." Then he goes on saying that "(t)he most exciting potential application of genuinely federalist principles seemed to me to be present in the European thrust toward effective political and economic integration. In 1990 I presented a paper in Paris, 'Europe's Constitutional Opportunity,' in which I outlined what seemed to be a once-in-history chance for Europe to establish a strong, and limited, central authority with competing national units and open internal markets." Things did, however, go other ways and later on (Buchanan, 1999 a, p 181 f) he deplores that "... Europe did miss out on a wonderful opportunity to introduce a really good monetary structure. It seems to me that Europe in the early nineties had the chance of adopting a proposal for competitive currencies. All that would have been needed would have been something in the treaties that would have allowed any citizen of any country in Europe to make contracts, including paying taxes, in any money that is issued by any bank in the structure. In that context, the separate central banks could still operate, and you could still have the local currencies, but in fact they would be in competition, so no central bank would dare inflate the currency because it would essentially lose out, and therefore you would have discipline imposed by competition on the separate banks. At the same time, people could have still retained their traditional currencies. Instead, Maastricht tore up that kind of possibility and they moved toward the Euro. I think Europe missed out on a wonderful opportunity."

In his recent proposal that the generality principle should be applied to politics Buchanan has also, together with Congleton, argued in favour of competition in policy, and for federations as fitting frameworks for harbouring such competition. The competition is, it should be noted, a "long-term competition for residents" (Buchanan & Congleton, 1998, p 141). These arguments are, however, less general than the ones quoted above, since they presume that the generality principle is in fact applied. At least for the moment this is a very special, and unrealistic, condition. I will come back to this point later on.

Another scholar who, in a way, has written about competition in policy is William Niskanen. According to him (Niskanen, 1971, p 19) "Even the most autocratic government would have to be approved by *every* resident if the costs of moving were zero. Effective popular control of government is more important, the greater the continuous territorial sovereignty of the government and the greater the restrictions on moving across the borders of the state, both of which increase the economic and psychic costs of moving. Unfortunately, the difficulties of popular control of government also increase with the size of the state. The superiority of ... local governments in providing certain services is due more to the lower cost of ... moving than to greater individual control—which, except in the smallest organizations, is still negligible. A purely autocratic government of a small area must be more responsive to each resident, if there are no coercive controls on moving, than the best conceivable democratic government of a large state." Niskanen thus argues that local government, for some public services, tends to be superior to national government. The reason is the low costs of moving from one governmental area to another, both due to the relative smallness of local government areas, and to the fact that the passing of borders between local governmental areas usually require much less formalities than the passing of national borders.

Another contribution to this field of thinking is Charles Tiebout's (Tiebout, 1956). His version of the ideas involved is less sketchy, and more elaborated, or formalized, than those of most other researchers. Since he specifies explicitly the premises of the results he deduces, he is in fact presenting a real theory or model and not just a mere suggestion.

Tiebout started with the well-known problem of determining the quantities of collective goods to be provided by public authorities. The conventional wisdom is that this problem has no exact solution, since, as Tiebout argues (Tiebout, 1956, p 417), "... there is no mechanism to force the consumer-voter to state his true preferences; in fact, the "rational" consumer will understate his preferences and hope to enjoy the goods while avoiding tax." Tiebout's treatment of this problem starts with the contention that some public goods such as "police and fire protection, education, hospitals, and courts" may be provided locally. These kinds of goods may thus be provided in different combinations by different local governments, and hence the individual consumer-voter may also move to "the community that satisfies his preference pattern" (Tiebout, 1956, p 420). "Moving or failing to move", says Tiebout (Tiebout, 1956, p 420), "replaces the usual market test of willingness to buy a good and reveals the consumer-voter's demand for public goods." The movement implies, it should be noted, both enjoying the public goods available *and* paying the concomitant taxes. In his account for the activities of the local authorities, Tiebout relies on the assumption that each community has an optimum size at which the average cost of the public goods is minimized. Then he says (Tiebout, 1956, p 419) "that communities below the optimum size seek to attract new residents to lower the average costs. Those above optimum size do just the opposite. Those at an optimum try to keep their populations constant."

Certainly this whole idea about competition in policy has some appeal, but there are also reasons for questions. In the rest of this chapter I will evaluate various aspects of the idea.

Deficiencies in the Market Analogy

A first point to be made is that the market analogy is halting. The clearest analogue, I think, is on the demand or customer side. Thus, in a lot of cases, it seems quite clear that people migrate from bad polities, because they are bad, and to good polities, because they are good. On the supply side, however, the analogy is much less clear. It is difficult to find correspondents to entrepreneurs and profits in the political context. This may be illustrated by a few examples.

Let us consider once again the following passage from Buchanan quoted above: "If there is an exit option, if there is a chance to leave, this necessarily imposes discipline on those who would exploit you through a political structure or a bureaucratic structure." At first we may note that the passage testifies to the tendency of citizens to move, if they can, from bad to good polities. So far everything is all right. Here, though, the passage is interesting mainly because it contains an uncommonly clear description of the incentives on the supply side. It says that the policy supplier exploits the citizens, and thus gets a profit. Now, if the citizens leave, there are two options available to the supplier. One, which is indicated in the quotation, is to make the exploitation less severe. The other is to strengthen the border control and thereby impede the emigration. The problem with the first strategy, as a market analogue, is that it does not increase the profit, rather the opposite. The problem with the second strategy is that it does not make the citizens' lives better, rather the opposite. With the incentives assumed in the example there is thus no correlation between a high profit for the policy supplier and good lives for the citizens.

Consequently the kind of profit-motive illustrated by the example does not work in a theory of policy competition. In the ideal economic market, we remember, the entrepreneurs gain their profits by developing and delivering products that the customers find attractive and therefore buy. Similarly in policy competition the profits, whatever their exact nature, should be a result of innovative policy-making that attracts citizens. The exploitation in the quoted example is rather the opposite. There the profit, to the extent that it exists, is a result of closed borders and trapped citizens. An equivalent comment may be made about Niskanen's example, quoted above. What, exactly, is the relationship between the interests of the "purely autocratic government" in that example, and the well-being of the citizens?

In Tiebout's theory there is a somewhat different problem on the supply side. In that theory, we remember, it was assumed that each community has an optimum size at which the average cost of the public goods is minimized. But do the actions of the authorities really lead in the direction of that optimal size? The problem is that in an ordinary commune, in the real world, the average costs are likely to hit the residents directly. Suppose, for instance, that we start with a population that is smaller than the optimum. If so, the residents will probably have to pay more than the optimal costs, and that is likely to induce some of the actual residents to leave the commune rather than to attract new ones, which, in turn, will cause more residents to leave, and so forth. In order to resist and reverse this mechanism, it seems necessary to leave the commune to a profit-making entrepreneur who, confident in his own judgement, sets the prices at the optimum level and suffers the losses in the short run. Certainly entrepreneurs like that are imaginable, but they do not usually appear in real communes. In fact, competition, although not far away, may be less important in Tiebout's theory, than often imagined. Another indication of this is that Tiebout primarily talks about a mechanism for separating the citizens into groups according to their true preferences of various public goods. The local governments just produce different mixes of public goods for different people. This is hardly competition.

Another problem with the market analogy is that it is unclear what the competition is about. The most common idea, I think, is that the competition is about citizens. The competition may, however, also be about capital or about tax-bases in general. These latter possibilities are, I think, in general more reasonable. It is, on the whole, easier to imagine competition about capital, and about tax-bases, than about citizens. Even so, however, I believe that the incentives related to migration are usually very complex and dependent on the conditions in the individual case. This may be illustrated by a problem in Sweden caused by the large cohorts born in the nineteen-forties. These people will soon become pensioners, which means that the burden of supporting them will fall heavily on younger, and smaller, cohorts. A solution proposed is to import labour. This import is likely to increase the GNP considerably since the 40-cohorts leave behind them a lot of real capital that may be highly productive but only, obviously, if utilized by some people. This GNP increase is crucial since it may contain the resources needed for the pensioners. In order to get those resources there the immigrants must however be taxed. Even with the very high

Swedish tax rates they may accept this if the wage level in their home countries is low enough. If so, they may still improve their lives a lot by moving to Sweden.

Here we thus have a case in which a polity, in a sense, tries to attract people. It is, however, more to the point to say that it tries to attract something which, when it gets into the country, becomes a fertile tax-base. The preconditions for this, in turn, is that there is an empty place in the population pyramid in the importing country, and that the original wages of those immigrating are low enough. These conditions are obviously special, complex and not omnipresent. Even if the example thus shows that there may sometimes be reasons for a polity to attract people, it obviously does not lend support to the idea of a general competition of that kind.

Still another problem with the market analogy is that the competing entities may not be as small, and thus as numerous, as sometimes suggested. Remember, for instance, that Buchanan and Tullock, in the Calculus of Consent, argued for the introduction of "market like alternatives into the political process" after having made the case for the smallest possible units of collective activity. But these small units, as we have seen, may not be as small, or as independent, as indicated by Buchanan and Tullock. They may rather be elements at the lower levels of governing hierarchies. If so, we again have a case of mistaking hierarchies for federations. Furthermore, this particular argument in favour of competition loses some of its edge.

The market analogy is thus deficient in some respects, and in particular the lack of an analogue to the profit-making entrepreneurs is a memento. Still this does not mean that the idea of policy competition is necessarily wrong. The conclusion, rather, is that the idea should be scrutinized on its own terms, and I will try to do so.

The Conditions of Variety and Mobility

Policy competition, according to it proponents, requires that two basic conditions are fulfilled—conditions which are practically always mentioned in discussions about these matters, on or between the lines. They are, for instance, obviously present in the examples given by Buchanan, Congleton, Niskanen and Tiebout in the first section of this chapter.

The first of these conditions is that there should be a supply of various policies. If any beneficial competition is to take place there must be a reasonable number of competing polities present, representing various policies or combinations of policies. We may call this the condition of variety.

The second condition is that the citizens can move easily between the polities. It is thus not considered enough that the politicians and citizens in the various polities just can look at each other in order to copy policies that appear beneficial elsewhere, and avoid those that appear harmful. It is required that the citizens actually can move easily and cheaply to the polities they prefer. This we may call the condition of mobility.

When the two conditions of variety and mobility are fulfilled the individual citizen can freely move between the polities and settle, perhaps temporarily, in the one he or she finds best. The idea is that these movements will improve the policy-making, but that is not necessarily so. One important problem is that people move for a lot of other reasons than political ones, and perhaps even mostly for other reasons. People may, for instance, move because they have got a new job, because they are marrying, because they can afford a more expensive living, or because they want to change something else of a non-political nature. These kinds of non-political movements are also primarily taking place within sovereign nations, and for the same reasons as political movements, namely that it is easier to cross intranational borders than international ones.

Now, if people's movements within a country are dictated more by non-political reasons than by political ones, the incentives created for local governments may be just the opposite to the ones imagined by the proponents of competition in policy. These governments, since they are the representatives of people who come and go, *i e* short-term residents, may rather find it rational not to bother too much about their communes. In contrast to Niskanen's claim, there may thus be a real risk that local public affairs are badly run rather than the opposite. And if local governments fail in that way, this also indicates the importance, locally, of the central government and of private enterprises.

This argument is in fact honoured by both Tiebout and by Buchanan and Congleton. Tiebout thus notes that "there has been very little empirical study of the motivations of people in choosing a community" and he acknowledges that people may move for a lot of other reasons than political ones, and that this is a problem. In order to make his theory work he has to eliminate these non-political incentives. He excludes, for instance, movements dictated by the labour market by explicitly making the rather extreme assumption that "all persons are living on dividend income". According to Buchanan and Congleton (Buchanan & Congleton, 1998, p 140), "Tiebout-type mobility is often characterized as voting with one's feet. Here, location reveals that one prefers the services, amenities, and job prospects associated with one location over all others—net of moving costs. The smaller are these moving costs, or threshold costs generally, *and the smaller are the variations in other nongovernmental services*, the more location itself can be interpreted to imply consent." The italics, which are mine, confirm my point.

Experiments

Another idea sometimes expressed by the proponents of political competition is that a federation may be very suitable for conducting policy experiments. Oates, for instance, writes that (Oates, 1999, p 1132) "(i)n a setting of imperfect competition with learning-by-doing, there are potential gains from experimentation with a variety of policies for addressing social and economic problems. And a federal system may offer some real opportunities for encouraging such experimentation and thereby promoting 'technical progress' in public policy." Besides underlining this possibility Oates also claims that "laboratory federalism" actually has proved its value in a number of cases. "There are", he writes, "a number of important and intriguing examples of policies whose advent was at the state or local level and that later became fixtures of federal policy", for instance unemployment insurance and tradeable emission rights in environmental policy.

These ideas are obviously interesting. Still there is a comment that is important, although it is basically terminological. Again it is the confusion between federations and hierarchies which is at issue. The point is that if we are really talking about conscious experimenting, the experiments have to be designed and enacted by someone, and that someone may reasonably be the national government. But if that is the case we are, strictly speaking, not dealing with a federation, since in a real federation the states are free to do what they want within their legally determined limits—they could not be given orders by the national government. Rather we are dealing with a hierarchy that in fact, is an excellent instrument for experimentation. A case in point is the current Swedish experiment concerning the rules for selling liquor. The general rule has been that liquor stores should be closed on Saturdays. Now, however, the stores are open on Saturdays in some local communes on instruction from the national authorities. This, by intention, is a clear-cut experiment. The basic idea is to compare the effects in the two groups of local communes, the ones with closed stores and the ones with open stores.

A federation is not a proper place for experimentation in this sense. In a federal context we will rather find another mechanism for policy innovation which, although it is not experimenting in the strict sense, still is quite interesting. The characteristic trait of a federation is that the states, individually and on their own initiatives, are free to implement various policies. In such a context, other states, and perhaps the federation itself, may adopt a policy that has proved good in some state, and avoid a policy that has proved bad somewhere. This, of course, is interesting and valuable, but it is not experimenting in a strict sense. Rather we are dealing with a multi-actor, trial-error process. From the central or federal point of view, the process can be considered stochastic. The federal authorities just have to sit waiting for what might happen, they cannot steer the process. Still the mechanisms described may give rise to a lot of innovative thinking, they may be quite fertile. If so, the proponents of competition in policy would say this is likely to be a result of the competition between the states of the federation.

Present India offers an interesting example. There, the three southern states of Karnataka, Andhra Pradesh and Tamil Nadu exhibit economic growth nearly twice the national rate. The cities of Bangalore, Hyderabad and Madras in these states harbour India's booming software industry, which enjoys the benefits of free-market reforms enacted by the state governments. The enterprises continually enter into new alliances with Western companies like Microsoft, and the stock markets flourish. As a consequence, the three states are quickly becoming models for other states, and for the nation as a whole.[10] State-level initiatives and referendums in the US give other interesting examples. There, successful policies pioneered by one state are often taken up in other states as well. (Moberg, 1999)

Innovation processes of the kind discussed here, in which successful policies are reproduced elsewhere and unsuccessful policies are avoided, are however also present in other contexts than in federal ones. The same kind of mechanisms may also work between independent nations. Such nations may observe each other in search of policy guidance, and they certainly do so to a large extent.

Thus, the conclusions in this section are that real experiments require hierarchies rather than federations, and that innovative trial-error processes may occur between independent nations as well as between the states of a federation.

The Framework for the Competition

I have already mentioned the idea that a federation is a particularly suitable instrument for competition, and that therefore the competition between the states in a federation may be more effective, and bring more benefits, than the competition between independent nations. One might for example imagine that rich variety and high mobility in a federation works in that direction. A memento, however, is that real federations, as we saw in chapter III, never have been created for the purpose of competition. The competitive federation is thus, at least to a large extent, just an intellectual idea. In this section I will try to bring the comparison between competing states within a federation, and competing independent nations, a bit further.

At first a point of terminology should be clarified. Hitherto, I have spoken quite generally about competition in policy, but obviously policy may include very different matters. I will therefore make a distinction between decisions about law, *i e* legislation, and decisions about other things. The distinction is important since legislation is about general rules, which people should follow whenever they apply, whereas decisions concerning other matters are usually about individual things, such as the building of a school. The consequences of legislation are thus different from, and usually much more far-reaching, than the consequences of other decisions. Decisions about laws specify the borderlines between actions permitted and prohibited. Decisions regarding other things are usually about the selection of a particular action within a permitted area. From now on I shall not talk about competition in decisions about individual matters of various kinds. I will confine myself to competition in legislation, or in law. Rules about taxes, I should make clear, are considered to be laws.

So let us consider competition in law in a real federation, that is in a two-level system. A first point is that such a system has a propensity for redistributions, between the competing states, at the federal level. Such redistributions, combined with competition, may easily result in races to the bottom as described in the section "Problems with two-level systems" in the preceding chapter. The proponents of policy competition are certainly aware of this danger, and they may also prescribe cures for it. Buchanan and Congleton (Buchanan & Congleton 1998, p138) thus say that the federal government itself should be "constrained by the generality principle", which means that it is obliged to treat all constituent states equally. Even so, however, it seems obvious that the risk of this kind of redistributions is always present in a federation, whereas it is basically non-existent between independent unitary states.

Furthermore, it seems most likely that a two-level system is more difficult to understand than a uni-level system, and hence less transparent. This, of course, is bad. A legal system should be as transparent as possible. With low transparency follows system-manipulation, rent-seeking and tricky behaviour in general. Migration, for instance, may very well be selective. If they are able to do so, people may like to be citizens in one state where the public social services are generous, to live in another one, for example where the climate is good, and to pay taxes in still another one where the tax rules are favourable. Such behaviour is likely to thrive in a system characterized by legal variety, easy movements and low transparency. In addition to being transparent a legal system should also be as stable as possible. And again a competitive two-level system may easily lead in the opposite direction. In such an environment laws may vary more over time than in other systems. If so, this conflicts with the norm which is often expressed in Sweden, and possibly in other countries as well, that rules should be firm.

A somewhat similar argument rather focuses on mobility. A precondition for the competition in law to work, it seems to me, is that good laws attract people and that bad laws repel them. This however presupposes, at the very least, that people's decisions about movements are taken behind a "veil of ignorance". If that is not case, and if short-term interests thus are able to influence the decisions fully, the competition is certainly not only beneficial. Under such conditions a criminal is, for instance, not attracted by the good law that punishes him, but rather by the bad law that lets him go. Or, in other words, if there is no "veil of ignorance", good laws may very well repel people, and bad laws may very well attract them. But how, and that is the problem, is decision-making behind a veil of ignorance to be reconciled with easy and high mobility?

More generally, it may be said that a society characterized by the "rule of law" has rules which are transparent, firm, easy to accept behind a veil of ignorance, and unavoidable. Federal competition in law, I think, tends to lead to results being in conflict with this ideal.

Another problem with two-level systems is related to the collection of taxes. This problem may be illustrated when starting from a discussion among economists about mobile tax-bases and tax evasion. In this discussion, which was started by Musgrave (Musgrave, 1959), two distinctions are made, the one between different tax-bases according to their mobility and the other between benefit and non-benefit taxes. Starting with the latter distinction benefit taxes are taxes which can be regarded as payments for goods received or utilized, for example taxes used for providing public goods. The taxes used for macro-economic policy, *e g* for overbalancing the public budget, and for income redistribution, are, on the contrary, called non-benefit taxes, since they cannot be considered to be payments for anything that the taxpayer receives or uses. Now, it is argued that the incentives to tax evasion are essentially stronger for non-benefit taxes than for benefit taxes. The argument, as it seems, is that without benefit taxes there will not be any benefits either, for example no public goods. Therefore benefit taxes could use mobile tax-bases without much harm. Non-benefit taxes on the contrary, and since mobile tax-bases easily escape taxation, should only be taken from relatively immobile tax-bases. Or, in Musgrave's words (Buchanan & Musgrave, 1999 a, p 170): "Immobile land must accept whatever burden is imposed upon it. Labour, still relatively immobile, comes next while capital (and particularly financial capital) is free to move. As a result, capital can be taxed on a benefit basis only."

It should be added that the mobility of tax-bases in this kind of argument not only depends on the nature of the base, but also on the area considered. The assumption is usually (Oates, 1999, p 1125) that "...there exists a nation state with a central government, where there is little or no mobility across national borders; at decentralized levels, in contrast, economic agents, goods, and resources have significant mobility across jurisdictional boundaries with the extent of this mobility increasing at successively lower levels of government." And again the conclusion is "that decentralized levels of government should avoid *nonbenefit* taxes on mobile units."

This reasoning may seem plausible but it contains, I submit, a flaw in the part dealing with benefit taxes. It is, of course, true that there will not be any benefits, such as public goods, without taxes, but only at an aggregated level. From the point of view of the single individual there may still be a tempting possibility of avoiding the taxes and still have access to the public goods. This, in fact, is what the whole discussion on public goods and free-riding (Olson, 1965) is about, and this discussion thus seems ignored in the reasoning presented here. We must therefore conclude that even benefit taxes should avoid mobile tax-bases, and that they should preferably be collected centrally.

Having drawn that conclusion I have also come to my own main point here. If benefit taxes for local public goods, say public goods in the states of a federation, are federally collected, they have to be sent subsequently to the states, to whom they belong. Already for this reason the federal level thus has a certain amount of control over the financial resources of the states. This being so, it is easy to imagine that the federal authorities when returning the money to the states adjust the sums according to some kind of redistributive policy. That, however, brings us very close to the redistributive races to the bottom described above.

Consequently, there are some considerable problems associated with policy competition within federations. At the same time it should be noted that mobility between independent nations is not necessarily that low. Measures, which increase the mobility of human beings and of other things as well between independent nations, could in fact, to a large extent, be undertaken by such nations in ordinary non-federal cooperation, and that also happens. Rules about passports, visas, and so forth, tend for instance to be less and less severe in many countries. From this point of view, policy competition between independent nations is therefore perfectly possible.

It is, by the way, interesting to consider Buchanan's argument concerning competition in money, which was presented above, in this context. Buchanan strongly favoured, we remember, a system with competitive European currencies to the Euro-system, which eventually was established. It is arguable, I think, that the Euro-system is a real two-level system in the sense that the Euro is hardly possible without a real federal level, whereas the system with competing currencies is quite realistic in a context with collaborating independent nations. "All that would have been needed", as Buchanan said, "would have been something in the treaties that would have allowed any citizen of any country in Europe to make contracts, including paying taxes, in any money that is issued by any bank in the structure. In that context, the separate central banks could still operate, and you could still have the local currencies, ... " This, as it seems, is perfectly possible in an ordinary one-level international environment, whereas the solution which finally emerged, to Buchanan's regret, is a typical two-level solution.

The conclusion of this section is thus that at least some of the beneficial effects, which often are attributed to competition within federations, may be obtained by competition between independent nations as well. On the other hand, competition within federations is associated with some severe problems, which do not appear in the competition between nations.

Competition in Law through Fission and Fusion

It should be clear by now that I am doubtful about the merits of competitive federalism. Even so, however, it may matter how such federalism is brought about. From the point of view of a single unitary nation, say Sweden, there are two totally different ways available. The one is fission, which means splitting one's own nation into a federation. The other is fusion, which means creating a federation together with some other independent nations. In the first case the mobility is there from the beginning, and the function of the fission is to create variety. In the case of fusion it's the other way round. The variety is there from the beginning and the function of the fusion is to pave the way for mobility. In this section I will compare these two possibilities.

First, fission entails legislation in many areas, which are much smaller than the homogenous cultural-linguistic areas described in chapter II. This necessarily entails large costs for learning the laws. In a federation created through fusion there is no correspondence to this. On the other hand the external costs, or the decision-making costs, may be very high in that case. That can, however, be avoided by limiting the federal legislation to areas where there are no cultural conflicts. All arguments for these statements are already given in chapter II. Considering the costs related to legislation we might therefore conclude that fusion is preferable to fission.

Second, the risk of central government redistributions as described in the section "Problems with two-level systems" in chapter III, and in the section "The framework for the competition" in this chapter, is reasonably much greater in a federation created through fission than in one created through fusion. The reason is that the original level is likely to remain powerful, and faithful to its traditions, for a long time after the creation of a federation. In a federation created through fission the federal level will therefore remain strong for long, whereas the same is true for the state level in a federation resulting from fusion. In a fissioned Sweden it is therefore likely that the central government, still quite strong and faithful to its habits, would continue to redistribute resources between the constituent parts. Thus, and again, fusion is preferable to fission.

Whatever the merits of competitive federalism, I therefore conclude that a federation created by fission is hardly an attractive alternative, particularly not for a small country like Sweden.

The Creation of Good Societies

I said above that the main deficiency in the market analogy is the lack of correspondents to entrepreneurs and profits in the political context. I will now turn to the implications of this deficiency. Competition in policy relies, as we have seen, on the idea that citizens move from bad to good polities. This is often called to "vote with one's feet" and certainly people may do so. Still there is the problem with the appearance of good societies. How do they come about, and through which mechanisms? It is here that the lack of profit-making entrepreneurs is a problem. If there are no actors like that, how are the good societies, to which the individuals are supposed to move, created?

The discussion of that question can depart from some ideas about voting. The expression to "vote with one's feet" indicates that political migration has similarities with the ordinary voting at the ballot-box. The expression is, however, also misleading since it overemphasizes the similarities, and disregards the differences, between the two kinds of voting. In Hirschman's (Hirschman, 1970) terminology voting with the feet is an exit-reaction, whereas voting at the ballot-box is a voice-reaction. Hirschman maintains that if exit is easy, the voice-option is not very important, whereas if exit is difficult or impossible, the voice-option becomes important. He does however not maintain the opposite, that exit becomes unimportant if the exercise of the voice-option is easy, and for a very good reason. The two kinds of acting are very different in the sense that voting with the feet is essentially an individual act, whereas voting at the ballot-box is (part of) collective action. The effects of voting with the feet are certain, total and immediate for the individual concerned, whereas the effects of ballot-box voting are, at best, uncertain, indirect, and most likely partial. From the individual voter's point of view everything depends on the extent to which other people vote in the same way as he himself. For this reason voting at the ballot-box can never substitute voting with the feet, whereas voting with the feet certainly can substitute voting at the ballot-box, at least for the individual and in the short run.

This last reservation is, however, crucial. A basic democratic idea, or perhaps even the basic democratic idea, is that a society should be built by its members. This means, in other words, that society-building is by necessity a collective undertaking. It is to a large extent dependent on stationary citizens exercising their citizenship. Therefore, and in spite of its attractions to the individual, voting with the feet does not build societies. Society-building is fundamentally dependent on the voting at the ballot-box and other essential democratic processes. The ideas of policy competition are therefore, to a considerable extent, at odds with basic democratic thinking.

Conclusions

My main conclusions from the discussion above about federalism and competition in government are as follows:

I. The idea of creating federations in order to obtain competition in government is not well founded. One reason is that a federation, which means a two-level system, is a bad instrument for that purpose. True, federations may certainly combine internal variety with high mobility, which are attractive features, but they are also full of hazards. Federal redistributions between the competing constituent parts are likely to take place. Furthermore, a federal structure has low transparency, and will probably provide incentives to various kinds of tricky behaviour. Federations created by fusion are, however, likely to be better in these respects than those resulting from fission.

II. Another reason is that the basic idea of competition in government is also inadequate. This, in turn, depends on the fact that the market analogy breaks down on the supply side. There are no profit-making entrepreneurs competing for citizens. Good societies, according to fundamental democratic thinking, are rather built by the people living in them. Citizens exercising their citizenship, including ballot-box voting, are the society builders. From this point of view voting with one's feet cannot substitute voting at the ballot-box.

III. But even if the market analogy does not hold on the supply side it has a substantial amount of realism on the demand side. People do to some extent migrate between polities, such as independent nations, and to some extent for political reasons. This migration of people, and of capital too for that matter, is not to be deplored—rather there are good reasons for making it easy. One such reason is that these movements constitute valuable signals to the democratic decision-makers, voters as well as politicians, in the countries concerned. These signals correspond to various kinds of signals from customers to producers in a market, and they can be used for making the "product" better. If people emigrate that is a warning to be taken seriously, and if people want to immigrate that may be taken as an encouragement. Similar conclusions hold for movements of capital and enterprises.

Notes

1. I want to thank Niclas Berggren, Nils Karlson, Björn Molin, Birgitta Swedenborg and Carl-Johan Westholm for valuable comments and suggestions. The responsibility for the final text with its opinions, and shortcomings, is still entirely mine.
2. There exists a fairly well developed theory about hierarchies. Main contributors to the theory of hierarchies are Simon (Simon, 1961), Tullock (Tullock, 1965), Downs (Downs, 1967), and Niskanen (Niskanen, 1971). Moberg (Moberg, 1994), chapter 7, contains a presentation in Swedish of these theories. It may also be noted that hierarchies are usually contrasted to markets rather than to federal systems. An example is Williamson (Williamson, 1975).
3. It is interesting to note how well an important idea of Friedrich Hayek fits into this rationale for hierarchies. What I am thinking about is Hayek's distinction between scientific or general knowledge, and "knowledge of the particular circumstances of time and place". In making this distinction he argues that the importance of the latter kind of knowledge is often seriously underestimated. He writes (Hayek, 1945 and 1980, p 80) that "practically every individual has some advantage over all others because he possesses unique information of which beneficial use might be made, but of which use can be made only if the decisions depending on it are left to him or are made with his active cooperation."

4. There are many works dealing with federalism and its various aspects. A main reference in this essay is Riker (Riker, 1964). Another important reference is Oates, 1999. Federalism as a mechanism for providing institutional competition is discussed by Berggren (Berggren, 1997), which also contains further references.
5. A confederation is a group of sovereign states with a common purpose, usually defensive or economic, allied by a treaty. In a confederation there is thus no federal level with a federal government (Bealey, 1999, the entries "confederations" and "federal government").
6. Riker, in fact, again and again emphasizes that there is no connection between federalism and freedom.
7. For a further explanation of the concept, see Buchanan & Tullock, 1962.
8. See for instance Gerholm, 1999, or, in Swedish, Gerholm, 1998.
9. In spite of its name the Swiss confederation is, according to the established terminology, a federation and not a confederation (Bealey, 1999, the entry "confederations").
10. The example is taken from the article "Reform grabs more seats in Delhi—Tech-savvy free marketeers won big in the October election" in *Business Week*, October 25, 1999.

References

Bealey, F, 1999, *The Blackwell dictionary of political science*. Oxford: Blackwell Publishers Ltd, 1999.

Berggren, N, 1997, "Social order through constitutional choice : a contractarian proposal" in Berggren, N, *Essays in constitutional economics*, Stockholm School of Economics, 1997.

Buchanan, J M, 1999, "Discussion of political science and economics: three research programs in constitutional political economy", in *Competition & cooperation : conversations with nobelists about economics and political science*, (ed Alt, J E, Levi, M & Ostrom, E). New York: Russell Sage Foundation, 1999.

Buchanan, J M & Congleton, R D, 1998, *Politics by principle, not interest : towards nondiscriminatory democracy*. Cambridge: Cambridge University Press, 1998.

Buchanan, J M & Musgrave, R A, 1999, *Public finance and public choice*. Cambridge, Massachusetts: The MIT Press, 1999.

Buchanan, J M & Tullock, G, 1962, *The calculus of consent, logical foundations of constitutional democracy*. Ann Arbor: The University of Michigan press, 1962.

Downs, A, 1967, *Inside bureaucracy*. Harper Collins Publishers, 1967.

Friedman, M & R D, 1998, *Two lucky people : memoirs*. Chicago & London: Chicago University Press, 1998.

Gerholm, T R (ed), 1998, *Klimatpolitik efter Kyotomötet*. Stockholm: SNS förlag, 1998.

— (ed), 1999, *Climate policy after Kyoto*. Bentwood: Multi-Science Publishing Co Ltd, 1999.

Hayek, F A, 1945, "The use of knowledge in society", in *the American Economic Review*, XXXV, September 1945. Also reprinted in Hayek, F A, *Individualism and economic order*, the University of Chicago Press, 1980.

Hirschman, A O, 1970, *Exit, voice and loyalty : responses to decline in firms, organizations, and states*. Cambridge [MA]: Harvard University Press, 1970.

Lijphart, A, 1999, *Patterns of democracy, government forms and performance in thirty-six countries*. New Haven: Yale University Press, 1999.

Moberg, E, 1994, *Offentliga beslut : en introduktion till den ekonomiska teoribildningen inom statsvetenska*pen. Lövestad: Mobergs Publikationer AB, 1994.

—, 1999, "Positive and normative aspects of direct democracy : the case of Sweden in a general context", in *Makt utan motvikt : om demokrati och konstitutionalism* (*eds* Berggren, N, Karlson, N & Nergelius, J). Stockholm: City University Press, 1999.

Musgrave, R M, 1959, *The theory of public finance*. New York: McGraw-Hill.

Niskanen, W A, 1971, *Bureaucracy and representative government*. Chicago, Aldine Publishing Company, 1971.

Olson, M, 1965, *The logic of collective action, public goods and the theory of groups*. Cambridge, Harvard University Press, 1965.

Oates, W E, 1999, "An essay on fiscal federalism", in *Journal of Economic Literature*, XXXVII, September 1999.

Riker, W H, 1964, *Federalism: origin, operation, significance*. Boston and Toronto, Little, Brown & Company, 1964.

Simon, H A, 1961, *Administrative behaviour : a study of decision-making processes in administrative organization*. New York, The Macmillan Company, 1961.

Tiebout, C M, 1956, "A pure theory of local expenditure", in *Journal of Political Economy*, 64, October 1956.

Tullock, G, 1965, *The politics of bureaucracy*. New York, University Press of America, 1987.

Williamson, O E, 1975, *Markets and hierarchies : analysis and antitrust implications*. New York, The Free Press, 1975.

Contributing authors

Niclas Berggren, PhD, is a research fellow in constitutional economics at the City University of Stockholm. He presented his doctoral thesis, Essays in Constitutional Economics, at the Stockholm School of Economics in 1997 and has published articles on constitutional issues in, *e g*, Public Choice and Constitutional Political Economy.
E-mail: niclasb@cityuniv.se

James Buchanan is Holbert L Harris University Professor and Advisory General Director of the Center for Study of Public Choice at George Mason University, and recipient of the Nobel Prize in Economic Science in 1986. He received his PhD at the University of Chicago. His most recent book, co-written with Roger Congleton, is *Politics by Principle, Not Interest: Towards Nondiscriminatory Democracy* (Cambridge University Press, 1998).

Sverker Härd, PhD, is a political scientist. His doctoral thesis builds a bridge between abstract social choice theory and empirical election and electorate research. He is Director of Education at the National Agency for Education. At the National Agency he is currently National Research Coordinator for the Swedish project in the IEA Civic Education Study, an international evaluation of school democracy and pupils' democratic competence.
E-mail: sverker.hard@skolverket.se

Nils Karlson, PhD, is a political scientist who presented his doctoral thesis, *The State of State*, at the University of Uppsala in 1993, and the President of the City University of Stockholm. He has edited and co-authored several books.
E-mail: nilsk@cityuniv.se

Wolfgang Kasper, PhD, is Professor Emeritus of Economics at the University of New South Wales, Australia, and Senior Fellow, Centre for Independent Studies. Among his publications, the book *Institutional Economics: Social Order and Public Policy* (Edward Elgar, 1998), co-written with Manfred Streit, can be mentioned.
E-mail: wkasper@cis.org.au

Peter Kurrild-Klitgaard, PhD, was educated at Columbia University and the University of Copenhagen and is now Assistant Professor, Department of Political Science, University of Aarhus. He is the author of *Rational Choice, Collective Action and the Paradox of Rebellion* (Copenhagen Political Studies Press, 1997) and co-author and editor of several other books.
E-mail: PKK@ps.au.dk

Mats Lundström, PhD, is Associate Professor at the Department of Government, Uppsala University. He wrote his doctoral thesis on the political philosophy of F Hayek: *The Moral Space of Politics: An Analysis of the Political Philosophy of F A Hayek* (Almqvist & Wiksell International, 1993).
E-mail: Mats.Lundstrom@statsvet.uu.se

Erik Moberg, Ph Lic, is a political scientist who, as an independent scholar, has developed a theory about the characteristics and effects of democratic constitutions. He has published a textbook in Swedish on the economic theory of politics, and his most recent book manuscript is entitled *Democracy: Constitutions, Politics, and Welfare Effects.*
E-mail: erik.moberg@mailbox.swipnet.se

Joakim Nergelius, LLD, is Associate Professor of Constitutional Law at the University of Lund. He presented his doctoral thesis, *Konstitutionellt rättighetsskydd*, in 1996 and has published

books on the institutional set-up of the EU and on Swedish administrative law. He served at the Court of Justice of the European Communities in Luxemburg in 1997-98.
E-mail: joakim.nergelius@jur.lu.se

Aleksander Peczenik, LLD & PhD, is Professor of Jurisprudence at the University of Lund and has published widely on the philosophical dimensions of constitutionalism and the rule of law. He is Vice President of the International Association for Philosophy of Law and Social Philosophy.
E-mail: aleksander.peczenik@jur.lu.se

For Product Safety Concerns and Information please contact our EU
representative GPSR@taylorandfrancis.com
Taylor & Francis Verlag GmbH, Kaufingerstraße 24, 80331 München, Germany

www.ingramcontent.com/pod-product-compliance
Ingram Content Group UK Ltd.
Pitfield, Milton Keynes, MK11 3LW, UK
UKHW040106200926
475702UK00011B/1272
9780765809247